Reprints of Economic Classics

VIEW

OF THE

PROGRESS OF POLITICAL ECONOMY

IN EUROPE

SINCE THE SIXTEENTH CENTURY

VIEW

OF THE

PROGRESS OF POLITICAL ECONOMY

IN EUROPE

SINCE THE SIXTEENTH CENTURY

A COURSE OF LECTURES

BY

TRAVERS TWISS

[1847]

AUGUSTUS M. KELLEY • PUBLISHERS
CLIFTON 1973

First Edition 1847

(London: Longman, Brown, Green & Longmans,
Pater Noster Row, 1847)

Reprinted 1973 by
AUGUSTUS M. KELLEY PUBLISHERS
Clifton New Jersey 07012

Library of Congress Cataloging in Publication Data

Twiss, Sir Travers, 1809-1897.
View of the progress of political economy in Europe since the sixteenth century.

(Reprints of economic classics)
Reprint of the 1847 ed. published by Longman, Brown, Green & Longmans, London.
1. Economics--History. I. Title.
HC51.T97 1974 330'.09 68-58035
ISBN 0-678-00850-7

PRINTED IN THE UNITED STATES OF AMERICA
by SENTRY PRESS, NEW YORK, N. Y. 10013

VIEW

OF THE

PROGRESS OF POLITICAL ECONOMY

IN EUROPE

SINCE THE SIXTEENTH CENTURY.

VIEW

OF THE

PROGRESS OF POLITICAL ECONOMY

IN EUROPE

SINCE THE SIXTEENTH CENTURY.

A

COURSE OF LECTURES

DELIVERED BEFORE

THE UNIVERSITY OF OXFORD

IN MICHAELMAS TERM, 1846, AND
LENT TERM, 1847.

BY

TRAVERS TWISS, D.C.L. F.R.S.

PROFESSOR OF POLITICAL ECONOMY,
AND FELLOW OF UNIVERSITY COLLEGE, OXFORD.

LONDON:
LONGMAN, BROWN, GREEN, AND LONGMANS,
PATERNOSTER-ROW.
1847.

PREFACE.

The regulations of the professorship of Political Economy impose upon the Professor the duty of publishing some portion of the Lectures delivered in each year, and as the nature of the present course would hardly allow me to select a separate portion for publication without risking an appearance of inexcusable incompleteness in the treatment of the subject, I have ventured to publish an entire course, being at the same time the last, which I am permitted by the tenure of my office to submit to the attention of those who feel an interest in the science. My object on the present occasion has been to exhibit Political Economy teaching its most important truths by example, and so to show, that its leading doctrines are the conclusions of an enlarged experience, and are not, as many persons suppose, mere deductions from arbitrary premises skilfully assumed. The course of such an inquiry has unavoidably led to the discussion of many popular principles, which have been from time to time arrayed against those conclusions, and of which the fallacy has been repeatedly demonstrated by some disastrous experiment. At the same time, it has been thought, that the elucidation of those fallacies by facts might serve to recommend the opposite truths more strongly to practical minds, which are indisposed to acquiesce in any general principles, unless they are certified of their having been submitted to the touchstone of particular experience. The following pages, therefore, although perhaps the inquiry may be thought by some to be too brief for the purpose, will, it is hoped, satisfy the majority of such minds, that the doctrines of Political Economy are in no way repugnant to the dictates of an enlightened common sense.

No novel views have been set forth in the course of these Lectures; nor can I lay claim to much originality of statement, having availed myself of the labours of many writers, wherever I have felt satisfied with their accuracy, and could agree with their opinions. Mr. Macculloch's Introductory Discourse to the "Wealth of Nations" is, as far as I am aware, the only historical sketch in the English language of the progress of the science. In the French language there is an abridged history at the conclusion of M. Jean Baptiste Say's "Cours d'Economie Politique," and there have issued from the French press, of late, several valuable publications, such as "L'Histoire de l'Economie Politique en Europe," by Professor Adolphe Blanqui, to which work I have been much indebted, and "L'Histoire de l'Economie Politique," by Le Vicomte Alban de Villeneuve Bargemont. The latter treatise contains what the Author considers to be the catholic view of the subject. In the Italian language we have Count Pecchio's "Storia della Economia Publica in Italia," comprising a series of brief notices of the chief Italian authors, whose works have been published by the Baron Custodi, in his collection of "Economisti Italiani." In addition, I may notice the "Collection des Principaux Economistes" in the course of publication at Paris, chez Guillaumin.

In selecting the subjects of the following Lectures, I have taken in successive order what appeared to be the leading economical fact of each period, and endeavoured in each case to show how the anticipations of a sound theory have been signally confirmed by the experience of statesmen.

The First Lecture exhibits Political Economy in its cradle in Italy, struggling against the stifling policy of the prohibitive system of Charles V. The Second Lecture shows the mischievous effects in France of Sully's protection of agriculture at the sacrifice of manufactures and commerce, and sets forth the origin of the mercantile system. The Third Lecture exhibits the evil results of Colbert's encouragement of manufactures and commerce at the expense of agriculture, based upon erroneous ideas of the value of manufactured produce. The object of the Fourth Lecture is to explain the nature of the great financial experiment in France, known as the Mississippi scheme, and to illustrate the confused notions of that day as to capital and credit, in reference more especially to banking transactions. The Fifth Lecture exhibits the reaction against Colbertism in France, and sets forth the agricultural theory of M. Quesnay, and the School of the French Economists. The Sixth Leeture contains an analysis of the chief doctrines of Adam Smith, and explains the importance of their bearings upon the subject of national wealth. In the Seventh Lecture the subject of population is discussed, in reference more particularly to the writings of Mr. Godwin and

Mr. Malthus. The Eighth Lecture is occupied with M. Say's theory of commercial outlets and various questions incidental to liberty of commerce. The currency question may be said to form the subject of the Ninth and concluding Lecture, extending over a period of about sixty years, from the first issue of assignâts in France to the Bank Charter Act of 1844.

I have attempted in the course of the above inquiry to assign to the chief writers their due shares respectively in furthering the progress of sound opinions, but I have purposely omitted the names of many authors of eminence, who have struggled to retard that progress, although they may have indirectly furthered it by the controversy which they have provoked. This circumstance will account for many names being passed over in the following pages. If, however, I had undertaken professedly to write in full a history of Political Economy, I should have attempted to find a suitable niche for each; but the limits of these Lectures would not allow me to do them justice, except at the expense of writers more deserving of the gratitude of posterity.

T. T.

University College, Oxford,
June 15, 1847.

CONTENTS.

LECTURE I.

LECTURE II.

LECTURE III.

LECTURE IV.

LECTURE V.

LECTURE VI.

LECTURE VII.

LECTURE VIII.

LECTURE IX.

VIEW

OF THE

PROGRESS OF POLITICAL ECONOMY

IN EUROPE

SINCE THE SIXTEENTH CENTURY.

LECTURE I.

LECTURE I.

It was observed by a distinguished French mathematician of the last century, that, during the preceding three hundred years, the middle period of each century had been the epoch of a revolution in the human mind. The fall of Constantinople, for instance, in the middle of the 15th century, led to the revival of letters in Western Europe: the assembling of the Council of Trent, in 1545, A. D., brought about a more complete examination of the principles at issue between the Church of Rome and the Reformed Churches, and so contributed not merely to the advancement of theological learning, but to the diffusion of light over subjects foreign to the controversy: whilst the middle of the 17th century ushered in the new philosophy of Descartes, whose system indeed has been rejected, but whose method has laid the foundation of a new era in science.

D'Alembert.

The epoch itself, at which D'Alembert made the above observations, was marked by appearances of a similar nature. A change had come over the ideas of men in the middle of the last century, the result of which none could venture to foretell, excepting so far

LECTURE I.

as its rapid progress seemed to imply that it was the prelude to a still mightier revolution. In like manner, if it were desirable to follow up the parallel, we might observe that our own lot is cast in a period of signal transition, which, though operating with more calm and stillness, promises to be as remarkable in its effects as the more showy periods which have preceded it.

In no department of thought, however, has so great an impulse been received, or is so great a change of ideas every where preceptible, as on subjects which fall within the province of political economy. The simplest doctrines, indeed, of the science were vigorously and earnestly controverted during the earlier part of the present century; whereas all the great principles are now readily acquiesced in, and at the same time that the improved intelligence of the age enables it to appreciate more correctly the bearings of those principles upon ancient traditions of state policy, the increased complication of our social system enforces a more scrupulous attention to them. It must not, however, be supposed that the victory has been lightly earned; on the contrary, the patient research of several generations of writers had undermined the foundations of the popular system, before Adam Smith assailed the fabric of it, and his followers achieved its downfal. Under these circumstances it is proposed, in the course of the following lectures, to review the successive labours of those writers who have combated the false doctrines and specious fallacies which enthralled the understanding of the great mass of mankind in the 17th and 18th centuries, and who have contributed to elucidate the simple truths which are at the foundation of the science.

Such an inquiry, however, will be essentially defective, if it does not take notice by the way of the more remarkable errors which have led earnest minds astray, not merely because an acquaintance with such errors will save their successors much profitless investigation, but because the merits of those who have kept to the right path will be better appreciated, according as we have a clearer notion of the temptations to go astray, which they successfully resisted. Again, many writers have contributed indirectly to promote the cause of the science by overthrowing the idols of their day, whose positive views have been hardly less exceptionable, and have in their turn been superseded by subsequent analysis. Thus the advocates of the mercantile system combated successfully the prohibitive system, whilst the errors of the mercantile system were in their turn exposed by the school of Quesnay. The theory of Net Produce, on the other hand, which the French Economists set up, was subsequently shown to be untenable by Adam Smith. Again, Adam Smith's doctrine of Rent has in its turn given place to the more scientific statement of later writers. Hence, the history of the science of Political Economy cannot but embrace some account of doubtful opinions, antiquated controversies, and even exploded errors, though, in proportion to the progress of our knowledge, the task of the historian will be in a certain sense lightened, from the circumstance that, as truths accumulate, crude and erroneous speculations lose both their interest and importance. Still, as in all but the pure sciences, plausible fallacies may from time to time be revived under some new modification of statement adapted to the altered condition of things, it may be as well to be familiar with the old forms under which they presented themselves in other times, and with the false principles which they involved, inasmuch as we shall thereby be enabled to detect them more readily, and to expose their true character to those who might otherwise be misled by them.

LECTURE I.

The commencement of the 16th century is generally regarded as the era of that decisive change in the direction of the human faculties, which has led to the great discoveries which separate modern science from the ancient philosophy. The impulse, however, which the study of facts then received in the various branches of natural science, did not at once extend itself to the phenomena of wealth, and to the laws which regulate its production and distribution. Few individuals would, at that period, have had sufficient intelligence to trace up to their true causes the evils which were so generally experienced from vicious systems of public administration, and still fewer would have had the courage to conceive and propound new doctrines at variance with the received practice of statesmen. As far as governments were concerned, their attention was mainly directed to fiscal expedients, which might enable them to meet the expense of almost uninterrupted warfare; and the public officer, who could but devise a new tax that would be immediately productive, irrespectively of all considerations as to its ultimate effect upon the sources of national wealth, was held to furnish thereby conclusive evidence of the highest administrative ability. Nor was the learning of the age likely to advocate a more enlarged view of the subject. For at this time, when the moral and political writings of

Aristotle's Economics.

Aristotle were exercising a dominant influence in the universities of Europe, a treatise on Public Economics was circulated under the authority of that great master's name, as supplemental to his Treatise on Politics, but most undeserving of a place by the side of that noble work. Camerarius, in the dedication prefixed to his Latin translation of the work, in 1564, writes thus: In exemplis historicis callidæ et astutæ atque etiam malitiosæ industriæ, quâ pecunia conficiatur, permultum negotii mihi exhibuit scriptura depravata librariorum inscitiâ atque negligentiâ. Sunt autem exempla illa ejusmodi, ut nostra ætas, hac in parte, antiquitati nequaquam cedere videatur. Cumque et his temporibus auferri simpliciter et aperte aliena nihil alicubi prohibeat, quæruntur tamen et reperiuntur colores, quibus vis injuriaque manifesta oblinantur. Sed boni honestique et pii talia legentes oderunt, cæteri nimirum quandam se imaginem consiliorum actionumque suarum conspicere lætantur.

When it is stated that this treatise comprises little more than a series of base and unworthy expedients, which unscrupulous rulers had employed under circumstances of pecuniary embarrassment, we might despair of the age which could merit the opprobrious comparison which Camerarius institutes. "In regard to the examples which this work furnishes, our own age does not in any way yield to antiquity; and although in these days open spoliation is universally and unhesitatingly practised, yet men seek to give some colour to their violence and injustice. Such persons rejoice to find in this work a mirror of their own schemes and actions; but the good and the honest will not peruse its contents without loathing." Camerarius.

The authority of such a work, although some more acute critics might dispute its genuineness, could not but tend to confirm the prevalent error of the day, which identified fiscal art with the science of public economy, and made the great end of that art to consist in raising the largest amount of revenue with the least inconvenience to the government, rather than in distributing the burden of taxation in the mode least calculated to impair the sources of revenue.

The work, to which I have just alluded, has long since been stripped of its usurped character, and is generally published as the production of an unknown writer. Its origin, indeed, cannot be decisively determined; but there are good grounds for supposing it to

LECTURE I.

have been written at a period certainly subsequent to the death of the founder of the Peripatetic School of Philosophy, and to have been compiled, most probably, for the use of the Persian satraps in Asia Minor, as a book of precedents in matters connected with the public revenue.

In addition to this, the great event with which the fifteenth century closed, and the sixteenth opened, namely, the discovery of the two Indies, was calculated in its more immediate effect to confirm the false prejudices of the age as to the nature of wealth. Spain, after the discovery of the mines of Mexico and Peru, finding herself suddenly rendered independent of all other countries for her supply of the precious metals, conceived that the maintenance of her unlooked for and unrivalled opulence would be best secured by closing up the outlets of commerce, and so preventing her stores of silver from leaving the country. For as the exchangeable value of this metal in Spain would diminish with the increased facility of procuring it, silver, being cheaper in Spain than elsewhere, would become a profitable article of exchange with other countries, and its exportation would be inevitable, if trade with other nations were not checked.

Prohibitive system of Spain.

Hence it seemed to be for the interest of Spain, if she wished to retain her newly acquired treasures, that her subjects should trade as little as possible with foreign countries; and with this object we find Spanish statesmen labouring to prohibit foreign commerce, and, by consequence, to restrict the growth of domestic industry. Hence exorbitant duties were imposed upon the importation even of raw produce, and the exportation of manufactured articles; the practice of an art in Spain was now made subject to a licence, and the exercise of a trade became a matter of privilege. Spain, however, in spite of her precautions, found her treasures imperceptibly drained away by the wasteful wars, in which Charles V. was engaged. In the mean time, her ruthless expulsion of the Jews had driven from her cities a most important body of capitalists; her merciless persecution of the Moors had deprived her of the services of the most industrious and intelligent portion of her agricultural population; and the financial embarrassment of Charles V., consequent upon his insatiable thirst of warlike aggrandizement, led him at last to lease out to foreigners the monopoly of the trade with the Indies, and, still further, to barter away to them the undeniable birthright of his subjects, the very commerce of the interior of Spain. The restrictions, which originated with Charles, were continued, and even extended, by Philip II., and they gradually become incorporated with the laws and usages of the Spaniards, until at length writers stepped forward to reduce these fatal financial experiments into a system, and to base general doctrines upon them, which found a more ready acceptation in other countries, as they appeared to be practically sanctioned by the administrative wisdom of the leading state of Europe.

The disastrous effects, however, of the prohibitive system of Charles V. and his successors, as experienced in the Italian dependencies of Spain, could not but form a striking contrast to the prosperity which had attended a very different policy, whereby Venice, Genoa, and Florence had successfully opened out for themselves a way to opulence and power. That the received notions as to the nature of wealth should at once be assailed and overthrown was hardly to be expected; but, that the best means for increasing the supply of the precious metals should become a subject of discussion, was an obvious consequence of the unexpected results, which the Spanish policy had entailed. Without impugning, therefore, the general belief, that wealth consisted exclusively

LECTURE I.

of gold and silver, the earliest writers ventured to question the wisdom of prohibiting the exportation of the precious metals.

Antonio Serra.

Amongst these Antonio Serra is, I think, justly entitled to be considered as the originator of the new order of ideas on questions of economical science. A native of Cosenza, in Calabria, he appears to have been involved in the unsuccessful enterprise of Tomaso Campanella to rescue the two Calabrias from the yoke of Spain. The work to which he may appeal as establishing his title, was dated from the prison of the Vicaria at Naples, in 1613, and was dedicated to the Conte di Lemos, the Spanish viceroy. It is entitled "Breve Trattato delle Cause che possono far abbondare li regni d' oro e d' argento dove non sono miniere;" and the first place has been assigned to it in the valuable collection of the works of the Italian economists, which the Baron Custodi edited at the commencement of the present century.

Abbé Galiani.

Of this work the Abbé Galiani, in a note to his Treatise on Money, published in the middle of the last century, thus writes:—"Whoever reads this treatise will certainly be surprised to find such clear and just views in a writer who lived in an age of complete darkness as to the first principles of economical science. His style, it must be admitted, is dry and obscure; but, in spite of these defects, I should not hesitate to rank him as the earliest and most ancient writer on the science of political economy, and to concede to Calabria the glory of having produced him. Yet this man, whom I would compare to Melon in France, and Locke in England, surpassed them both, from having lived at a period so much earlier, and in an age of such total darkness in respect of the subjects upon which he wrote. This man, whose understanding was so clear, and whose judgment so sound, was despised during his lifetime, and since his death has remained forgotten with his work. No one has ever cited it, and perhaps the only existing copy is the one which Bartolomeo Intieri has presented to me, and by which his memory will be rescued from oblivion."

The title of Serra's work does not fully explain the scope of it, and has led most writers on political economy, I might almost say all with the exception of Florez-Estrada in Spain, to neglect it as being merely a treatise on money, and to class it with the writings of Scaruffi, Davanzati, and Turbolo, who confined their attention to the exposure of the existing abuses in the monetary systems of their day, consequent on the debasement of the coinage, and to the suggestion of suitable remedies. Serra, on the other hand, assuming, at the very onset of his work, that all men would admit it to be advantageous to a country to be well supplied with the precious metals, proceeds forthwith in the first part to examine into the causes which make gold and silver to be abundant in countries where there are no mines; in the second part he combats the erroneous notions of his contemporaries as to the causes which make gold and silver to be scarce; and he concludes the third part with exposing the fallacious character of the expedients usually suggested by way of remedy.

The causes which, he maintains, will produce an abundance of gold and silver in a country where there are no mines, are either peculiar or common. The peculiar causes are — 1st, the fertility of the soil, which, bearing more than is necessary for the wants of the inhabitants, places at their disposal a surplus, which may be exchanged away with other countries for gold and silver; 2nd, the situation of the country itself, when it lies in the line of traffic between other states, as was the case with Venice when it was the *entrepôt* of the trade between Europe and Asia. The peculiar causes are evidently beyond the control of

LECTURE I.

statesmen; not so the common causes, which he divides under four heads. The first of these is an abundance of clever artizans, skilful in producing the necessaries, and conveniences, and luxuries of life, and to the working of this cause, he attributes greater results than to the fertility of the soil: 1st, because its operations are independent of the seasons; 2d, because the amount of its produce is capable of an unlimited increase, whereas to the produce of the soil there must be a limit; 3d, because the manufactured article is more durable and more portable than the raw material, and so may find access to a greater number of markets; 4th, because states generally export a larger quantity of manufactured articles than of raw goods. By this last statement, he seems to mean, that more merchants deal in manufactured articles fit for consumption than in raw materials; and Venice is instanced as an example.

The second cause, according to his classification, is traced to the character of the people, if they are industrious, inventive, and enterprising. In the order of priority, under this head, he places Genoa first, then Florence, lastly Venice.

The third cause is an extensive trade. When trade is extensive, he says, you need not prove that money must be plentiful, since trade cannot go on without money, and money is made for the purpose of trading. The fourth and last cause is the order and security which a government based upon principles of justice alone guarantees; and, as an instance of this, he cites the extraordinary prosperity of Rome under the just and enlightened administration of Sixtus Quintus.

Sixtus Quintus.

With respect to the erroneous notions of the day as to the causes of gold and silver being scarce, Serra, in the second part of his work, directs his attention chiefly to the examination and refutation of the views of Marco Antonio de Santis, who seems at that time

LECTURE I.

Antonio de Santis.

to have been the oracle of the Neapolitan exchequer. De Santis had apparently maintained, that the abundance of gold and silver in every country was the effect of the exchange in that country being low, and a scarcity of those metals the effect of the exchange being high; and that the high rate of the exchange in Naples, as compared with the other towns of Italy, was the sole cause of the country being drained of the precious metals; the reason being, as he alleged, that the high rate of exchange in Naples caused bills, and not specie, to be sent to Naples in return for Neapolitan produce, and specie and not bills to be sent out of Naples in return for foreign merchandize. In confirmation of this view, De Santis appealed to the experience of a period about twenty or thirty years previous, when the exchange was low and specie was abundant. Accordingly he proposed, by way of remedy for the scarcity of money, that the rate of the exchange in Naples should be reduced by a state ordinance.

Now the exchange is said to be high in one place as compared with another — in Naples, for instance, as compared with Venice — when a bill drawn by a merchant of Venice upon a merchant of Naples is at a discount on the exchange of Venice, or when a bill drawn by a merchant of Naples upon a merchant of Venice is at a premium upon the exchange of Naples.

Par of exchange.

The exchange, on the other hand, is said to be at par between two countries, when a bill of exchange, bought in one country with a certain amount of gold and silver of a given fineness, will, when paid in the other country upon which it is drawn, produce the same quantity of gold and silver of the same fineness. Consequently, if bills payable in Venice were at a premium at Naples, the exchange was evidently unfavourable to Naples; and the price of such bills, as of any other article of commerce, would continue to rise, according as the demand for them increased:

LECTURE I.

and the demand for them would increase in proportion, as Naples had to pay a larger balance to Venice than Venice to Naples, in consequence of having imported commodities from Venice of greater value than she had exported in return to Venice; in other words, the credit of Venice would be at a premium on the exchange of Naples, in proportion as the debt of Naples to Venice was augmented.

Serra, in combating the proposal of De Santis, did not think it necessary to discuss the relation between the high rate of exchange and the deficiency of specie, but contented himself with observing that the fluctuation in the exchange was an accident of commerce; whereas the scarcity of money might be the result of certain measures of the government. But the true cause he did not fail to point out, why specie did not flow into Naples; a truth, as he said, not sufficiently appreciated, namely, the excessive importations of foreign produce, and the total neglect of industry at home. Nor did he omit, in answer to De Santis, to appeal to the experience of the past as conclusive against the efficacy of the remedy which he suggested, from the fact that the Conde di Olivarez, the immediate predecessor of the Conde di Lemos, had during his viceroyalty issued an ordinance to lower the rate of the exchange in Naples, but had recalled it, as the merchants of the great trading cities of Italy refused to regulate their transactions by it.

In the third part of his work, Serra exposes the inefficient character of the remedies usually advocated; such as prohibitions against the exportation of specie; ordinances to limit the rate of exchange; and bounties upon the importation of foreign money, by allowing it to circulate at an advanced nominal rate. The ostensible object of restricting or prohibiting the exportation of specie, he observes, is to keep the money which flows into a country from flowing out, and so to produce a redundancy of it; but, he continues, the prohibition to export money is not only not advantageous to states, but, on the contrary, is detrimental to them. No merchant will export specie except with the view of making a profit by the transaction. He will export it for one of two reasons, either for the purpose of buying goods abroad, or because it is of more value in foreign countries than at home, and the exchange will be profitable. If the goods are wanted for consumption at home, no loss can result, because they must be paid for. But, it may be urged, why not pay for them with bills of exchange, or with other commodities instead of exporting specie? The answer is, that we ultimately arrive at the same result; since, in order that the bills of a merchant should be cashed in a foreign country, specie must have been sent there either before or after the transaction; and, on the other hand, in order that we should have commodities to exchange, we must already have given value, and probably specie, for them in some other market. If, on the other hand, the goods are not wanted for the home market, they will be carried elsewhere, and sold for more money than they cost, and this will bring back a greater amount of specie than was exported. Again, whenever money is exported because the exchange is unfavourable, it will return with profit as soon as the opposite cause comes into operation; but its exportation will reduce the rate of exchange on other countries, and it will cease to be exported as soon as the exchange is depressed to a certain level. The opposite cause will then come into action, and the current will set the other way. Again, he observes, the liberty of exporting specie encourages commerce, for it does not always answer the purpose of a merchant to take bills of exchange; and he may sometimes find it desirable to be paid in ready money,

LECTURE I.

so that, when money itself is allowed to be an article of commerce, it furnishes an additional element of trade. He then proceeds to illustrate his principles, by pointing out the very different results which attended the different policies of Naples and Venice. Thus at Naples neither foreign nor Neapolitan money was allowed to be exported under a penalty of treble the value exported; whereas from Venice, Venetian money to any amount might be exported, and five millions of coin, at least, were annually exported to the Levant; yet Venice had her coffers full of specie, whilst the Neapolitan treasury was drained empty.

It can hardly be denied, after this brief analysis of Serra's work, that this writer, though he may have limited his investigation to certain branches of the science, such as the laws which regulate commercial exchanges, and the rules which should guide the administrative department of government, in respect of commercial and monetary questions, is entitled to the position which the Abbé Galiani assigns to him. It is curious, indeed, that whilst his just meed has been withheld from Serra, the authors with whom it has been customary to class him, such as Scaruffi, Davanzati, and Turbolo, have attained a reputation apparently beyond their desert, as to them is generally assigned the credit of having first exposed the mischievous results of a debased currency, and of laying down the principles which should regulate a sound monetary system.

Monetary questions had at this time forced themselves more immediately into notice from the growing practice in all the states of Europe of adulterating the coinage; and at the very time when the New World was pouring unprecedented stores of specie into the Spanish treasury, Charles V. was reckless enough to hazard the overthrow of the entire system of commercial credit, which had been built up slowly on the wise administration of the banks of Venice and Genoa, by inundating his Italian dominions with a flood of base gold coin. The disorder consequent on these immoral expedients had attracted the attention of thoughtful observers; and we find the Count Scaruffi, the director of the mint at Reggio, suggesting, as a remedy against the frauds which were universal in all dealings in specie, that the guarantee of a generally recognised stamp should be affixed to articles of pure gold, and that an European diet should be convoked to agree upon an uniform general coinage. His project was reduced into writing in 1579; but not published till 1582. The talents and method of the author could not fail to arrest the attention of men of science; but the execution of a scheme on so enlarged a basis was evidently at that period impracticable.

Scaruffi.

The merit, however, of originating a more correct system of ideas upon the nature of money is not unfrequently assigned to Bernardo Davanzati of Florence, who addressed a short treatise upon the subject to the Academy of Florence in 1588. The Abbé Galiani, indeed, did not hesitate to assail the established reputation of this author, and to charge him with complete ignorance of the subject-matter about which he wrote. That Davanzati was ignorant of the fundamental principles which determine the value of money, is evident from the definition which he adopts, "Moneta — e oro, ariento, o rame, coniato del publico a piacimento, fatto dallè genti pregio e misura delle cose per contrattarle agevolmente."

Davanzati.

"Gold and silver," he says, "being found to be of no use for supporting human life, have been adopted, by the agreement of mankind, as the measure of all other commodities, and as the instruments of circulating those commodities, and so we may call them the secondary causes of human happiness."

LECTURE I.

Again, he says, "they are employed as the price and measure of all things, because mankind have agreed so to employ them, and not because these metals have any natural value."

Davanzati then proceeds to illustrate this fact. "An egg," he says, "the price of which may be half a grain of gold, sufficed (valeva) to keep the count Ugolino alive in the Tower of Famine for eleven days, whilst all the gold of the world would not suffice (no'l valeva) to do so.

Again; "what is of more importance to life than wheat? yet 10,000 grains of wheat sell for a grain of gold. How happens it, then, that things by nature so valuable are worth so little gold? And upon what does it depend that one thing is worth so much more than another, or is worth this rather than that quantity of gold? Can this be really accidental? All mankind labour for their own happiness, and they expect to find happiness in the satisfaction of their wants and desires. To this end nature has adapted all things on the surface of the globe, and the aggregate of these is, by the universal consent of nations, worth all the gold and silver which is produced. The value, therefore, of any given article measured in gold is determined by the respective proportions of the part which each represents in relation to the whole."

The ingenuity of this view cannot be denied; but it is clear that Davanzati had not the most remote notion of the distinction between value in use and value in exchange.

The distinction, however, between the utility and value of commodities is so fundamental, that writers who confound them can hardly be expected, except from the merest accident, to arrive at correct conclusions. It may be true that Locke and other distinguished writers, at a much later period, clung to the same idea which Davanzati advocated, as to the value

LECTURE I.

of the precious metals being merely conventional, and therefore he may be entitled to greater allowance: but he must be content to renounce all claim as the discoverer of the true principles by which monetary questions should be regulated. His theory answered the purpose which he had in view, of showing the mischievous effects of debasing the coinage. "The baser the coin," he observes, "and the more reduced its weight, the greater the loss to the state as well as to private creditors, for they receive a less quantity of gold and silver in a given amount of coin, and have a less quantity of metal to exchange for commodities suitable for their consumption; for it invariably happens, that where money is reduced in value, other commodities become enhanced in price. Commodities are ordinarily given in exchange for the metal which is supposed to be contained in the coin, and not for a certain number of tokens or pieces of money. If in 109 pieces of money there is now only as much silver as there was formerly in 100, must we not give 109 pieces of money for what we could formerly purchase with 100?"

Having thus briefly criticised Davanzati's treatise, I shall proceed to show that more clear and correct views on the subject of money than any which were made public in Italy during the sixteenth or seventeenth century are to be found in an English work dedicated to Queen Elizabeth, in the year 1581, entitled "A Briefe Conceipte of English Policy." The initials of W. S., gentleman, on the title-page of the original edition, printed in London by Thomas Marshe, afford the only clue to the author's name. It was, however, reprinted in 1751 by some adventurous bookseller, as the work of William Shakspeare, Gent. But Watt, in his Bibliotheca Britannica, under the head of our great dramatic poet's name, states that

Briefe Conceipte.

LECTURE I.

Mr. Farmer has now proved it to be the production of William Stafford, gentleman.

William Stafford.

The work is cast into the form of a dialogue, in which the interests of the landowners are represented by a knight who has served in parliament, the tenant-interest by a husbandman, commerce by a merchant, handicrafts by a master-hatter, and learning by a doctor of divinity. The dialogue is conducted with considerable spirit and intelligence, the object of each speaker being to show that the interest which he individually represents, is the most depressed by the circumstances of the times. They seem all to have agreed that, though there was plenty of food and other commodities in the country, there was a wonderful dearth of all things, prices having risen on all hands: they could not agree, however, as to the cause of this, and ultimately refer the decision to the learning of the doctor. The doctor, having traced the origin of the rise of prices to the adulteration of the coinage in the preceding reigns, accounts for the continued dearth in two ways; first, that the landholders, in respect of the rise of prices from the debasement of the coinage, found themselves obliged to raise their rents, and so the husbandman was enforced to raise the price of his produce, and so food becoming dearer, the wares of artificers rose in price, &c.; secondly, although the coin of the country was now restored to its proper purity, yet such infinite sums of gold and silver had been imported from the Indies, that an income of 30*l.* or 40*l.*, which formerly was sufficient to entitle a man to be accounted rich and wealthy, so far from constituting in common opinion a man of wealth, in the present day, would not relieve him from being reputed next neighbour to a beggar.

Rise of prices.

My object, however, in referring to this dialogue is not so much to represent the general scope of it, as to

LECTURE I.

exhibit the soundness of the views set forth in it on the subject of money. Having shown that the quality and weight of the coin determine its exchangeable value, and not its name, as, for instance, that a silver coin of the sixth part of an ounce, and a silver coin of the twelfth part of an ounce, though they both may be called by the same name, *i. e.* a grote, can never bear any other relation to each other than that of two and one, the whole thing and the half, the doctor observes, —

"We must consider, though gold and silver be the metals commonly wherein the coin is stricken, to be the tokens for exchange of things between man and man, yet it is the wares that are necessary for man's use that are exchanged in deed, under the outward name of the coin, and it is the rarity and splendour of such wares that makes the price thereof higher or baser."

The knight thereupon inquires, "What makes these metals to be of more value than other?"

Value of gold and silver.

To this the doctor replies, "That it is partly their natural qualities, partly their rarity. When I told you," he continues, "the rarity commends the said metals of gold and silver, yet more than this. For as they do excel in qualities, so Dame Nature seems to have laid them up in a further ward than her other gifts, to show us that all fine things be rare, and that the fairest things, as they are the hardest to be obtained, so they be most to be esteemed. If a glass, as Erasmus saith well, were as rare as silver, it would be as dear as silver, and not without cause. Who could glaze a window with silver so as he might keep out the injury of the weather, and yet nevertheless receive the commodity of the light through the same to his house, as with glass he might? and so I might commend other things for their use afore gold and silver, as iron and steel, with which we may make better tools for many necessary uses, than with gold and silver; but for the uses that we talk of, silver and gold do clearly excel all other metals. I pass over that matter: thus I have shown some reason why these metals of gold and silver are grown in estimation above other."

A distinction is here clearly drawn between the utility of a thing and its value. Thus iron and steel are spoken of as more useful than gold and silver, but gold and silver as of greater value. The value, as distinguished from the utility, is made to depend upon the rarity of a thing, in other words, upon its being hard to be obtained, and the value of the precious metals is determined by the same rule as that of other wares. This is a very different view from the conventional value, which Davanzati suggested.

System of enclosures.

With respect to agriculture, one of the acknowledged evils of the day was the system of enclosures, as it is termed, or in other words, the general conversion of arable land into pasture; and the popular explanation was that the dearth of prices had forced the landowners to take their land into their own hands, and that, as tillage required a greater outlay of capital and labour than pasturage, the landowners had betaken themselves to grazing in preference to husbandry. The doctor, however, admitting the influence of this cause, does not fail to point out another great cause, namely, that "whatsoever thing is reared upon grazing has free vent both over this side and also beyond the sea to be sold at the highest penny; whereas, if the market do arise either within the realm or without, the poor husbandman shall be so restrained from selling his corn, that he never after shall have any joy to set his plough in the ground." Another remedy which he suggests is, "that the husbandman might have as much liberty at all times to sell his corn either within the realm or without, as the grazier hath to sell his wool, which would make the husbandmen more willing to occupy their plough; and others seeing them thrive would turn their pasture into tillage. And though it enhance the market for the time, yet would it cause much more tillage to be used, and consequently more corn, within time of plenty within this realm, might bring in much treasure, and in time of scarcity would suffice for the realm, as I showed you before."

The author's views, as here stated, in relation to agriculture were more sound than his notions in regard to commerce. He was ready to condemn the attempt on the part of the state to keep down the prices of agricultural produce, by restricting access to any but the home market; but with respect to manufactures he fully shared in the popular prejudices of his age. It is obvious that if the state allowed the free exportation of wool, and restricted or prohibited the free exportation of corn, the effect would be the same as if it had granted a bounty on the exportation of wool to the exclusion of corn: for it would have enabled the wool stapler to resort to a foreign market where the demand was in excess of the supply, whereby he would obtain a higher price for his wool.

The merchant had complained of the decay of towns, which the doctor attributed to the decay of occupations.

"I believe that well," replied the merchant; "but what, I pray you, was the occasion of such decay of the occupations?"

Decay of occupations.

The doctor, therefore, proceeds to state, that "the decay of the occupations arose from the decay of the demand for the stuffs which were once made in the towns: and that this demand had decreased, because gentlemen now-a-days must have this gear come from London, and yet many things hereof are not there made, but beyond the sea, whereby the artificers of

LECTURE I.

our good towns are idle, and the occupations in London and especially of the towns beyond the seas, are well set a-work even upon our costs. Wherefore I would wish some stay were devised for coming of so many trifles from beyond the sea, and especially of such things as might be made here amongst ourselves."

Foreign wares prohibited.

He then proposes that no commodity which could be made out of raw materials produced at home, should be allowed to be imported from foreign places, but should all be wrought within this realm, so that all the profit upon working it might be saved. "I would have those occupations most preferred and cherished that bring most commodity and treasure into the country, as ye must consider three sorts of occupations, one that carrieth out treasure, the second that merely spendeth in the country what it getteth, the third that bringeth in treasure. The first sort are those who sell us wares made beyond the sea, for they do but exhaust the treasure of the realm, such as mercers, vintners, grocers, &c.; the second, bakers, butchers, brewers, &c., which like as they convey no money out of the country, so they bring none in, but where they get it, they spend it. Of the third sort be these, clothiers, cappers, worsted makers, pewterers, tanners, which be all that we have of any art which I can now reckon, that brings into the realm any treasure. Therefore these arts are to be cherished, whereas they be used, and where they be not, they would be set up, &c." As for the first class, the doctor observes, "I cannot see what they do to a town, but find a living to five or six households, and instead thereof impoverish ten times as many; but since men will need have silks, wine, and spice, it is as good that men do spend their money upon such in their own town, as to be driven to seek the same further." In a word, "by these two means chiefly, i. e. first by staying of wares wrought beyond sea, which might be wrought within us, from coming in to be sold; secondly, by restraining of our wools, tins, felts, and other commodities from passing over unwrought, I would think our towns might be soon restored to their ancient wealth."

Exportation of gold and silver.

In regard to the exportation of silver and gold, which was prohibited at that time in England, the knight observes, "it was never lawful, nor yet is expedient, that strangers should have any from us," and therefore he infers that the adulteration of the coinage in the previous reigns could not have affected the prices of foreign products in the English markets. But to this the doctor replies, "that he might have answered again, that it chanced not all ways together, that when they had wares which we wanted, we had again all those wares that they looked for; and therefore they having perchance more wares necessary for us than we had of such wares as they looked for, would be glad to receive of us such stuff current in most places, as might buy that they looked for elsewere at their pleasure. And that, they will say, was not our coin (being debased). And as for our laws of not transporting over sea any gold or silver, they passed not thereof, so they might have the same once conveyed them, as they had many ways to have it so, which I have before remembered."

It will have been seen that the learning of the age, which the doctor represents in this dialogue, suggested, as the most obvious course for raising the price of corn, and so encouraging tillage, that corn should be allowed to be exported as freely as wool, the chief produce of the pasture lands. But, as a secondary remedy, another way is proposed: "To abate the commodity of grazing, as when any taxe is requisite to be granted to the prince, if lands be chargeable thereto, to charge one acre of pasture as much as two of arable. Or else to burden wools, and felts, and such things as are reared by grazing, that pass to the parts beyond the sea unwrought, with double tollage over any corn transported, and so by enhancing the profits of tillage and abating of the profits of grazing, I doubt not but husbandry would be more occupied and grazing much less."

And elsewhere he says, that "a way to make tillage to be as well cherished of every man as pasture, would be to make the wool to be of as base a price to the breeders thereof as the corn is; and that shall be if ye make a like restraint of its passing over sea unwrought, as ye make of corn; another is, to increase the custom of wool that passeth over unwrought. And by that the price of it shall be abated to the breeders, and yet the price over sea shall be never the less: but that which is increased in the price thereof on strangers shall come to the Queen's Highness, which is as profitable to the realme as though it came to the breeders, and might relieve them of other subsidies."

Increase of custom duties.

The merchant, however, in reply, suggests that men would send less wool over sea than they do now, and by that way the Queen's custom should be diminished;—to which the doctor answers, "I think not so; for the one way as much as she should have for the more wool at little custom ventured over, so much should she have for the less wool at a greater custom ventured. And the other way as much as her Grace should lose by her custom of wool, so much or more should her Grace win by the custom of cloths made within the realme."

It is strange that the doctor should have overlooked the inevitable consequence of restricting the exportation of wool by increasing the duties upon it, which he anticipates would fall upon the producer, it being assumed that the price of wool in the foreign market was to remain the same, when he expressly pointed out the prejudicial operation of analogous restrictions upon tillage; namely, that the diminished profits would discourage pasturage, and so diminish the quantity of wool, which might be available for the purposes of the clothier, and thus limit the increase of the custom upon cloth.

But the doctor does not fail to state, that he considers the raising of the price of corn, by opening new markets to the corn grower, to be a better way for bringing husbandry up than the basing the estimation of wool and felts.

The artizan, however, objects to the enhancement of the price of corn, "as every man hath need of it; but not so in the case of other wares."

The doctor replies—"Wherefore the more necessary that corn is, the more be the men to be cherished that rear it: for if they see there be not so much profit in using the plough as they see in other feats, think ye not that they will leave that trade and fall to another that they see more profitable?"

"How then," says the knight, "would ye have them better cherished to use the plough?"

"To let them have more profit by it than they have, and liberty to sell it at all times, and to all places as freely as men may do other things: but then, no doubt, the price of corn would rise specially at the first more than at length; yet the price would provoke every man to set the plough in the ground, to till waste grounds; yea, and to turn the land that is now enclosed for pasture to arable; for every man will the gladder follow that whereby they see more gains, and thereby must needs ensue both greater plenty of corn within the realm, and also much treasure should be brought into the realm by reason thereof; and, besides that, plenty of all other victual increased among us.

LECTURE I.

"Ye have heard," he continues, "that, by this free vent and sale of corn, the husbandman's profit is advanced; then it is shewed that every man naturally will follow that wherein he sees profit ensue: therefore men will the gladder occupy husbandry, and the more do occupy husbandry, the more plenty of corn must needs be; and the more plenty of corn there is thereof the better cheap, and also the more will be spared over that which shall suffice for the realm. And then that may be spared in a good yeare shall bring us again either corn, or else the commodities of other countries necessary for us. Then the more husbandry there is occupied, the more universal breed should be of all victuals of neat, sheep, swine, geese, hens, capons, and chickens, for all these are reared much on corn."

Duties on exportation of corn.

When it is remembered that the duties upon the exportation of corn were not repealed in this country until the accession of William III., and that as late as 1662 the duty was so very high as to be almost prohibitory, it must be admitted that the writer of this dialogue displays, in respect of the corn trade, an intelligence far in advance of his contemporaries. He refutes with equal vigour the popular objection that the exportation of corn would lead to a scarcity at home, by showing that if a scarce year should fall after a plentiful year, the corn of so many ploughs as in a good year would be more than enough, in an unfruitful year would at the least be sufficient to find the realm, and so should the realm be served with enough of corn in a scarce year, and in a plentiful year with more than enough, which might be sold over for great treasure or greater commodities; where now in a plentiful year we seek to have but as much as may suffice the realm. Then if a scarce year should happen, we must needs lack of our own to serve, and should be driven to buy from beyond the sea, and then if they were as envious as we be, might not they say, when we required any corn of them (that seeing they could get none from us when we had plenty), why should they let us have any corn when we have scarcity?

Mutual dependence of countries.

"Surely common reason would that one region should help another when it lacks, and therefore God hath ordained that no country should have all commodities, but which that one lacks, another brings forth; and that the one country lacketh this year, another hath plenty thereof, commonly the same year, to the intent men may know that they have need of another's help and thereby love, and society to grow among all men the more; but here we would do as though we had need of no other country on earth, but to live all of ourselves, and as though we might make the market of all things as we lust ourselves, for though God is bountiful unto us, and sends us many great commodities, yet we could not live without the commodities of others."

We have here a surprising largeness of view in a writer of the sixteenth century, though he is disposed to limit this natural interchange of commodities between country and country to substantial wares and necessaries. For elsewhere, he says, that "if we keep within as much of our commodities as would be the result of a heavy duty on exporting wool, we must spare many other things that we have now from beyond sea, for we must always take heed that we buy no more of strangers than we do sell them, for so we would impoverish ourselves and enrich them. For he were no good husband that had no other yearly revenues but of his husbandry to live on, that would buy more in the market than he sells again. And that is a point that we might save much by our treasure in this realm if we would; and I marvel no man takes heed to it, what number first of thinges come

LECTURE I.

hither from beyond the sea, that we might either clean spare, or else make them within our realm, for the which we either pay inestimable treasure every year, or else exchange substantial wares and necessary for them, for the which we might receive great treasure."

Germ of mercantile system.

In this passage, on the other hand, as in other parts of the work, we have the germ of the theory, which was in the next century developed in the mercantile system, namely, that the balance of trade was in favour of the country that sold to strangers more commodities than it bought from them, receiving the difference in specie or treasure.

It was reasonable to expect that the bearings of commerce upon agriculture would be appreciated, more readily than its bearings upon manufactures, because the former were more immediate and direct than the latter; and thus we must not be surprised to find that whilst it was proposed to grant to agriculture a "free vente," in order that commensurate profits should attract labour and capital to it, it was suggested that the importation of foreign commodities should be limited by restrictive duties, or absolutely prohibited, in order that our own people might be set to work upon the raw material, and the profit of the work be saved within the realm. And elsewhere he says, "Yet it were better for us to pay more to our own countrymen for these wares," (admitting that when made at home they would cost more than when made abroad) "than to strangers less, for how little gaines so ever goeth from one of us to another, it is all saved within the realm."

"Then," says the knight, "you would have a law made that no such ware should be brought from beyond the sea, to be sold here, of such things as could be made here, as well as there." "Yea, forsooth," says the doctor, "so would I wish." "Then," says the knight, "such a thing was once moved in Parliament, but only for cappers, and then it was objected, that the passing of such a law was contrary to treaties with foreign powers. But," he continues, "what if they should make a like law beyond the sea, that wares made within this realm should not be sold there, as they made of late, when we devised a law that no wines should be carried hither in strangers' bottoms?"

Foreign wares not necessaries.

The doctor, in order to meet the objection that prohibitions might be retaliated, is obliged to have recourse to a common fallacy. "Yet they would be enforced rather to dissolve their law than we ours, for our stuff is necessary for them that is made here, theirs be to us more to serve pleasure than necessity."— "Yea, their chief commodities might be better spared of us than retained of them."—"I would to God we would follow the example of a poor haven town in the marches of Wales, called Carmarthen—when there came certain vessels out of England all laden with apples, the town commanded that none should buy the said apples upon a great pain, and so the boat stood so long in the haven without sale or vent that the apples were putrified and lost, and when the owner demanded of the bailiff of the town why he had stayed his sale and vent, the bailiff answered again, 'that the said vessel came thither to fetch the best wares they had in the country, as friezes, broad cloths, and wool, and instead thereof, he should leave them in their country but apples, that should be spent and wasted in less than a week.' And said, 'bring unto us corn and malt as ye were wont to do, whereof the country hath need, and ye shall be welcome at all times, and ye shall have free vent and sale thereof in our port.' Think ye that the cities of London, Southampton, Bristol, Chester, &c., might they not learn a good lesson of this poor Welsh town in this doing? Might they not say when ships full of

Bailiff of Carmarthen.

LECTURE I.

oranges, pippins, and cherries come in, that if they would again take plums, damazins, and strawberries for them, they should have free exchange. And when they bring in glasses, puppets, rattles and such like things, they should have like trifles for them, if any such were to be had within their realm, as there be many; but if they come for our wools, for our cloths, kerseys, corn, tin, lead, yea, our gold and silver, and such substantial and necessary things, let them bring in again flax, tar, tiles, fish, and such like; and not to use them like little children, give them an apple for the best jewel that they have about them. And thus we are impoverished of our treasure and chief commodities, and cannot perceive it. Such is the fineness of strangers' wits and the grossness of ours."

I have quoted this passage at length, as it is curious to observe how difficult it is for the human understanding to disenthral itself from prejudices which our feelings dispose us to cling to. The doctor, in various parts of the treatise, displays his disapprobation of the growing taste of the day for luxuries—

"Ætas parentum, pejor avis, tulit
Nos nequiores."

Hence, indeed, the consumption of luxuries was regarded by him as wasteful, and a man who should have exchanged a necessary of life for a luxury was held by him to have made a bad bargain, as the consumption of the luxury would be an unproductive consumption. Again, the exchange of a durable for a perishable article would appear to him to be an unequal exchange. He seems in this respect to have imagined utility to be an absolute, not a conditional quality, and to have forgotten that it is not the capacity of satisfying natural wants or ends alone which limits the idea of utility, but that whatever is capable of satisfying any want or end, is relatively to the satisfaction of that want or end useful; and that men are led to exert their energies for the attainment of ap-

LECTURE I.

Prohibitions entail waste.

parent good, and their desire of such apparent good requires satisfaction as intensely as any natural desire.

It seems not to have occurred to the bailiff of Carmarthen that there was any national waste in the apples being allowed to putrify and be lost. Had the trade of the apple merchant not been interfered with, he would have been the medium of transferring the broad cloths of Carmarthen to some other part of England, where they would either have been made up for use at home, or exchanged for commodities from abroad. The apples would have been consumed partly by the clothiers of Carmarthen, partly by the wool growers, with whom the clothiers would have exchanged a portion either directly or indirectly which they did not themselves wish to consume; and the clothiers with the wool which they would receive for a portion of the apples, would have continued their occupation, and prepared a fresh stock of cloth for the merchant, when he should return on a future occasion with corn. As it was, in the first place there was an absolute loss of so much produce: in the second place the merchant would have no produce at his command to take to another market and procure another cargo; he would therefore not return to Carmarthen, and the clothier not having sold his cloth, would have had no means of buying more wool, and would thus remain unrequited for the past, and unoccupied for the future. The interference of the bailiff would thus be prejudicial to all the individuals whom he restrained from trading, with no advantage to the commonwealth; on the contrary, the commonwealth would have suffered from the operations of the clothier's industry being suspended. Yet the worthy doctor was anxious that the example of the good town of Carmarthen should be imitated by all the great commercial cities of the kingdom.

In contrasting this writer with Davanzati, he

LECTURE I. seems to have perceived all the commercial consequences of a debased coinage as fully and clearly as the Florentine, and to have had much sounder notions as to the principles which determined the value of money, and in this respect I have no hesitation in placing him on a higher pedestal than his contemporary; but when we compare his views on the subject of manufactures and general commerce with those of Serra, the palm of intelligence must be awarded to the Calabrian. In both writers we see the elements of that preference for manufactures over agriculture, which lay at the foundation of the system, which has been subsequently denominated Colbertism from the great minister of Louis XIV. Serra considered one of the great elements of national wealth to consist in an abundance of artizans skilled in producing the necessaries, and conveniences, and luxuries of human life, in this respect rising above the sumptuary prejudices of the English author: and such a condition of things, he conceived, for the various reasons above enumerated, to be more advantageous for a country than superior fertility of soil; the English author, on the other hand, was not unwilling that heavy duties should be imposed upon the exportation of wool to discourage pasturage, whilst he suggested that the example of the Venetians might be followed with good results, "who, if they may hear of any cunning craftsman in any faculty, will find the means to allure him to dwell in their city." But Serra's great merit consists in the clear view which he took of the course of the exchange between countries, and his bold suggestion, that specie ought to be allowed to be exported, because it would never be exported except it was profitable to do so, and that it would return in due course of time through the natural operation of the exchanges.

It has been already observed that Serra's treatise seems to have exercised no effect upon the policy of the Neapolitan viceroy. In regard to the English treatise, which was dedicated to Queen Elizabeth, if any attention was paid to it, that attention was bestowed on the errors and not on the sound and more intelligent views of the author. Thus the suggestions as to the prohibiting the exportation of undressed cloth, and of wool, were actually put into practice by the statesmen of King James's reign. Rapin informs us that "Alderman Cockaine and some rich citizens, having, as was said, promised Rochester, Northampton, and the Lord Treasurer, great sums of money to procure them a patent for the dressing and dying of cloths, and that the king would seize into his hands the charter of the Merchant Adventurers for transporting white and undressed cloths; Cockaine pretending that besides the enriching of the nation, multitudes of poor people might be employed to the benefit of the nation, which now were a burden to it. Hereupon the king seizes upon the Merchant Adventurers' patent, and grants to Cockaine and others a new patent for dressing and dying of cloths. But Cockaine's project succeeded both ways quite contrary: for the Dutch prohibited the importation of dressed and dyed cloths from England, and Cockaine and his company not only dyed and dressed cloths worse and dearer (which are ever the consequences of monopolies) than they were in Holland; but these being restrained to a company, they could not dress and dye the cloths made in England. Whereupon the making of cloth stood at a stand, and infinite numbers of poor people, which were employed in making cloths, lay idle and were reduced to a starving condition." The result was that, the Commons in the next Parliament voting Cockaine's patent to be a monopoly and grievance, it was recalled and cancelled,

Cockaine's patent.

LECTURE I.

and the vent of white cloths left free. Camden in his annals gives 1616 as the date of Cockaine's patent.

Experience on this occasion thus dissipated one error at least, viz. that strangers could not do without our cloths, "as being substantial wares and necessaries."

Six years afterwards, under the notion that foreigners could not make their cloths without materials hitherto exported from England, a royal proclamation prohibited the exportation of wool, woolfels, wool yarns, fuller's earth, and wood ashes. The avowed object of this was to prevent foreign clothiers from competing with English clothiers in the common markets of Europe, such competition having already been found to diminish both the quantity and the price of English cloth sold in those markets. In consequence of this measure the price of wool in England fell from 33*s.* to 18*s.* the tod, and under; and thus the end which W. S. had suggested as the alternative for the purpose of discouraging pasturage, was fully attained. We must not, however, suppose that this proclamation had the interests of the corn grower in view. On the contrary, it is generally considered that King James having determined to govern without the advice and aid of Parliament, had recourse to this and similar prohibitions, that he might exact, under the colour of licences, more money from such of his subjects, as should be desirous of exporting wool, than they would have been required to pay under the statute 1 Jac. 33.

Policy of James I.

The practical result of these two measures, which we have just examined, could not but tend to disabuse the public mind in England of its fond delusion, that English exports were necessary to the foreign consumer. The States General and the great commercial cities of Germany maintained most strictly their prohibitions against English woollen manufactures, and so far exposed the idleness of the notion, that "the Dutch could not subsist without our English cloth," which had been stoutly maintained by Gerard Malynes, in 1622. The other fallacy, that "the makers of cloth, beyond the seas, cannot make their cloth without our English wool," was similarly refuted by the fact, that the demand for English cloth did not in any way increase in foreign markets, although its price might well be reduced still lower, from the fall in the price of wool; on the contrary, it steadily declined, as was pointed out by E. Misselden, the opponent of Malynes, in his treatise, entitled "the Circle of Commerce," 1623.

Gerard Malynes.

E. Misselden.

LECTURE II.

LECTURE II.

DURING the greater portion of the sixteenth century, with which the inquiry in the previous Lecture was concerned, the condition of the leading states on the continent of Europe must be considered to have retrograded in an economical point of view, and the capacity of the statesmen, who directed their councils, was unequal to the task of reorganising the national resources. The seventeenth century opened with fairer prospects for France, but Spain was condemned to an accumulation of financial embarrassment with the accession of each new sovereign of the dynasty of Hapsburg. A total change had meanwhile taken place in the commercial relations of the various European states, consequent on the successful enterprize of Vasco de Gama, at the conclusion of the fifteenth century, and the weapons of monopoly, which Venice had so long wielded against the world, were now borrowed from her own armoury, and turned against her. The combination of the great abundance produced by Venetian commerce, with the great mercantile security resulting from Venetian credit, had, to a certain extent, reconciled Europe to the exclusive system which Venice had of late rigidly maintained; but the yoke was felt to be oppressive, and there existed a general disposition to shake it off, on the first favourable opportunity. The struggle was commenced immediately upon the accession of Charles V. to the Spanish throne, when he set an

Vasco de Gama.

LECTURE II.

Prohibitory System of Europe.

example to the other states of Europe, of retaliating upon the Merchant Queen of the Adriatic her own prohibitory laws. From this period we may date the origin of that systematic warfare which the various states of Europe have carried, and still carry, on with one another, by means of hostile custom-house regulations, from which there has resulted a series of what may be regarded as *Cadmean victories*, which have proved more exhausting to the conquerors than to the vanquished. On this occasion it was supposed that what had been employed so effectively by Venice, could not but be productive of similar advantages to other states. Venice, however, had established her greatness by the early freedom of her commercial and industrial institutions, and by that very greatness she had been tempted, as she had been enabled, to adopt an entire change of policy. Europe, on the other hand, beholding her great prosperity in later times, combined with a most exclusive system, connected them as effect and cause; and thus the various states, as they threw off the yoke of Venice, hastened to follow the example of Spain, and to fence themselves in with prohibitory regulations, as barriers against unequal competition. Henceforward the commercial policy of the European states centred in the attempt to achieve an impracticable result, viz., "the selling to strangers more than strangers sold to them." With this object, measures were devised in order to prevent gold and silver, reputed to be the sole elements of wealth, from being exported. The importation of foreign merchandise was restricted by heavy duties, or totally prohibited, as it might cause specie to leave the country; and even the exportation of raw produce, as supplying materials for foreign industry to work upon, was in many cases forbidden. The perfection of economical wisdom was held to consist in the combined attainment of these several results.

LECTURE II.

Spain had made greater progress than any other country towards the realization of an Utopian self-sufficiency, and before the termination of the sixteenth century, her Austrian rulers had almost isolated her in sombre gloom from the rest of Europe. In France, on the other hand, the dawn of a brighter order of events was discernible upon the accession of Henri of Navarre (IV.) to the throne.

Condition of England.

England, at this period, was somewhat in advance of her continental neighbour, as the reign of Elizabeth, which had opened under disastrous auspices, had concluded with most happy results to British industry and commerce. England had, besides, enjoyed a period of domestic repose, while France had been distracted by the wars of the League, and when Henri Quatre engrafted the Bourbon branch upon the inheritance of the House of Valois, he found the finances of the country in the utmost disorder, and the state on the verge of bankruptcy. Fortunately for France, and the monarch who was so suddenly called to guide her fortunes, the ability of the Marquis de Rosny, his minister of finance, better known as the Duc de Sully, was equal to the emergency, and by the happy combination of great discernment with an unconquerable firmness of purpose, he achieved the restoration of order and plenty in a department, which seemed but a short time before to be irretrievably embarrassed.

Character of Sully.

Sully, indeed, must not be regarded as a mere financier; he did not content himself with temporary expedients, or with measures devised solely with a view to the immediate replenishment of the state-coffers, but he fully appreciated the truth which arbitrary power so generally and so strangely overlooked, that the surest way to enrich the sovereign, was to enrich the subjects of the sovereign. In the dialogue which was referred to at length in the previous lecture, entitled, a "Brief Conceipte of English

Policy," the principle seems to have been almost for the first time recognised, "that the Queen's majesty cannot have treasure when her subjects have none;" and as for the subsidies, it is asked, "how can they be large, when the subjects have little to depart with? and yet that way of gathering treasure is not always most safe for the prince's surety; and we see many times the profits of such subsidies spent in the appeasing of the people that are moved to sedition, partly by occasion of the same." To a similar purport, Sully was aware "that if he made money pass through the hands of the people, there would necessarily flow into the public treasury a proportionate quantity, which no one would regret; if the people have little money, it can give up but little, and that little must be wrested from it."

The measures, therefore, which Sully adopted with a view to reanimate the dormant industry of France, and promote the growth of national wealth, as they were based upon a system, and were attended with striking results, will merit examination, the more so as Sully is considered to have been the first statesman in France entitled to the character of a political economist, and there are writers even in the present day, who would set him up as a fit model for statesmen of our own time to copy.

Sully's predilection for agriculture.

Sully was in an especial manner the friend of agriculture; his favourite saying is well known, that "tillage and pasturage were the nursing mothers of the state (les deux mamelles)," and his legislation left little to be desired in respect of its encouragement to agriculture. The abolition of the arbitrary and vexatious taxes, hitherto levied upon the cultivators of the soil, the removal of the ancient restrictions which the narrow jealousy of the provincial states or parliaments had imposed upon the transport of corn from one province to another, and the relaxation of the prohibitions against the exportation of grain and other raw produce to foreign countries, could not but lead to results as surprising as they were satisfactory to the French monarch. Within fifteen years Sully abolished five millions of direct taxes upon the cultivators of the soil (la taille); reduced by one half the amount of duties levied on the internal trade of the country, and yet the annual revenue had increased four millions. In the mean time one hundred millions of the state-debt had been paid off; thirty-five millions' worth of royal domains, alienated by the king's predecessors, had been repurchased, and upwards of forty-one millions of livres were accumulated in the state treasury.

He prohibits the exportation of specie.

In regard to monetary questions, Sully, fully participated in the popular prejudices of his age; and although the exports to Spain secured an influx of gold and silver, he did not hesitate to prohibit the exportation of specie and coin. A strong political motive most probably influenced him on this occasion, viz. a desire to accumulate the means of carrying on war at some future opportunity with Austria, without the necessity of increasing the taxes upon French industry. Sully, it may be remembered, had been brought up as a soldier, and his fame as an officer of artillery was hardly inferior to his reputation as a financier. Some allowance may therefore be made for him personally on this score.

Forbonnais, in his "Recherches sur les Finances de France," in discussing the economical bearings of this accumulation of treasure, one effect of which was to withdraw from general circulation a very large amount of coin, seems to have overlooked one consideration. The free exportation of corn and other produce to Spain entailed a continued influx of the precious metals, whilst the prohibition to re-export them necessarily restricted French merchants from dealing with other nations that exported manufactured goods, irrespectively of the direct impediments, which Sully on principle raised up against the introduction of them into France. The consequence was that the nominal prices of all commodities would have risen very considerably, and general inconvenience have resulted, had not a certain portion of the annual imports of silver been thus as it were absorbed. For instance, in the kingdom of Castile, according to Ortiz, a Spanish writer, the continued influx of silver had caused it to fall in the early part of the 16th century to one sixth of its value prior to the discovery of the New World.

Depreciation of silver.

What limit was to be assigned to such absorption, must totally have depended upon the rate of influx: thus it has been calculated by Forbonnais, that between 1492 and 1724, one half of the gold and silver, which America had supplied to Europe, was absorbed by the Levant, the India, and the China trade; and Mr. Jacob, in his work on the Precious Metals, (vol. ii. p. 213.,) calculates that during the 18th century, the quantity of gold and silver which was converted into other objects than coin, amounted to two-thirds of that which was left in Europe, after the part which was conveyed to Asia was subtracted from the total produce of the mines.

Under the circumstances, then, in which France was placed, it seems probable, that the withdrawal of a large amount of specie from circulating, as coin, neutralized some of the prejudicial results, that could not but attend the withholding it from commercial uses, as a commodity. That the influx of specie must have been very large, may be inferred from the fact that Sully was enabled to reduce the rate of interest from 10 and 8 to 6 per cent. "The pistoles of Spain," says Forbonnais, "were more common in France than in Spain, because we sold them freely our corn, our wine,

LECTURE II.

and our brandies, and because the interest of money with us was lower than in other states," i. e. because our farmers could procure money on easier terms. "Reciprocally the interest of money had fallen, because the trade in corn being free, attracted money."

Sully's discouragement of manufactures.

In respect of manufactures and commerce, Sully exhibited all the scruples of a Spartan legislator. Combining apparently an aristocratic aversion to artisans, as a class, with a philosophical indifference to the comforts and luxuries of life, he did not hesitate to engage in a resolute, though ineffectual, struggle against his sovereign, who was anxious to introduce the cultivation of the silk-worm, and the working of silk, into France. The king was persuaded that his own wealth depended on that of his subjects, and that to multiply the sources of individual occupation was to multiply the sources of national wealth. Sully, on the contrary, believing that the sedentary occupation of the artisan incapacitated him from the duties of a military life, held that the geographical situation and political state of France made it a question of the last importance to maintain the race of robust agricultural labourers. Whilst, then, the production of silk fabrics would enervate a portion of the people, the consumption of such articles of luxury would corrupt another portion. "Have we not already," he said, "in France, a sufficient number of useless citizens, who under robes of gold and scarlet hide all the feebleness of women?"

A Roman censor, as Mr. Blanqui justly observes, could not have expressed himself better, but a minister of agriculture and commerce ought to have entertained other views, when the 16th century was drawing to its close.

His aversion to foreign commerce.

In respect of foreign commerce, Sully regarded it simply in the light of a drain upon the specie of the country. Foreign fabrics he considered to be vicious superfluities, which good citizens should dispense with. The king, however, adopted a different view, and invited by large bounties workmen from Flanders and Holland to establish themselves in France, and bring with them the art of making tapestry.

Transit trade through France.

The greatest blot, however, in the system of Sully, seems to have been the indifference with which he permitted France to lose a great portion of the transit trade from the Levant to the north of Europe, by which the important cities of Marseilles and Lyons had formerly attained great prosperity. In 1540, Francis I. had established duties upon the importation of foreign silk fabrics into France from Spain and Italy, by the coasts of the Mediterranean. They were required to be brought to Lyons, and a duty of five per cent was levied on goods which were intended for home consumption, two per cent on those which were to be exported again to other countries. In 1554, the city of Lyons was allowed to levy a toll (*octroi*) in addition of 2½ per cent, which four years afterwards the Crown incorporated into the general customs. In 1585, Henry III. extended these duties to all commodities from the Levant, making no distinction between articles intended for home consumption and those for transit. French subjects could not avoid paying these duties; but foreign merchants hastened to relieve themselves from the obligation, by seeking another route. It is from this period that the commerce of Italy with England and Flanders quitted, once and for all, the overland route across the continent of Europe, and adopted the longer but surer course by sea. There were not wanting men of intelligence to discern the tendency of this policy, and men of courage to represent to the minister the disastrous workings of it. "Already," said a deputy from Lyons to the estates of Dauphiné, whose discourse has been thought worthy to be handed down to us by the historians of

Expostulations from Lyons.

LECTURE II.

that day, "since the passage of the Rhine has fallen into disrepute, and merchants prefer all other risks to the injustice to which they have been exposed, the city of Lyons, illustrious and flourishing as it has been, is hastening to become a desert, unless liberty is restored to traffic. Already the merchandise which came from the Levant to Marseilles, and thence to Lyons, has deserted its ancient course, and sought a more secure road. Let it not be supposed, however, that we have been taught so imperfectly the duty of obedience, the most precious lesson which a subject can have learnt, that we wish to thwart the intentions of the king or diminish his revenue. The burdens which nations bear, although they may be heavy, have ever been considered as sanctioned by Divine and human law; but they are intended to serve the same purpose for a state, which sails serve for a vessel, namely, to propel it in an onward course, and to keep it upright, not to overload and sink it."

Although similar complaints were heard in all parts of France, Sully's innate aversion to every thing connected with foreign commerce caused him to turn a deaf ear to them.

On the other hand, when the interests of agriculture were concerned, Sully was not dull to perceive the importance of promoting the circulation of produce by the improvement of the existing lines of communication, and by the creation of new ones. The canal of Briare, the first artificial line of water communication in France, was with this object projected by him to unite the Seine and the Loire rivers, though it was not completed until 1740, under the reign of Louis XV. "He was aware," says Forbonnois, "that money could not find its way into the interior of the country without the necessary means were established to facilitate the transport and consumption of agricultural produce. And with a

The Canal of Briare.

similar object he established a line of public passage-boats on the great rivers, and organised on the great roads a service of post-horses for travellers. These measures were but the complement of Sully's other reforms for the encouragement of agricultural industry in France.

New outlets for produce.

The key to his agricultural system was a very simple one; whilst with one hand he removed the ancient obstacles to production, with the other he opened new outlets for produce: whilst he relieved the agriculturist from an overwhelming load of direct taxes, which cramped the exercise of his productive powers, he secured for him access to new markets. We should, therefore, be prepared to expect the most favourable results from so simple and sound a policy, in respect of this branch of industry in a country like France, the soil of which is so well adapted for tillage; but when it is proposed to set up the general system of Sully as a suitable model for imitation in the present day, let it not be forgotten that the evil results of his erroneous views in regard to the operation of manufactures and foreign commerce upon national wealth, were not fully discovered, until he had ceased to be minister. The good effects of legislative changes, based upon sound principles of public economy, are, generally speaking, appreciated more readily and more immediately than the bad effects of erroneous measures; and the reason of this may be supplied by an illustration. A steel spring will unbend itself more readily than you can bend it. So it is with the industry of man. It exhibits an analogous elasticity and resistance to compression, and the removal of restrictions to its development has been invariably attended by an immediate increase of prosperity; whereas industry will struggle long and silently against the obstacles which an unwise policy has created or neglected to remove, and the tale of its

LECTURE II.

struggle will rarely be known, until it has terminated fatally.

It has been observed, that Sully participated in the popular prejudice of the day, as to the inexpediency of allowing the exportation of gold and silver. On the other hand, England set an example to the great states of Europe, of abandoning this ancient error: but this result was arrived at by an experimental and indirect process. The establishment of a direct intercourse with India by the Cape of Good Hope, as observed by Mr. Macculloch in his introductory discourse to Adam Smith's Wealth of Nations, seems to have had the greatest influence in effecting this change. The East India Company, on its earliest institution, in 1600, obtained leave to export annually foreign silver coin, or bullion, to the amount of 30,000*l.*, on condition of re-importing within six months after the conclusion of each voyage, which occupied generally rather more than thirty months, as much gold and silver as should, together, be equal to the value of the silver exported. It so happened, that a commerce of specie could be carried on with the East under great advantage, from gold being there more plentiful, and therefore cheaper than in Europe, and silver being rarer, and therefore dearer. The enemies, however, of the Company, to use Mr. Macculloch's words, "contended that this condition was not complied with, and that it was besides contrary to all principle, and highly injurious to the public interest, to permit gold and silver to be sent out of the country. The merchants and others interested in the support of the Company could not controvert the reasoning of their opponents without openly impugning the ancient policy of absolutely preventing the exportation of the precious metals. They did not, however, venture to contend, nor is there, indeed, any good reason for thinking that it really occurred to them,

East India Company in 1600.

LECTURE II.

that the exportation of bullion to the East was advantageous, on the ground that the commodities purchased by it were of greater value in England. But they contended, that the exportation of bullion to India was advantageous, because the commodities imported from thence were chiefly re-exported to other countries, from which a much greater quantity of bullion was obtained, than had been required to pay for them in India. Mr. Thomas Mun, the ablest of the Company's advocates, ingeniously compares the operations of the merchant, in conducting a trade carried on by the exportation of gold and silver, to the seed-time and harvest of agriculture. "If we only behold," says he, "the actions of the husbandman, in the seed-time, when he casteth away much good corn into the ground, we shall account him rather a madman than a husbandman. But when we consider his labour in the harvest, which is the end of his endeavours, we shall find the worth and plentiful increase of his actions."

Mr. Thomas Mun.

It was thus attempted, as it were, by a side blow to introduce the wedge into the ancient fabric of commercial restriction. Men required first of all to be persuaded to allow the precious metals to fulfil, under limitation, the same office in regard to foreign commerce, the need for which, in respect of the home market, they had long since admitted. They could not deny that at home the precious metals facilitated the exchange of commodities, and that such exchange in some way or other was advantageous to individuals and the state: they were now asked to allow the Company to employ in an analogous manner a limited amount of specie to facilitate the interchange of commodities in the foreign market, the Company undertaking that by the transaction the stock of specie in the country should not ultimately suffer a diminution. Even so slight an advance towards sounder opinions

LECTURE II.

in commerce could not but provoke frequent attacks from the partisans of the ancient system, and the supporters of the Company thought it advisable, not so much to meet these attacks with arguments, as to parry them with facts, by pointing out the gain to the nation upon the quantity of cloths and other woollen goods exported to the East, and the saving in the price of the spices and other produce of India, imported by the Company. Such are the topics on which Sir Dudley Diggs, in his pamphlet entitled 'The Defence of Trade,' published in 1615, lays the chief stress.

Sir Dudley Diggs.

One step was decidedly gained; namely, by the concession of the Charter it was admitted in theory that the exportation of bullion might be productive of advantage to the state; and a petition, embodying the same views as those put forth by Mr. Mun in his 'Treasure by Foreign Trade,' above cited, was presented by the East India Company to Parliament in 1628. The returns of the Company, which had been published by Mr. Mun in 1620, fully confirmed the truth of the theory. He shows in his 'Discourse on Trade,' reprinted in Purchas' Pilgrims, that the exports to India, during the first twenty years, had amounted in value to 840,376*l.*: that the produce brought from India had cost 356,288*l.*, and had produced here the very large sum of 1,914,600*l.*: that the quarrels of the Dutch had caused a loss of 84,088*l.*, and that the Company's stock in hand amounted to 400,000*l.* In the face of such facts, it was hardly possible to maintain that the permission to export gold and silver had so far been prejudicial to the national interest: on the contrary, a new order of ideas, which has been called the Mercantile System, came into vogue, the supporters of which, without abandoning the received notions as to the precious metals being the only real element of wealth, allowed the field of their employment, as the medium of facilitating exchanges, to be enlarged under certain conditions. These were, either, that the commodities obtained in exchange for them should realise in some other foreign market a larger amount of specie, or that the value of the increased exports of native produce should more than equal the value of the increased imports of foreign commodities, whereby the balance must necessarily be made good by importing specie.

Waiving for a moment our examination of this system, let us review the progress of ideas in England in reference to the exportation of specie. The supporters of the East India Company, having successfully impugned the ancient notions, began gradually to inculcate more enlarged views of the part which the precious metals fulfilled in the circle of commerce. They at last boldly maintained that specie was nothing but a commodity, and that its circulation should be as unrestricted as that of any other commodity. The success of the Company in their commercial transactions could not but give countenance to any doctrines, which they might put forth on the subject of trade, and merchants unconnected with the Company began to distrust the ancient maxims of commerce, and to lend a ready ear to wider and more comprehensive views. "The new ideas," as Mr. Macculloch observes, "ultimately made their way into the House of Commons, and in 1663, the statutes prohibiting the exportation of foreign coin and bullion were repealed, and full liberty given to the East India Company, and to private traders, to export those articles in unlimited quantities."

Progress of ideas in England.

In regard to other economical questions, there had been great vacillations in the public policy of England during the first half of the seventeenth century, owing to the antagonism of the two first sovereigns of the Stuart dynasty and their Parliaments. The latter body was certainly the reforming body in

The Stuart Dynasty.

LECTURE II.

matters of finance; but the determination of both these monarchs to govern without the aid of Parliament led to apparent inconsistencies of conduct on both sides. James I., by virtue of his prerogative, imposed prohibitions upon various branches of the export trade, in order that merchants might buy licences from the Treasury. He granted monopolies of the import trade, in order that he might make money by the sale of letters patent. In a similar manner Charles I., by royal proclamation, prohibited the exportation of wool and all raw materials employed in woollen fabrics in 1630; restricted the transportation of corn and other agricultural produce from one county to another in 1632; confined the exportation of woollen cloths into Germany and the Netherlands in 1634 to the company of the Merchant Adventurers, contrary to the resolution of the Commons House of Parliament, which had thrown open the trade, in 1624, to all merchants indiscriminately; but licences to trade might still be purchased. So that during the reigns of both these monarchs we must consider that the relief of financial embarrassment was paramount to all other considerations of general policy. As long as the Parliament was not convoked, no one ventured to point out the evils of such a system, for the fear of the Star Chamber was before his eyes; but with the assembling of the Long Parliament in 1640, the general dissatisfaction found a vent. It is curious, however, to observe, how even in the case of the Parliament, similar considerations of finance controlled their decisions. Thus we learn from Whitlock's Memorials, that in 1643, although a petition against the monopoly of the Merchant Adventurers was referred to a committee of the House of Commons, an ordinance was passed to continue their charter in return for a loan of 30,000*l.*, to enable the Parliament to make war upon the Sovereign.

LECTURE II.

The mercantile system.

The new order of ideas, called the mercantile system, to which I have above briefly alluded, as having now come into vogue in England, obtained general acceptation in Europe in the course of the 17th century. To what writer, or to what country, the origin of this system is rightly to be referred, is still a matter of discussion. M. Blanqui, in his Histoire de l'Economie Politique, refers the invention of the theory to the Spaniards; and quotes, in illustration of the ideas of the latter part of the 16th century, a passage, which M. Ustaritz, an ex-minister of Spain, published in 1740, in his treatise on the theory and practice of commerce. "We must rigorously adopt those means which will enable us to sell to foreigners more of our productions than we buy from them of their productions: herein consists the sole secret and sole advantage of commerce." Florez-Estrada, on the other hand, a Spanish writer, considers that the Italians are entitled to claim for Antonio Serra, what was at one time held to be the merit of the discovery. No writer has been more unfortunate than Serra. His treatise seems to have been neglected or forgotten till the Abbé Galiani brought it into public notice more than a century after it was written: and now that his name is to be found in the pages of most histories of the science, he is praised by one writer, or blamed by another, for views which he really did not maintain. The object of Serra's treatise was simply and solely to persuade the Neapolitan government to allow the free exportation of gold and silver. He assumes, at the commencement of the treatise, that it is advantageous for a country to be well supplied with gold and silver; but he lays it down, that a country which has plenty of artisans who can produce the luxuries, and comforts, and necessaries of life, will never want gold and silver. Yet M. Blanqui, having alluded to Serra's

Ustaritz.

Serra.

LECTURE II. treatise, dismisses it with the observation, that its object was "to prove that gold and silver were the sole articles of wealth (et il s'attachait à prouver qu'à ses yeux les seules richesses étaient les matières d'or et d'argent)." On the contrary, Serra, having enumerated the various causes which operate to bring money into a country, proceeds to state the reasons why it should be allowed to be exported. "No merchant will export it, except with the object of making profit. He will make that profit either by buying goods to be sold again in the home, or the foreign market, or by the rate of exchange being favourable, and money being of more value in the country to which he imports it than in his own. If he buys goods for the home market, his own country has the benefit of consuming those goods, and they must be paid for somehow or other; and it is immaterial whether they are paid for with the produce of the country, or with money, not the produce of the country, but for which the produce of the country has been previously exchanged away. If he buys goods for the foreign market, he will sell them there for more money than he gave, and so the money which he brings home will exceed in amount what he exported. If the exchange on other countries is favourable, he will of course gain by exporting money thither; but repeated exports of money will in due course turn the exchange in favour of his own country; and then, for similar reasons, the merchant will import money back again." These views, if I do not here overstate them, for the style of Serra is obscure, and the idiom is antiquated, entitle him most decidedly to a place far in advance of the advocates of the mercantile system; although the principle on which the mercantile system was based did not escape his recognition.

Sully. France, on the other hand, under Sully, can hardly be considered to have reached that stage to which the mercantile system was applicable. Sully's policy was much more simple. He was content to limit French exports to agricultural produce; and his systematic opposition to the establishment of manufactures in France, excepting those of articles of the first necessity, precluded France from any varied trade with foreign countries: besides, he maintained the ancient prohibitions upon the exportation of specie, under all circumstances. It is, on the other hand, reasonable to suppose that such a system must have originated in a country which had not the command of mines; and, for this reason, Spain may be set aside. The claim of England remains, and Mr. Macculloch seems to be fairly justified in assigning to Mr. Mun the credit of having first popularised the principles, upon which was founded the celebrated doctrine of the Balance of Trade.

Mr. Mun.

"Although a kingdom," says Mr. Mun, "may be enriched by gifts received, or by purchase taken from some other nations, yet these are things uncertain and of small consideration, when they happen. The ordinary means, therefore, to increase our wealth and treasure is by foreign trade, wherein we must ever observe this rule, *to sell more to strangers yearly, than we consume of theirs in value;* for, suppose that when this kingdom is plentifully served with cloth, lead, tin, iron, fish, and other native commodities, we do yearly export the overplus to foreign countries to the value of 2,200,000*l.*, by which means we are enabled, beyond the seas, to buy and bring in foreign wares for our use and consumption to the value of 2,000,000*l.*, by this order duly kept in our trading, we may rest assured that the kingdom shall be enriched 200,000*l.*, which must be brought to us as so much treasure; because that part of our stock which is not returned to us in wares must necessarily be brought home in treasure."

LECTURE II.

According to this view, the annual excess in the money value of the exports over the imports would furnish the best evidence that a country was carrying on a prosperous foreign commerce, as such an excess could only be balanced by an importation of the precious metals, which would continually augment the real wealth of the country.

Balance of trade.

It must be admitted that this system was a step in advance of the old prohibitive system; for at all events, it allowed some interchange of commodities between countries hitherto entirely dissevered, so that its adoption could not but be beneficial to the general interests of mankind, though it might not be really advantageous in the manner supposed to particular communities. The Indian markets, for instance, received European exports by the route of the Cape of Good Hope to the value of 840,376*l.* during the first twenty years of the East India Company's trade. Upon these there must have been an immense saving of cost to the natives of India, if we look back to the prices previously required to compensate the merchant, for overcoming the obstacles of the overland route. On the other side, we find that there was imported into Europe by the same route, during that period, a quantity of Indian commodities at a cost of only 511,458*l.* 5*s.* 8*d.* in the Indian markets, which would have cost in the market of Aleppo or Alexandria no less a sum than 1,465,000*l.* 19*s.* 0*d.* The sacrifice therefore, required on the part of the consumers of such commodities, would be proportionately diminished, without any discouragement to the producers.

East Indian trade.

This modification of the old exclusive system, although it was opposed to the popular notions of the day in its mode of operation, accorded fully with them in respect of the end which it had in view; and the success which attended the commercial undertakings of the East India Company led men to suppose, that experience would sanction the general application of the principle to all foreign commerce.

In this we seem to have an instance of the very common mistake which men make, in confounding an essential condition with a cause. In order that the course of commerce between two countries should be attended by an influx of gold and silver, from one into the other country, as an exchange of equivalents is the foundation of all commerce, it is a necessary condition that one of the two countries should have imported general commodities of greater value than those which it has exported. In this case two alternatives present themselves; either it must employ the special commodities of gold or silver, as the universal merchandise, to make up the balance, or it must suspend its importations until the account is balanced by further general exports. If the former of these alternatives be adopted, the cause will be found in the circumstance, that the country has more than enough of gold or silver, and less than enough of other commodities. Overtrading, indeed, or rather, as it might with more propriety be said, over-purchasing, is the cause of one country getting into debt with another, but not of its paying its debt: the getting into debt is a circumstance necessary as a condition precedent to a country paying its debt, but it has no tendency to produce such a result. Public men, however, were led to suppose that the more that they raised impediments to the importation of foreign commodities, and gave encouragement to the exportation of their own goods, the more were they creating causes to make specie flow into their own country.

Thus there was an enactment in the reign of Edward III. (A. D. 1342) which ordained that "Whoso transporteth wool out of the realm shall bring in for every pack carried forth four nobles,

Edward III.

LECTURE II.

(1*l.* 6*s.* 8*d.*) in bullion, and so for all merchandise, according to the rate of the pack." Now the chief export trade of England in wool at this time was to Flanders, and Flanders had not more than enough of gold and silver; so the Duke of Brabant issued a prohibition against the exportation of gold and silver from Flanders, and the Commons of England found themselves obliged, in 1347, A. D., to petition the Crown for a repeal of the very statute, which had been passed five years before at their own request. Here then was an instance where it was attempted to cause gold and silver to flow into England by exporting her wool to Flanders. Now the importation of English wool into Flanders would most probably have been a necessary condition for the importation of Flemish bullion into England; but an adequate cause was wanting why Flanders should part with her gold and silver, and consequently the result anticipated by the Commons of England did not ensue. An excess of general exports over imports is thus not alone sufficient to account for an influx of bullion: bullion must be cheaper in other countries, or the alternative of a suspension of commerce will be adopted.

Influx of specie.

The mercantile system possessed one decided superiority over the old exclusive system; it had something positive about it as distinguished from the negative character of the latter. Whilst the exclusive system tended to check productive industry, the mercantile system tended in a certain manner to stimulate it. Whilst the former sought to prevent the exportation of gold and silver, the latter sought to promote its importation. Hence it was unavoidably calculated to encourage the spirit of tampering regulation, which under the garb of political sagacity loves to interfere in matters which should be left to individual discretion. It has thus commended itself

LECTURE II.

Evils of mercantile system.

to the notice of statesmen, and the most disastrous consequences to the welfare of nations have thereupon ensued. Attaching a peculiar value to the precious metals, and professing to ensure an abundance of them to the state which should listen to its suggestions, it has led nations to consider the welfare of their neighbours to be incompatible with their own, as all cannot have an increased share in a limited quantity of wealth. Hence has originated the mutual desire to hurt and impoverish one another: hence that commercial jealousy, the immediate or remote cause of most of the wars of later times. It is this system, which has multiplied obstacles to international communication, and kept on foot armies of custom-house officers, to be paid from the fruits of productive industry for the express purpose, not of facilitating, but of impeding its operations. It is this system, which, as M. Say has well observed, has prompted statesmen to employ force or stratagem to obtain from the fears or ignorance of neighbouring nations what they deemed to be advantageous treaties of commerce, in which, however, the dupers have been not unfrequently duped. It is this system, which regards colonies merely in the light of useful dependencies to the mother country, for the purpose of enabling her to have a monopoly of new markets, and of securing for her merchants a succession of new customers.

But in admitting these as *results*, we must not consider them to be, strictly speaking, the *effects* of the system, but of causes which were in active operation long prior to the system; namely, erroneous notions as to the nature of wealth, and the conditions of value, as well as the principle of exchanges. As long as men believed that gold and silver were the sole articles of wealth, that value and utility were identical, and, therefore, that an article of necessary use was more valuable than a luxury, and that a commercial exchange could never benefit both parties to it equally, but that the one party invariably gained something at the expense of the other, the results, which followed the general adoption of the mercantile system, would have attended any other system based on such fundamental errors. There might have been some little modification in the form of the results; but in whatever form the system might have been cast, it would have been equally prejudicial to the interests of nations.

Of these fundamental errors, the earliest that was assailed, as we have already observed, was the inveterate notion respecting the nature of wealth, that it consisted exclusively of gold and silver. We have seen that the English Parliament in 1663 permitted the free exportation of bullion, when it threw open the trade to India, and from this time bullion seems to have been regarded in England as a commodity. Still the exportation of it was vigorously contested. Thus in a debate in the House of Commons in 1680, on a petition being presented from the company of silk weavers against the importation of Indian silks, as destructive to their branch of manufactures, it was contended by one member (Mr. John Basset) "that the people in India are such slaves as to work for less than a penny a day, whereas ours here will not work for less than a shilling; and they have all materials also very reasonable, and are thereby enabled to make their goods so cheap, as it will be impossible for our people here to contend with them. And, therefore, because the said trade hath abundantly increased of late years, that we may not enrich the Indians, and impoverish our own people, I humbly move you that this petition may be referred to some Committee that may take particular care of it."

Free exportation of bullion.

Debate in House of Commons A. D. 1680.

The next speaker (Mr. John Parkhurst) maintained

"that the manufactures of this country were discouraged because Indian goods hindered the expense of our own woollen goods by serving instead of them here, and also by hindering the consumption of them in other parts too, to which we export them, and by obstructing the expense of linen and silks, which we formerly purchased from our neighbour nations in return of our manufactures. For when that mutual conveniency of taking off their goods in return of ours failed, it is found by experience that our trade in manufactures is failed also."

* * * * * * *

"But this," he continues, "is not all. This trade is carried on by the exportation of 5 or 600,000*l.* per annum in bullion, which is so useful a commodity as ought not to be exported in so great a quantity, especially seeing its exportation hath increased in some years from 200,000*l.* to 600,000*l.* per annum. For it may increase to millions, to the discouragement of the exportation of the products of our country, upon which the maintenance of our poor and rent of land depends; whereas by the exportation of so much bullion no immediate advantage redounds to the nation; and though it is usually affirmed, that the trade brings back as much money as it exports, yet, upon an inquiry, it will be found a mistake. And I think every nation, but especially this, which is so well stored with other commodities for trade, ought to be very jealous of a trade carried on by the exportation of our gold and silver, and to be very careful how to allow it, it being dangerous to make that which is the standard of trade merchandise itself."

A third speaker (Mr. William Love), to much the same purport, argued, "that the East India trade will in time ruin a great part of our manufactures, if not prevented. For the cheapness of wages

LECTURE II.

and materials in the Indies must enable the Indians to afford their manufactured goods cheaper than any we can make here, and, therefore, it is probable, the trade will increase prodigiously, which may be a good motive for you to take into your consideration that part of it, in which the consumption of our manufactures is concerned. They have already spoiled the Italian and Flanders trade with their silks and calicoes; now they will endeavour to spoil the Turkish trade, by bringing abundance of raw silk from the Indies; so that ere long we shall have no need of having silk from Turkey; and if not, I am sure we shall not be able to send any cloths or other goods there."

This petition was referred to the Grand Committee for Trade.

Arguments against East India Company.

Let us now examine from the eminence on which we stand in the nineteenth century, the nature of the arguments arrayed on this occasion against the East India Company. It may be admitted that the private interests of the Turkey Company, which the last speaker evidently represented, were certainly jeopardised by the trade of the East India Company; but as far as the English people were concerned, as consumers of silk goods, it was not for their interests that the merchant should continue to buy in the dearer market of Turkey what he could procure in abundance in the cheaper market of India.

Turkey Company.

We, i. e., the Turkey Company, he might have said, shall be undersold if the people of England allow the East India Company to trade as freely as it does at present; but let it be remembered, that if this happens, the clothiers will lose an excellent market, which we provide for them.

In other words, England cannot maintain her trade in the markets of both India and Turkey; and it is better for her to deal in the dearer markets of Turkey, where she will get rid of a greater quantity of cloth, than in the cheaper markets of India, where she will get rid of less in exchange for the same quantity of silk; otherwise the clothiers will suffer, because the demand for cloth would not be so great: that is, it is better for England to give away a quantity of cloth without an equivalent, than to consume it at home, and be none the poorer, inasmuch as the merchant in both cases would bring back the same amount of silk.

Again, both the first and last speaker maintained that English fabrics could not compete with Indian goods, because wages were lower and raw material cheaper in India; and that if the English persisted in buying in the cheapest market, they would impoverish themselves and enrich the Indians.

One speaker only lays stress upon the exportation of bullion; and although he admits it to be a commodity, and that it may possibly find its way back, yet he urges that we can spare plenty of other commodities (just as if other nations must perforce take what we choose to send to them), and the allowing bullion to be merchandise will confound men's notions of value, as there would then be no fixed measure of value.

It will be seen that in the place of the old prejudices against the exportation of specie, a new prejudice against the importation of foreign products was growing up on the ground of their discouraging domestic manufactures; in other words, the circle of incomplete truths was revolving, and before the mercantile system had as yet reached its zenith, the dawn of the protective system was discernible.

Sir Josiah Child.

The resolution of the House of Commons on this occasion was not allowed to pass unnoticed. Sir Josiah Child, who on previous occasions had stood forward as the champion of the East India Company, published a treatise in the following year, in answer to most of the arguments of the supporters of the

LECTURE II. petition. The Turkey merchants had ventured to assert, that the bringing in of so much silk, and so cheap, was a public nuisance, and destroyed their trade, which depended wholly on the woollen manufacture, whereas the East India Company send out little manufacture and much bullion.

To which he answers, "It is strange, if making a material cheap, that is to be manufactured at home, or re-exported to foreign countries, should be the public damage to a country;" but "the question is not now which company sends out most woollen manufactures, but which is most profitable to the nation. Now the East India Company, by re-exporting to foreign countries above two-fifths of the commodities imported from India, brings back from those countries more than treble the bullion which was first exported to India: again, it saves the kingdom at least 500,000*l.* per annum, in respect of the prices of East India commodities which England consumes, whilst, as a matter of fact, there is a quicker vent and export of woollen manufactures than ever was remembered, and the manufacture of silk, resulting from our import trade, has furnished already employment for about 40,000 families. In addition, many articles which are now exported directly to India, and find a ready demand in the markets there, would not be exported at all, if we left the trade in the hands of the Dutch, as we know that they exclude English manufactures from their dealings with the Japanese."

So far Sir J. Child met directly the arguments of his opponents by calling in the evidence of a favourable balance of trade; but to their further objection, "that besides raw silk, the Company imports wrought silk, to the prejudice of the silk manufacture of England," he replied, "that the objection lay as much or more against all other wrought silks imported into

England from Italy, Holland, or any other part of the world. 2. That the class of silk goods brought in were such as were not usually made in England, but imported from Europe; so that this importation works upon our neighbours, preserves the balance of trade, and consequently increases the capital of our nation. 3. That the mass of silk goods imported were shipped again for the continent of Europe.

The third argument might be thought to be at variance with the second one. However, Sir Josiah no doubt felt that the principles upon which the mercantile system was based, would not furnish him with a complete answer to this objection; and, therefore, before using it, as a matter of courtesy to his adversaries, he appealed to their own experience, which had never impugned the advantage of an analogous trade between England and Europe.

The British Merchant.

It might perhaps be questioned whether Sir Josiah Child at this time adhered to the principles of the mercantile system, further than as weapons against the adversaries of the East India Company, when occasion required, for in a pamphlet published in the same year by Φιλόπατρις, which "The British Merchant" says was either written, or superintended by Sir Josiah, it is most explicitly maintained, that "Silver and gold coined or uncoined, though they are used for a measure of all other things, are no less a commodity than wine, cloth, stuff, &c., and may in many cases be exported, as much to national advantage as any other commodity, and that no nation ever was or will be considerable that prohibits the exportation of bullion."

It was, however, perfectly possible for a writer at this period to regard bullion as a commodity; yet to attach superior importance to it above other commodities from its durability and other natural qualities, and so to support heartily the doctrine of the balance

LECTURE II.

Sir W. Petty.

of trade, as the safest criterion of a nation's progress in wealth. Thus we find Sir W. Petty giving, in 1667, a clear exposition of the conditions of value in his work on "Taxes and Contributions;" yet in 1691 maintaining, in his "Political Arithmetic," the advantage of foreign trade, from its bringing in not wealth at large, but particularly abundance of silver, gold, and jewels, which are not perishable nor so mutable as other commodities, but are wealth at all times and all places; whereas abundance of wine, corn, fowls, flesh, &c., are riches but *hic et nunc;* so as the raising of such commodities, and the following of such trade, which does store the country with gold, silver, jewels, &c., is profitable before others. But the labour of seamen, and the freight of ships, is always of the nature of an exported commodity, the overplus whereof, above what is imported, brings home money, &c.

It will be better perhaps to refrain from entering on the question of value in this lecture, as the analysis of it was only commenced towards the latter part of the seventeenth century, and it will deserve more than a cursory notice. The great practical result of the conflict of ideas in the seventeenth century was the establishment of the doctrine that gold and silver were commodities, and were not exclusively articles of wealth; but the question remained still undetermined, viz. under what conditions a commodity like the precious metals became the measure of the value of other commodities — in fact, what were the constituent elements of value?

Progress of ideas in the 17th century.

In other respects, the distance was still very great, which separated the seventeenth from the nineteenth century. It was then believed that the precious metals passed from one country to another as money, for the payment of balances; it is now understood that they are transferred as commodities, according as

Distance from the 19th century.

their market value rises or falls in different countries. It was then believed that you could sell your own commodities to foreign nations without purchasing any of their goods; it is now understood that every nation must discharge its debts with the produce of its own soil and labour: it was then believed that the excess of the value of exports over imports was the best evidence of a prosperous commerce with other nations; it is now understood that a profitable trade with foreign countries is shown by the superior value of the goods brought home as compared with the commodities sent abroad : it was then believed that gold and silver were the most profitable articles of importation; it is now understood, that it is immaterial what kinds of commodities are imported, provided they are of equal value: it was then believed that the gain of one nation was the loss of another; it is now understood that "an exchange of equivalents is the foundation of all commerce, from the simple barter of the untutored Indian to the most complicated and extensive operations of the London merchant."

LECTURE III.

LECTURE III.

THE antagonism and rivalry of the Chartered Trading Companies, established during the reign of Elizabeth, had materially contributed to the great progress towards sounder opinions, which England had made during the seventeenth century, and which was alluded to in the previous Lecture; whilst the termination of the struggle between the House of Stuart and the Commons House of Parliament, in favour of the latter body, led at once to the removal of many practical obstacles in the way of further advancement. In France, on the other hand, after the death of Henri IV., and the retirement of Sully from public affairs, the ancient elements of disorder, which the firm hand of that minister had restrained, resumed their disastrous influence, and the good effects of his wise administration were obliterated within a brief interval, in the struggle which soon ensued between the crown and the great nobles. The Wars of the Roses had fortunately released England from the trammels of feudalism; the Wars of the League, however, had not accomplished this desirable result for France, inasmuch as the accession of Henri IV. had effected a compromise, rather than a conclusion of the conflict, and with the death of that sovereign it recommenced. It was on this, the last occasion, indeed, with the exception of the more memorable one of the year 1789, that the Crown of France called in the aid of the third estate (tiers état) of the kingdom, and in 1614, a meeting of the States General was convoked. The constitution, however, of this body was very different from that of the English Parlia-

Disorders in France after death of Henri IV.

ment, and the two privileged chambers of the nobles, and the clergy respectively, could hardly be expected to assent to the reforms which were suggested by the third estate, upon which, almost exclusively, the public burdens pressed; and the third estate in France could not venture to speak with the same boldness, as it had not the same privileges, with the Commons in England. Nothing, therefore, was accomplished on this occasion, and the successive administrations of Richelieu and Mazarin were too anxiously occupied with foreign and domestic warfare, to admit of their attention being directed to the interests of peace. With the termination of the quarrels of the Fronde, the struggle for supremacy between the Crown and the Nobles may be considered to have concluded, and with the death of Mazarin in 1661, the monarchy in France once more resumed, in the person of Louis XIV., its long abandoned duty of governing the country.

Accession of Louis XIV.

A new era now dawned upon French industry. Mazarin's last act had been to recommend to the confidence of Louis XIV. a man, whose name has since been identified with a system, and whose spirit has apparently never ceased to influence the councils of his country. Colbert, the intendant of the late minister, brought with him into the king's service the habits of a laborious and plodding man of business, to use Adam Smith's own words, combined with great integrity and great clearness of intellect. But the very ability which fitted him so well for the task of introducing order into the collection and expenditure of the public revenue, was likely to engender a spirit of system, and a disposition to apply its rules to other subjects than those of finance. Sismondi, in his *Histoire des Français*, c. xxviii. says, that in the great encouragement which Colbert gave to manufactures and commerce, he merely executed the measures which his predecessor, Fouquet, had designed. It is

Colbert's administration.

LECTURE III.

immaterial whether the whole credit be due to Colbert or not, as most assuredly the execution of a great political measure has always been deemed a more trying test of statesmanship than the conception of it.

His predilection for manufactures and commerce.

After having re-established order in the public finances, Colbert directed his attention to the sources of revenue. His views, in regard to the best mode of developing the national resources, were diametrically opposed to the previous system of Sully. As the grandson of a wool-merchant at Rheims, Colbert might be expected to have a bias in favour of the pursuits of his ancestor, and accordingly we find his ruling idea to have been, that the promotion of agriculture might justly be made subordinate to the encouragement of manufactures and commerce: that the manufacturer and merchant were more efficient pioneers of national wealth than the cultivator of the soil; and that the welfare of the two former classes would entail, as a necessary consequence, the prosperity of the latter, by increasing the demand, in the home market, for agricultural produce. Having, therefore, relieved the cultivator of the soil from a portion of the oppressive burden of direct taxes, which since Sully's time had been once more recklessly heaped upon him, Colbert did not hesitate to prohibit the exportation of corn. In this respect his discernment of the connexion between cause and effect was not so clear as that which Sully had shown. The latter had fully appreciated the principle, that if we would encourage production, we must open outlets for produce. Colbert, on the other hand, seems not to have formed a correct estimate of the extent to which, from the nature of the relations between supply and demand, production would be discouraged by closing up the existing outlets for produce, and to have overlooked the fact, that the cost of production would be increased with every diminution in the quantity of the produce.

Exportation of corn prohibited.

We learn from Forbonnais, that since Sully's administration, the price of wheat in France had now more than doubled; but at the same time the burdens upon the cultivator had been more than doubled. In addition, the troubled state of the country, during the administration of the two cardinals, must have interfered with the pursuits of agriculture; so that we should not be surprised to find that the supply of the home market occasionally fell short of the demand. Instead, however, of attributing the rise in the price of corn to the circumstances just alluded to, which seem quite sufficient to account for it, since most assuredly had there not been some such obstacles in the way, the agriculturists would have readily met the growing demand with increased supplies, where the price was apparently highly remunerative; the consumers at once referred the occasional dearths of corn to the incautious policy of Sully in according freedom to commerce in grain, and raised their voice against allowing any longer the exportation of corn. Colbert had thus the popular feeling in favour of his regulations, and he may probably have conceived that the reduction which he had made in the direct burdens upon agriculture was altogether a boon to the producers, and would enable agricultural industry to maintain its ground against a temporary depression of prices. In the mean time, the diminished cost of maintenance would encourage the growth of a manufacturing population, and its increasing consumption of agricultural produce would in time replace the extinguished demand of the foreign consumer.

The pursuits in which Colbert had been trained, disposed him to overlook the operation of disturbing causes, for which a statesman, no less than an engineer, must make allowances. Accustomed to superintend the department of a public office, and to see his own

LECTURE III.

well-adjusted system of checks and counter-checks work with admirable precision, he conceived it possible to regulate the industry of a great nation upon a similar model. But his first experiment with agriculture signally failed. The immediate effect of his measures was, that the price of wheat fell one half. This he had most probably foreseen; but he could not have contemplated the consequences which ensued upon this great reduction of price; namely, that one half the land would be immediately put out of cultivation, and that the ultimate result would be a return of the very dearth, which his measures were intended to counteract, and with that dearth again an increase in the cost of food for the manufacturer.

Effects upon Tillage.

"What were the effects," writes Forbonnais, i. p. 293., "of this unwise policy? Tillage was everywhere reduced, but more especially on the indifferent or bad soils, which required a considerable outlay. Marsh lands remained undrained, and it seemed useless to put the plough into fresh land, upon a very simple calculation. The highest price, which the cultivator could expect to obtain for his produce, would not compensate him for the expense of cultivation."

Such was the result of tampering with commercial outlets. Similar results have invariably attended similar experiments. Thus, confining our attention to France, we find, in 1714, the exportation of turpentine and pitch prohibited, upon which the cultivation of the pine tree was abandoned in the district of the Landes, and the ruin of the population was only averted by the trade being again made free. The cultivation of the teazle, likewise, the use of which in manufactures is well known, had for a similar reason been abandoned; but it was once more revived upon the substitution of a moderate export duty in lieu of the attempted prohibition.

Colbert's next measure was to abolish or reduce the transit duties on the rivers and great roads, and thereby facilitate the internal commerce of the country. He then applied himself to his favourite task, the encouragement of the manufacturing industry of France. With this object he combined under one system the custom duties, which had hitherto been farmed out in five departments, and then drew up his tariff of 1664. The object of this tariff was to promote, by a reduction of duties, the exportation of French raw materials and manufactured goods, and the importation of such foreign raw materials as were needed for French manufactures, but to discourage by heavy duties the importation of foreign manufactured goods. The combination of these two results constituted the distinguishing feature of Colbertism, according to the friends of the system. The scale of duties was at first comparatively moderate, but within three years they were raised enormously, and the amended tariff of 1667 was equivalent to a declaration of war against the Dutch. Actual hostilities, however, were deferred for a short time, whilst retaliatory measures of exclusion were adopted by the Dutch against the wines and brandies and manufactured goods of France; but after a series of ineffectual negotiations, war ensued, and it was not until the peace of Nimeguen, in 1678, that France allowed some modifications to be introduced into the later tariff.

Tariff of 1664.

Peace of Nimeguen in 1678.

"It was about the same time," observes Adam Smith, "that the French and English began mutually to oppress each other's industry by the like duties and prohibitions, of which the French, however, seem to have set the first example." He might have gone back as far as 1649, when the King of France having prohibited all trade with England, the House of Commons prohibited in return the importation of wine, wool, or silk, from France.

"There may be good policy," says the same author, "in retaliations of this kind, when there is a proba-

LECTURE III. bility that they will procure the repeal of the high duties on prohibitions complained of. When there is no probability that any such repeal can be procured, it seems a bad method of compensating the injury done to certain classes of our people, to do another injury ourselves, not only to those classes, but to almost all the other classes of them. When our neighbours prohibit some manufacture of ours, we generally prohibit, not only the same, for that alone would seldom affect them considerably, but some other manufacture of theirs. This may no doubt give encouragement to some particular class of workmen among ourselves, and by excluding some of their rivals, may enable them to raise their prices in the home market. Those workmen, however, who suffered by our neighbour's prohibition, will not be benefited by ours. On the contrary, they and almost all the other classes of our citizens, will thereby be obliged to pay dearer than before for certain goods. Every such law, therefore, imposes a real tax upon the whole country, not in favour of that particular class of workmen who were injured by our neighbour's prohibition, but of some other class."

M. Blanqui, in discussing the modifications which the system of Colbert underwent after the peace of Nimeguen, observes, "that the prodigious development of the manufacturing interest of France under the encouragement which it afforded to them, has contributed more than any thing else to propagate the mischievous doctrine of the natural enmity of manufacturing nations." Hence have originated the senseless, though proverbial, expressions of "of becoming tributary to the foreigner," "allowing our markets to be invaded by foreign merchandize," "letting our gold be taken from us," and such like. These, and similar metaphorical phrases, with which we are still familiar in the 19th century, are gradually losing their influence over the imagination of men. They are an instance of that subtle abuse of language by which the whole question is assumed in the selection of the nomenclature, and it would be idle to discuss the wisdom or folly of Colbert's system, if its supporters are to be allowed, without question, the use of the vocabulary which they have invented.

Vocabulary of Colbertism.

Thus, if we were discussing the question, whether the use of foreign products was advantageous or prejudicial to a nation, the Colbertist would at once assert it to be prejudicial to a country, that it should pay *tribute* to foreigners; and thus the introduction of the word *tribute* would at once settle the question, unless we dispute the application of it to the relations of commerce. Let us see then what the real fact is, which the word *tribute* is employed to denote. Let us suppose France to have purchased a thousand pieces of cotton goods from England, and to have given in exchange 10,000 francs in silver or wines. According to the language which we have been discussing, the Colbertists would declare that France had paid tribute to England for the cotton. But England has not received the 10,000 francs for nothing, as men do who receive tribute, but has given 1000 pieces of cotton in exchange for 10,000 francs in silver or wines. England has thus paid a tribute of cotton goods to France for her silver or wines, as the case may be. But this reciprocal payment of tribute on both sides is equivalent to a receipt of tribute on neither side. In other words, there has been no payment of tribute at all, in the proper sense of the term, which signifies a gratuitous offering, but there has been simply an exchange of produce for mutual convenience. The term *tribute* may probably have crept into use at a very early period of the mercantile system, when bullion had not yet come to be regarded as a commodity, and when the exchanging it for foreign

LECTURE III.

commodities might with some plausibility be represented as equivalent to the payment of tribute.

Encouragement of commerce.

The next great object of Colbert was to devise measures for the revival of commerce, and the establishment of a mercantile marine. Of the 20,000 vessels which were at this time supposed to be employed in the general commerce of the civilized world, it was computed that the Dutch alone possessed from 15,000 to 16,000, and the French not more than 500 or 600. Colbert applied the system of bounties to navigation, as he had already done to manufactures. In a memoir presented to the king in 1681, which Forbonnais has preserved, the minister's views in respect of the policy of bounties are made to accord with those of the supporters of the mercantile system. "The principal point in finance," he writes, "consists, according to my notion, in employing every year at least 100,000 francs, and whenever it should be possible, at least 500,000 francs, in gratuities to those who carry on maritime commerce, who form new companies, and introduce new manufactures: because these means serve to maintain and preserve money within the realm, to make that which goes out of the country return, and to keep foreign states always deficiently supplied with money." *

In furtherance of the same object, he permitted the free exportation of gold and silver; he abolished the Droit d'Aubaine at Marseilles, in order that opulent foreign merchants engaged in the Levant trade might be induced to settle there; and by an edict in 1669, the king declared the occupations of commerce to be an honourable profession, compatible with nobility. Free ports were now established where foreign mer-

* Le principal point des finances consiste, selon moi, à employer tous les ans au moins cent mille livres, et lorsqu'il sera possible, au moins cent mille écus pour gratifier ceux qui font le commerce de mer, qui entreprennent de nouvelles compagnies, de nouvelles manufactures; parceque ces moyens servent à maintenir et conserver l'argent dans le royaume, à faire revenir celui qui en sort, et à tenir toujours les états étrangers dans la nécessité et le besoin d'argent où ils sont. —Vol. i. p. 529.

chandise might be deposited, and whence it might be re-exported free of duty; and the transit dues on foreign products passing overland through France were reduced. The canal of Languedoc was now projected to unite the Mediterranean with the Atlantic; and finally, the Code of Commerce, known as L'Ordonnance de la Marine, was drawn up in 1672. These were all admirable measures, consistent with sound principles, and their ultimate results were in harmony with their immediate effects.

L'Ordonnance de la Marine.

It was observed in the review of Antonio Serra's treatise in the first lecture, that that writer, in his classification of the causes which make gold and silver to be plentiful in any country, gives a preference to the common cause of *an abundance of skilful artisans* over the peculiar cause of *an extraordinary fertility of soil:* on the grounds that the operations of the manufacturer are not dependent upon the seasons, and are capable of being carried on to an unlimited extent, and that his produce finds access to a greater number of markets, and is in more varied demand. These are very different notions from those which the supporters of Colbertism put forward, who contended that the profits upon manufactures were fifty fold or a hundred fold greater than those of agricultural industry, and that therefore a manufacturing country, if it can only contrive to secure markets for its manufactures, must make much more rapid strides in wealth than an agricultural country. These notions were directly combatted by Mengotti, in his treatise on ('Il Colbertismo') Colbertism, to which in 1792 the prize was awarded by the Royal Agricultural Society of Florence. He contended therein "that the value of a piece of cloth is determined by precisely the same considerations as the value of a sack of wool. Thus, the price of a piece of cloth is composed of the price of the raw materials, and the price of the corn,

Mengotti. Il Colbertismo.

LECTURE III. the wine, the oil, the meat, the fruit, and other things which have been consumed by the scourer, the carder, the spinner, the dyer, the weaver, and the rest who have taken any part in the preparation of the cloth. The prices of all these commodities heaped up one upon another, like stratum upon stratum, will form the value of the manufactured article. The wool, itself, has not increased in value, as some believe, but has merely served as a nucleus round which other values have been accumulated, until at last the whole value is concentrated in one object, the price of which is but the sum of all the expenses of the workmen which has been added on day by day, until the completion of the work. Consequently, the price of the cloth is only the aggregate of many values, which already existed in their own peculiar and separate forms, and now are combined in the manufactured article, and under a different form.

"Instead, however, of the cloth being exported, let us suppose that the wool, the corn, the oil, the wine, the fuel, and the other articles, which would have been consumed by the manufacturer, have been exported. The return to the nation will be nearly of the same value. I say, nearly so, since the manufacturer does not create new values, which did not before exist, but only adds to the first value of the raw material, a second value of the bread, a third of the meat, a fourth of the fruit; and so from day to day, by repeated additions of expenditure upon expenditure, and of consumption upon consumption, he at last succeeds in combining in one form the value of the linen, or the stuff, or the jewellery, or the porcelain, or whatever the manufactured article may be. But during this process, the nation loses on the one hand the value which it gains on the other, and in proportion as a piece of cloth or embroidery advances towards completion, the mass of products continues to diminish. At the very moment, therefore, that we sell to foreigners a certain portion of our manufactures, we sell to them in a compendious form and under a different aspect, our raw produce; and when a ship sails from our shores with a rich cargo of linen, and stuffs, and cloths, and crapes, and mirrors, we may rest assured that we are witnessing the departure of our grapes and our grain, our milk and our butter, our fruits and our vegetables; in short, of the various products of our soil encased as it were in a shell, and converted into the form of manufactures. The advantage of this change is very great, since, by compressing into a narrower space the raw products of the soil, which are often heavy and bulky, we render the transport of them less expensive, and the saving of this expense becomes to us a source of profit. But this falls very far short of the enormous multiplication of value which has been attributed to manufactures."

Mengotti's theory of value.

It will be hardly necessary to observe that Mengotti's own theory of value is in its turn essentially defective, though his dissertation is interesting, and will repay the perusal of it. The term value is apparently used in the above passages to denote the original cost of a commodity, or what Adam Smith distinguishes as its natural price, in which average profits are included. In this sense it is obvious, that the value of manufactured goods is determined by no different considerations from those, which regulate the value of agricultural produce. In the case, therefore, of equal values, there cannot be more profit upon manufactured articles, than upon raw materials. If, however, the profits of the manufacturer, as a fact, exceed in the aggregate the profits of the agriculturist, it is not by reason that the mode in which the industry of the former is employed, creates a superior kind of value to that which results from the industry of the latter, but by reason that the manufacturer has a wider field for

LECTURE III.

the operations of his industry, and has consequently greater opportunities of making profit by the employment of a large capital.

Colbert's encouragement of manufactures.

Let us now consider briefly the mode, in which Colbert's measures for the encouragement of manufacturing industry must have affected the growth of national wealth in France. He had prohibited the exportation of corn in order that the manufacturer should have provisions cheap. The result, as we have already seen, was, that half the arable land in France was thrown out of cultivation. In that proportion then there was a diminution in the amount of national wealth, as far as agricultural produce was one of the elements of it. But to compensate for this loss, France was no longer *tributary* to foreigners for manufactured goods: these were now made at home; and the value which France had hitherto been obliged to part with to other countries in exchange for them was saved to the nation, to which was to be added the value which France would receive in return for such of her manufactures as were exported.

The aggregate of these two values, namely, the value saved, and the value created by reason of France becoming a manufacturing country, it was contended, would more than counterbalance the value lost by reason of France ceasing to receive foreign commodities in exchange for her agricultural produce.

In regard, then, first of all, to the value saved by France ceasing to pay for foreign manufactured goods, it is obvious that France under the previous system, where gold and silver were not allowed to be exported, obtained those goods either directly or indirectly in exchange for a portion of her agricultural produce. But that portion of her agricultural produce which ceased to be exported, ceased also to be raised, inasmuch as the former demand for it no longer existed.

France, therefore, gained nothing by this arrangement: on the contrary, the supposed saving was a clear loss to her, for she had no more agricultural produce than before, for her own consumption; and, in addition, she had lost the enjoyment of so much foreign manufactured produce.

But the gains from her domestic manufactures, it may be supposed, more than made up for this loss. If, indeed, through the natural advantages of climate, water, mineral wealth, &c. France was enabled to produce at home manufactured goods at a less cost of labour and capital, than the agricultural produce which she had previously exchanged away for foreign manufactures, she would evidently be a gainer by the alteration. She would both save the cost of what she herself consumed, and gain by the profit of the sale of her goods in the foreign market, as she would be able to undersell other nations. But if this system of manufactures was kept alive by bounties and drawbacks, without which the manufacturer could not bring his goods into the market at a price at which he could find purchasers, the state would be losing whilst the position of the manufacturer himself might be stationary; for the state would be taking money out of the pocket of the nation to enable the manufacturer to continue working at a loss. The state would be likewise encouraging the manufacturer to send goods into the foreign market to be sold at less than their cost of production; and by every transaction between the French manufacturer, to whom the state gave a bounty, and the foreign consumer, the French nation would part with a certain amount of produce without an equivalent, and would so far be the poorer. France would thus be really tributary to the foreigner, at the moment when she conceived herself to be levying a tribute.

As far, then, as the export of manufactures was concerned, the bounty upon production would evidently Bounties.

LECTURE III.

operate in the same way as a bounty upon exportation. By means of this bounty the French manufacturer would be enabled to sell his goods as cheap, or cheaper than his rivals in the foreign market. A greater quantity would thus be exported, and the balance of trade, according to the views of those who supported the mercantile system, would be turned more in favour of France. France could not of course give her workmen a monopoly of the foreign market, nor force foreigners to buy her goods; but in order to promote their consumption, she might pay them for buying them; in other words, pay her manufacturers to let foreigners have the articles at less than the cost price.

"Those trades only require bounties," says Adam Smith, "in which the merchant is obliged to sell his goods for a price which does not replace to him his capital, together with the ordinary profit, or in which he is obliged to sell them for less than it really costs him to send them to market. The bounty is given in order to make up this loss, and to encourage him to continue, or perhaps to begin, a trade of which the expense is supposed to be greater than the returns, of which every operation eats up a part of the capital employed in it, and which is of such a nature, that if all other trades resembled it, there would soon be no capital left in the country."

Prejudicial to national wealth.

"The trades, it is to be observed, which are carried on by means of bounties, are the only ones which can be carried on between two nations for any considerable time together, in such a manner as that one of them shall always and regularly lose, or sell its goods for less than it really cost to send them to market. But if the bounty did not repay to the merchant what he would otherwise lose upon the price of his goods, his own interest would soon oblige him to employ his stock in another way, or to find a trade in which the price of the goods would replace to him, with the ordinary profit, the capital employed in sending them to the market. The effect of bounties, like that of all the other expedients of the mercantile system, can only be to force the trade of a country into a channel much less advantageous than that in which it would naturally run of its own accord."

It will be seen then that Colbertism, embodied as the peculiarities of the system are considered to have been in the tariff of 1667, was based upon two distinct errors; the one connected with the balance of trade, the other with the profit of manufactures. That France should exhibit signs of revived prosperity and augmented wealth, under the administration of Colbert, was to be attributed to similar causes to those which had operated under the system of Sully; viz., the re-establishment of order in the finances of the country, and the removal of various obstacles which impeded the operations of certain branches of industry. Sully, as we have seen, had freed agriculture from its fetters; but he forged new chains for manufacturing industry and commerce. Colbert set the two latter branches free; but he reimposed upon agricultural industry its ancient shackles. France throve in spite of the restrictions of Sully, not by virtue of them: in a similar way she prospered under Colbert's system; but it was in spite of its peculiarities.

Causes of revived prosperity in France.

In the very year in which Colbert's revised tariff of 1667 was put forth, we find a writer in England, Sir W. Petty, taking the lead in impugning the current notions respecting value, and laying down, in a clear and original manner, the principle upon which price is regulated. In his treatise on Taxes and Contributions, he says, "If a man bring to London an ounce of silver out of the earth in Peru, in the same time that he can produce a bushel of corn, the one is the natural price of the other: now, if by reason of

Sir W. Petty on value.

LECTURE III. new and more easy mines, a man can get two ounces of silver as easily as formerly he did one, then corn will be as cheap at ten shillings the bushel as it was before at five shillings, cæteris paribus."

Again, " Let a hundred men work ten years upon corn, and the same number of men the same time upon silver: I say, that the net proceed of the silver is the price of the whole net proceed of the corn, and like parts of the one the price of like parts of the other."

These views were very different from those entertained by the author of the Brief Conceipte of English policy nearly a century before, where he says, " I think not so little as a hundred thousand pounds a year is fetched of our treasure, for things of *no value* of themselves, but only for the labour of the workers of the same, which are set a work all on our charges."

As long as the utility and value of a commodity were confounded, a false theory of exchanges could not but prevail, and the true principles of commerce were inevitably kept out of sight. Each nation at one time supposed its own exports to be necessaries; whereas it held its neighbour's exports to be superfluities: so that commerce with foreign nations was but a continued repetition of losing exchanges, by the barter of highly useful commodities for trifles, which might easily be dispensed with.

Prevalent error as to value.

We cannot therefore be surprised that, as long as men were ignorant of the fundamental doctrine, that *the value* of all commodities was determined by one and the same consideration, they should be ignorant that commerce might consist in the exchange of equivalents, and should overlook the fact that it would be impossible for commerce to be carried on for any length of time, if one party always surrendered up a certain amount of value in the exchange. " It were better," says a writer in the 16th century, " for us to pay more to our own countrymen for these wares, than to strangers less; for how little gains so ever goeth over, it is lost to us clear, but how much soever the gain is that goeth from us to another, it is all saved within the realm."

It is here evidently supposed that the greater value of the manufactured article, as compared with the raw material, was so much gain to the workman, and so much loss to the consumer who purchased it from him, and that the loss would be saved to the nation by an interchange of products in the home market; whilst, if the consumer became a customer in the foreign market, that loss must be incurred. There is the same confusion in this notion, as in the idea, that the profit on manufactures was much greater than that on agricultural occupations: as if profits in any one branch of industry can be maintained at a higher rate than in others, except there be a monopoly, or some artificial obstacle exist to prevent capital and labour flowing into their natural channels.

Opposed to the doctrines of the school of Colbert, as to the natural enmity of manufacturing nations, in which prejudice several English writers fully participated, we find an able statement of the true principles of commerce, in the Discourses on Trade by Sir Dudley North, published in 1697. This writer had passed a considerable portion of his time in Russia and Turkey, and was intimately conversant with the details of the Russian and Levant trades. On his return home he held an official situation in the Customs, and thus had ample opportunities of observing the operations of commerce.

Sir Dudley North.

The tract itself, which had been long consigned to oblivion, has been recalled to public notice of late by Mr. Macculloch, in his Introductory Discourse on the Wealth of Nations:—"That the whole world, as to trade, is but as one nation or people, and therein

LECTURE III.

Discourses on trade.

nations as persons," is one of the first propositions maintained in it; the truth of which is only, in our own times, beginning to be recognised. "That to force men to deal in any prescribed manner may profit such as happen to serve them, but the public gain not, because it is taking from one subject to give to another," was another proposition, quite at variance with the prevalent notions of Sir Dudley's own time, in regard to the gain which would accrue to nations by fostering artificial branches of industry; and the statement "that money is a merchandise, whereof there may be a glut as well as a scarcity, and that even to an inconvenience," was a direct assault upon the popular doctrine of the balance of trade.

This treatise, as Mr. Macculloch states, does not seem ever to have obtained any general circulation, or to have been referred to by any subsequent writer on commerce. It may be observed, in corroboration of this, that no reference to it is found in Watts' Bibliotheca Britannica.

We have seen that, as far as the constituents of wealth were concerned, the ancient notion of gold and silver being exclusively entitled to consideration as such, had been successfully assailed; but with the new views as to the precious metals being only commodities, the problem of the laws which regulated the proportions in which commodities should be exchanged—in other words, from what sources commodities derived their exchangeable value—would at once demand solution. The philosophers of olden days had not fathomed this question. Aristotle had certainly drawn a distinction between the exchangeable quality and the useful quality of commodities. He was aware that commerce consisted in the exchange of equivalents; but he conceived the value of a commodity to be measured by the demand for it, and that money by convention was made the repre-

LECTURE III.

sentative of demand: Δεῖ ἄρα ἑνί τινι ταῦτα μετρεῖσθαι, ὥσπερ ἐλέχθη πρότερον· τοῦτο δ' ἐστὶ τῇ μὲν ἀληθείᾳ ἡ χρεία, ἣ πάντα συνέχει· εἰ γὰρ μηθὲν δέοιντο, ἢ μὴ ὁμοίως, ἢ οὐκ ἔσται ἀλλαγὴ, ἢ οὐχ ἡ αὐτή. Commodities must be measured by some one common measure, and this common measure is in truth demand, which is the great connecting link; for if man do not want any thing, or do not want it equally, there will either not be any exchange at all, or there will be an exchange not on the same terms. In the "Politics," however, though Aristotle adopts the same view as to money being by convention a symbol of value, yet he expressly allows it to be a commodity: Διὸ πρὸς τὰς ἀλλαγὰς τοιοῦτόν τι συνέθεντο πρὸς σφᾶς αὐτοὺς διδόναι καὶ λαμβάνειν, ὃ τῶν χρησίμων αὐτὸ ον εἶχε τὴν χρέιαν εὐμεταχείριστον πρὸς τὸ ζῆν, οἷον σίδηρος καὶ ἄργυρος κἂν εἴ τι τοιοῦτον ἑτέρον.

Aristotle's Politics.

From this and other passages it would appear that Aristotle had no idea of the exchangeable value of commodities depending on other considerations than their utility, the word χρεία, which was held to be the true measure of the value of all commodities, signifying demand founded on utility. On the other hand, in regard to money, so far was he from considering it to be the only article of wealth, that he held its value to rest entirely upon opinion: thus in the "Ethics" he writes οἷον δ' ὑπάλλαγμα τῆς χρείας τὸ νόμισμα γέγονε κατὰ συνθήκην καὶ διὰ τοῦτο τοὔνομα ἔχει νόμισμα, ὅτι οὐ φύσει, ἀλλὰ νόμῳ ἐστὶ, καὶ ἐφ' ἡμῖν μεταβάλλειν καὶ ποιῆσαι ἄχρηστον. And in accordance with this view we find him in the "Politics," i. 3., exposing the erroneous principles upon which the κάπηλος, who practised the empirical trade of making gain by exchanges, sought to accumulate an abundance of money, as identical with wealth. Yet, as he observes, the fable of Midas should have taught mankind a different lesson. Had Aristotle lived in later time, it might have been expected he would have been a most vigorous assailant of the mercantile system, which, as we have seen, sought to convert the whole science of exchanges (ἡ μεταβλητικὴ) into the science of money making, and to degrade the ἔμπορος to a level with the κάπηλος.

A philosophic mind, as acute as Aristotle's, however, though perhaps not so comprehensive, was led, in the process of analysing the nature of civil government, and the origin of property, to discriminate between what he terms the natural intrinsic value or usefulness of things, and what may be called their actual value, and to ascribe the difference, not to the demand or desire of possessing them, but to the labour bestowed on their production. "Nor is it so strange," to quote from Locke's Essay on Government, b. ii. c. 5., "as perhaps, before consideration, it may appear, that the property of labour should be able to overbalance the community of land; for it is labour, indeed, that puts the difference of value on every thing: and let any one consider what the difference is between an acre of land planted with tobacco or sugar, sown with wheat or barley, and an acre of the same land lying in common without any husbandry upon it, and he will find that the improvement of labour makes the far greater part of the value."

Locke's Essay on Government.

Again, "Let us but trace some of the ordinary provisions of life, through their several progresses, before they come to our use, and see how much of their value they receive from human industry. Bread, wine, and cloth, are things of daily use, and great plenty: yet, notwithstanding, acorns, water, and leaves, or skins, must be our bread, drink, and clothing, did not labour furnish us with these more useful commodities: for whatever bread is more worth than acorns, wine than water, and cloth or silk than leaves, skins, or moss, that is wholly owing

LECTURE III.

to labour and industry; the one of these being the food and raiment which unassisted nature furnishes us with; the other, provisions which our industry and pains prepare for us; which, how much they exceed the other in value, when any one has computed, he will then see how much labour makes the far greater part of the value of things we enjoy in this world: and the ground which produces the materials is scarce to be reckoned in as any, or at most, but a very small part of it; so little, that even amongst us, land that is left wholly to nature, that hath no improvement of pasturage, tillage, or planting, is called, as indeed it is, waste, and we shall find the benefit of it amount to little more than nothing."

In these and other passages, too long to quote, there may be perceived the germ of the doctrine of value, which was ripened and matured under the hand of Adam Smith; but it may be doubted whether Locke was on the verge of discovering the fundamental principle, upon which the industrial system of political economy was built up. Locke evidently means by the term value, the capacity of satisfying the wants of man: by natural intrinsic value, the capacity of satisfying his natural wants, in other words, of supporting man in a rude condition of life: by actual or acquired value, the capacity of satisfying his actual or acquired wants, in other words, of supporting him in a state of civilisation. Greater value, with him, was identical with greater usefulness. Bread was worth more than acorns, because it was a more useful commodity. Still the distinction was most important, more particularly in reference to the approaching reaction against Colbertism in France, when the most erroneous notions as to the origin of value obtained general circulation under the countenance of the agricultural school of M. Quesnay, the leader of the so-called "Economists."

Locke's idea of value.

LECTURE III.

Actual value, then, according to Locke, was a compound quality made up of what he terms real usefulness, the gift of nature, and acquired usefulness, the work of man's labour. But there were certain articles of little real use, but great actual value, such as gold, silver, and diamonds: these, he says, are "things that fancy or agreement hath put the value on, more than real use, and the necessary support of life:" that is, fancy or agreement have attached to the quality of durability a value, corresponding to the intrinsic value of goods, which are useful to the life of man; but the labour of man was held by him to be the measure of what we have called the actual value of these articles: for he elsewhere says, "Since gold and silver, being little useful to the life of man in proportion to food, raiment, and carriage, has its value only from the consent of man, whereof labour yet makes, in great part, the measure." Here, indeed, Locke seems to have had his hand upon the key, without being aware of the lock which it would open. Elsewhere, indeed, in his treatise on money, he says, "Money has a value, as it is capable by exchange of procuring us the necessaries or conveniences of life, and in this it has the nature of a commodity; only with this difference, that it serves us commonly by its exchange, never almost by its consumption. But though the use men make of money be not in its consumption, yet it has not at all a more standing, settled value, in exchange with any other thing, than any other commodity has, but a more known one, and better fixed by name, number, and weight, to enable us to reckon what the proportion of scarcity and vent of one commodity is to another." Here we certainly seem to have a distinction between value in use and value in exchange; the value of money in use being conventional, the value in exchange being determined by the same considerations as that of other commodities, which he elsewhere

Intrinsic and actual value.

explains, as the proportion which the quantity in the market bears to the vent, or, in other words, the proportion of the supply to the demand. Still we may seek in vain for that clearness of statement with which Sir W. Petty's original genius announced "that if 100 men work ten years upon corn, and the same number of men the same time upon silver, the net proceed of the silver is the price of the whole net proceed of the corn:" and again, "corn will be twice as dear when there are 200 workmen to do the same work which 100 could perform."

LECTURE III.

Sir W. Petty.

LECTURE IV.

LECTURE IV.

THE commencement of the 18th century may be considered to have been the transition period in Europe in respect of the science of wealth (ἡ χρηματιστική). The ancient notion of gold and silver being the sole articles of wealth had been successfully impugned, and these metals were now deemed by many persons to be commodities, more desirable, indeed, to possess than other commodities from their natural and conventional qualities, but still subject to variations and inequalities of value, as other commodities. Thus Locke, in his "Treatise on Money," writes: "In exchanging coined silver for any other commodity (which is buying and selling), the same measure governs the proportion you receive, as if you exchange lead, or wheat, or any other commodity." How, indeed, that proportion was determined, and whence commodities derived their value in exchange, remained still to be investigated. Some writers conceived that the value of money was purely conventional; that mankind had tacitly agreed to employ it as a common measure, by which they might reckon the proportion which "the scarcity or vent" of one commodity bore to that of another. For instance, where a commodity measured according to its bulk, as a hogshead of wine, had to be compared with a commodity measured according to its weight, as a hundred weight of iron, or with commodities measured according to their number, as a score of sheep, it is evident that a common measure would very much facilitate the determination of the proportions in value which given quantities, numbers, and weights, bore to one another. Such an office money was ob-

Locke's Treatise on Money.

served to fulfil, and as a system of tokens or counters might be agreed upon to discharge such functions, analogous to those which arbitrary symbols are employed to fulfil in mathematics, a large class of persons were content to acquiesce in such an hypothesis, to explain how money had come to serve as a common measure. Others, on the opposite hand, admitting the theory of a general tacit agreement to employ money as a common measure, still held that its value was not wholly conventional, but was partly influenced by similar conditions to those which determined the value of other commodities; but what those conditions were, was not yet settled. The most obvious explanation was, that they were the conditions of supply and demand, for it was on the surface of things that the market value fluctuated according to those conditions; but it could not escape notice that the market value continually as it were gravitated towards a standing settled value; and the reason of this remained to be discovered. Some few had perceived that the rarity of a commodity corresponded to the difficulty of procuring it; but how that difficulty was to be measured, and to what causes it was to be referred, eluded discovery. Whilst, therefore, this problem remained undetermined, there would be an opening for much unsound speculation, and we should not be surprised to find financial embarrassment, as it had been already the cause of the adoption of imperfect systems, now disposing statesmen to lend too ready an ear to the recommendations of plausible experimentalists.

The Regent Orleans.

An adviser of this character presented himself in the person of the well-known John Law, to the Regent Orleans in France, at a most critical period in the history of French finance. The gorgeous extravagance of Louis XIV. had exhausted all the resources, which the ingenuity of Colbert's successors

LECTURE IV. could devise, and had overwhelmed the treasury in debt, and the accompanying embarrassment was not confined to the state, but extended throughout all classes of society. The capital of the public debt on the demise of Louis XIV. amounted to 300 millions of French livres, and in the first council of state held by the Regent, it was proposed to sacrifice the creditors of the state, as being the smaller number, whose ruin might justly be a subordinate consideration to the preservation of the country. Law had previously appeared in Paris during the lifetime of Louis XIV., full of grand but visionary conceptions as to the extent to which public credit might be safely developed, and conventional values be substituted in the place of real values: but his plans, which he laid before the controller general Desmaretz, were rejected, as fraught with greater dangers than the difficulties which they were intended to obviate.

John Law.

Law had studied the operations of commerce and credit in most of the great cities of Europe; he had beheld great results apparently flowing from the establishment of banks of deposit, such as that at Amsterdam, of which the bank-money or credit in the books of the bank, representing the value of the deposits of gold and silver in its cellars, was current at a higher rate than specie money. He had seen the foundation of an incorporated bank of circulation in England, attended with most advantageous results to the state, through the assistance which the issue of a paper currency of 1,200,000*l.* enabled it to furnish to the government. He was likewise aware that the notes of the bank in Scotland, which, however, had not maintained itself for a very long time, had circulated at their nominal value, at a time when there was no gold or silver in the coffers of the bank, though their acceptance was voluntary. Law reflecting on these different facts, had come to the conclusion that it was by mis take that mankind had come to employ the precious metals as the agents of circulation, and that paper money, if made the representative of value, would fulfil all the purposes of a common measure, with much better effect, from not being a commodity, and so not being liable to fluctuation in its value. The bank in Scotland, to which allusion has just been made, had not succeeded, and it was proposed to establish one on a different plan. On this occasion Law submitted his views to the Parliament of Scotland, in a memoir, entitled "Money and Trade considered, with a Proposal for supplying the Nation with Money," published at Edinburgh in 1705, in which, as might be expected, there is a curious combination of acute perception with erroneous inferences.

Considerations upon Money and Trade.

"The value of things," says he, "is not determined according to their more or less necessary uses, but according to the greater or less quantity of them, in proportion to the demand. Water is of great use, yet of little value, because the quantity of water is much greater than the demand for it. Diamonds are of little use, yet of great value, because the demand for diamonds is much greater than the existing quantity of them."

This is a clearer statement of value, as distinguished from utility, than we meet with in any earlier writer.

Law in another publication objected to Locke's statement, referred to in a previous Lecture, namely, that the value of goods was "according to their quantity, in proportion to their vent," on the ground that the vent of goods cannot be greater than the quantity, but the demand may be greater. Certainly Law's terminology is more precise, and carries us a step farther than Locke's; but Locke's language was meant to denote the same fact, the vent being considered the index of demand. After all, the phrase, "demand

LECTURE IV.

for an article," is a conventional mode of expression, by which, in reality, the relative supply of other articles of exchange is denoted, the demand for any one article being governed by the supply of other articles.

Law's notion of value.

Law goes on to say, "the value of things varies from two distinct causes, the greater or less quantity of products, and the greater or less quantity of money. Of these two causes, the one is beyond the control of man, whilst the other may be subjected to his regulation. We cannot, indeed, secure that the quantity of corn, wine, &c., shall at all times be sufficient for men's wants; but we may provide, that the quantity of money shall always bear a proper relation to the demand, provided this money has no intrinsic value, does not consist of gold and silver."

The distinction here made between the general value, and the specific value of commodities, corresponds to the distinction made by Locke between value and price, which is obvious when enunciated; but Law was in error, in maintaining that prices would always fluctuate as long as money had any intrinsic value, for if the state could duly regulate the supply of it, its intrinsic value might be maintained at a constant level, equally as its conventional value. The experience of modern days renders it unnecessary to do more than state this fact.

"There would be," Law continues, "in such a state of things, an immense advantage, as money is the originating principle of labor, the cultivation of the soil, the growth of population. Rich countries are such as have plenty of money; poor countries, those where it is scarce."

The meaning of the first of these two sentences is made more clear elsewhere, in another work, where he says, "Domestic trade depends on money. A greater quantity employs more people than a lesser quantity.

A limited sum can only set a number of people to work proportioned to it, and it is with little success laws are made, for employing the poor and idle, in countries where money is scarce. Good laws may bring money to the full circulation it is capable of, and force it to those employments that are most profitable to the country, but no laws can make it go further, nor can more people be set to work, without more money to circulate, so as to pay the wages of a greater number. They may be brought to work on credit, and that is not practicable, unless the credit have a circulation, so as to supply the workman with necessaries. If that is supposed, then that credit is money, and will have the same effects on home and foreign trade."

Truth and error run side by side through this entire passage. With the labourer, indeed, money passes current, for so much food, clothing, or other necessaries, in the representative character which general usage has sanctioned; but the wages of the workman might be paid in those articles themselves, in lieu of which he accepts money. Money, doubtless, simplifies very much the relations of the workman to his employer; but it is not necessary to enable those relations to be maintained. Circulating credit would answer precisely the same purpose, where it is adequately guaranteed; but a similar guarantee will be requisite to enable credit to circulate, to that which causes money to circulate universally, namely, the assurance that it may be exchanged at any time for food, clothing, &c. Law might have said, rich countries are such as have plenty of credit; just as he said, rich countries are such as have plenty of money; but countries are not rich because they have credit, or because they have money; but they have credit and have money because they are rich.

Functions of money.

"Nothing," continues Law, "is more appropriate

LECTURE IV.

Advantages of paper money.

for the purposes of money than paper. In addition to the advantages which recommend the precious metals, it has qualities which they do not possess. 1. It is more easy to count, and to transport. 2. The material costs nearly nothing, whilst gold and silver are very dear. 3. It is consequently not exported, and the supply may be always regulated to suit the demand. This is a most important consideration!

"In fact, there is a perpetual struggle between the proprietors of commodities and the holders of money. The former impose conditions on the latter, when produce and manufactures are scarce; and they submit to them, on the other hand, when they are plentiful. Yet justice, and the public interests, require that the value or the price of things should never exceed the limit of the cost of production. There is, however, only one way of attaining this result: namely, by securing that the quantity of money should bear a constant proportion to the quantity of commodities: which condition will be realized, as soon as all who require it may be furnished with money upon real guarantees. If such a desideratum is unattainable whilst money retains a metallic form, nothing would be more easy than its accomplishment with money in the form of paper."

Commerce, according to the above view, is little else than a game between monopolists; and the mystery of trade consists in dealing out wares in such proportions as should create a notion of their scarcity, and so stimulate the competition of those who might wish to obtain them. "Yet justice and the public interests require that the value or the price of things should never exceed the limit of their cost of production." A most sound principle is here enunciated, that the enhancement of the exchangeable value of commodities, by artificial means, is prejudicial to the public interests, and inconsistent with justice. For justice will surely be best satisfied where the exchangeable value corresponds to the natural price, i. e. where the remuneration secures the return of the outlay, and average profits upon it; and the public interests will be most furthered, where the consumer is enabled to enjoy the necessaries and comforts of life, with no greater sacrifice on his part than is required to compensate the cost of production, in which profits are included. It is obvious, however, that such a result will not be attainable, if a fluctuating common measure is made use of. But on the other hand, the use of an invariable common measure will not alone secure the desired end. It will produce one good effect, namely, the price of commodities will be an invariable index of their value, and so far exchanges will be facilitated, and inasmuch as the returns will be measured by the same standard as the outlay, the proportion which the exchangeable value bears to the cost, would be more readily determined.

Bank of Amsterdam.

Bank of England.

Law was fully aware in the cases above alluded to, that the credit of the bank of Amsterdam rested on the deposits of money supposed to be in its coffers, and ready to be paid out on demand; that the credit of the Bank of England was based upon a parliamentary fund, pledged to it by the Government, as security for the money lent to the Crown; and that the credit of the Bank of Scotland was destroyed by its specie being exported, and its consequent inability to meet the demand upon it for money in exchange for its notes. He must consequently have perceived that "credit that promises a payment of money, cannot well be extended beyond a certain proportion which it ought to have with the money," and that "where a country had little money, no considerable credit could be given upon it." The problem, therefore, which he undertook to solve, was, whether any other goods than the precious metals, or rather silver, for that metal was in more general use, could be made money with the same safety and convenience. The solution of such a problem was evidently of the last importance to a country, which had little silver, but which had great resources, requiring, as it was then supposed, money to develop them. Of course in this latter supposition there was involved the great mistake of confounding money with capital, and this seems to have been the fundamental error of Law's entire system. Capital, as is well known, is the accumulated produce of man's industry, which is available at once for his support, or in its turn will facilitate the appropriation or production of other commodities. Without some capital, therefore, the resources of a country would be very slowly developed; for it would be impossible for the people to engage in any branch of industry, where the return was not immediate, or where the labour required was not of the simplest sort. How could the husbandman venture to commit the seed to the earth, unless he had an accumulated stock of food to support him until the coming season of the harvest, or how could he prepare the soil to receive the seed, unless he were already provided with a spade or a plough? It is obvious, then, that a country will be able to develop its resources more rapidly according as it has capital; but the growth of its capital is not conditional on its possession of money. Wages, for instance, may be paid in kind, profits may be stored away in the same form, and exchanges may be carried on by barter. Now money, according to Law, is, in the first place, "the measure by which goods are valued, the value by which they are exchanged, and in which contracts are made payable." 2. It "is not a pledge, as some call it; it is a value paid or contracted to be paid, with which, it is supposed, the receiver may, as his occasions require, buy an equal quantity of the same goods he has sold,

Law's idea of money.

or other goods equal in value to them; and that money is the most secure value, either to receive, to contract for, or to value goods by, which is least liable to a change in its value." In other words, money is a common measure of other commodities; and the commodity, whose general value is less variable than that of other commodities, will best serve the purposes of money. The money, therefore, of a country will be that part of its capital which is exclusively employed in facilitating the exchange of other portions of its capital, just as the loom of the weaver, or the saw of the carpenter, are portions of the capital of a nation employed in facilitating the production of clothes and dwellings, which become, again, other portions of its capital.

General depreciation of silver.

The frequent tampering with the quality and quantity of the silver coin on the part of almost every state, had subjected the value of silver money to an artificial uncertainty, which deprived it in many respects of its chief recommendation. Of this Law took advantage, for the purpose of his argument, which was to show that, as a matter of fact, the combination of defects in silver money disqualified it from answering the true purposes of money, and that as the general value of silver was likely to continue falling from the Spaniards importing great quantities into Europe, there was a tendency in silver to become every year more unfit to serve as money. If, therefore, any other article could be found, having the qualities required in money, and not liable to such fluctuations in its general value as silver, it might be substituted with advantage in the place of silver for the purposes of money. Such qualities Law considered land to possess, and he proposed to make "money of land equal to its value."

"Any goods," he writes, "that have the qualities necessary in money, may be made money equal to

LECTURE IV.

their value. Five ounces of gold is equal to 20*l.* (of silver), and may be made money to that value. An acre of land, rented at 2 bolls of victual (the victual at 8*l.*, and land at 20 years' purchase), is equal to 20*l.*, and may be made money equal to that value, for it has all the qualities necessary in money. But that acre of land cannot be coined to the value of 50*l.*, no more than the five ounces of gold; and though the five ounces of gold, the 20*l.* silver money, and the acre of land be now equal in value, yet they cannot well continue so; for, as I have shown already, any disproportioned change in the quality, quantity, or in the demand of either of them, will make the same quantity of the one equal to a greater or less quantity of the others. Land is what, in all appearance, will keep its value best; it may rise in value, but cannot well fall: gold and silver are liable to many accidents whereby their value may lessen, but cannot well rise in value."

The grounds why Law considered land must rise in value, seem to have been, that it was capable of improvement, and that the demand for it would daily increase, whilst the quantity would remain the same.

Law proposed to issue notes on security of land.

Law accordingly proposed to the Parliament of Scotland that 40 responsible commissioners should be appointed by it, having power to coin notes, and to lend them on the security of land under certain restrictions, the land to be assigned to the commissioners, but to be redeemable within a term of years. The land was to be valued at 20 years' purchase, according to what would be given for it in silver money. The commission was to receive no other money than these notes, and no person who had contracted for these notes should be obliged to receive silver or metal money.

It was contended that this proposed paper money would be equal in value to silver, as it would have a value of land pledged equal to the same sum of silver money that it was given out for, and that it would not fall in value like silver money, because the commissioners giving out what sums were demanded and taking back what sums were offered to be returned, the supply would be always uniformly proportionate to the demand, and there would be always as much money as there would be occasion or employment for, and no more. In other respects land would have a more certain value than any other goods, for it could not be increased in absolute quantity, nor was it liable to lose any of its uses like other goods: on the contrary, whilst these goods would be liable to lose a part of their value, if the use of them by custom should be taken away, land could always be turned to produce whatever was most used, and would therefore always maintain its value; and if it at all varied, it would increase in value. It was further contended that the superior qualification of paper, when it has a value, to serve the purposes of money, was shown by the practice of most trading nations: in Holland, for instance, silver was pledged, and paper used for money; but land is undeniably a better pledge than silver. If it should be objected that paper passed current in Holland, because silver could be got for it when demanded, or at a certain time, it might be replied that the value of silver itself might, in the mean time, fall, so that the security pledged for that paper money could not be depended upon; whereas the security pledged for the proposed paper money would be land, and land, if it changed at all, would increase in value; so that whilst paper money issued on the security of silver money, might fall below the value of other goods, paper money issued on the security of land would, in all appearance, not only keep equal to other goods, but rise above them.

Experience of Holland.

Let us now, for a moment, consider, what is the

LECTURE IV.

difference between paper money issued on the security of silver, and paper money issued on the security of land. Silver, like any other commodity, is so much accumulated produce, it is therefore a portion of the capital of the country. Land, on the other hand, is an instrument of production which nature has furnished to man's hand, like the air or the sea; but of itself it forms no part of the capital of a country.

Silver, realised capital.

The security of silver, therefore, is the security of so much actual produce, the result of past labour; the security of land is the security of an instrument of production, the efficient operation of which is contingent on the combined employment of actual produce, such as seed and tools, and man's labour, subject even then to the influences of natural disturbing causes. Realised capital, whatever be its form, will always possess value, as its use will save labour to a purchaser, and so long it will always be exchangeable, and silver, like other commodities, is so much realised capital. But men exchange produce for produce, with a view to the ultimate consumption of some commodity, which will contribute to their support or comfort. Land, on the contrary, does not, under all circumstances, possess value, for its use will not always save labour: labour itself, either rude, or combined with capital, must be applied to it, before it can possess value. When these conditions have been fulfilled, it may become an article of exchange, because its use will save so much labour to the purchaser; the use of cleared land, for instance, will save the labour of clearing it; the use of enclosed land will save the labour of enclosing it. The improvements of the land are thus so much realised capital. It is not, however, all realised capital, which will answer the purposes of money. One most important qualification, is the absence of any tendency to deteriorate in quality by the influence of natural causes. From such a tendency the improvements of the land are least exempt of all realised capital, as without the continued application of fresh labour and fresh capital they will rapidly deteriorate; they will thus lose the quality of saving labour; they will consequently lose their exchangeable value.

Capital commands money.

As long as a country has plenty of capital, it will have no difficulty in procuring silver for the purposes of money: the fact of its having no silver is evidence that it has little or no capital: it has exported its silver to other countries in exchange for foreign commodities: its silver has not returned, because it has no other commodities to export in their turn in exchange for it. A country is wealthy which has plenty of capital, that is, plenty of accumulated produce suitable for consumption, or applicable to further production. But a country which has plenty of accumulated produce will need some commodity to employ as a medium of exchanging commodities; it will therefore exchange away some portion of its capital for such a commodity, which will replace that portion of its capital. A rich country, therefore, as it requires money, and as it can purchase silver with its produce, will always have plenty of silver money: its wealth will thus be the cause of its having silver money. The use of such money will facilitate exchanges, but those exchanges are exchanges of labour and capital: such exchanges will in their turn accelerate the growth of wealth. Where money does not follow in the train of capital, it cannot contribute to the growth of wealth in a country, for it is not the exchange of money, as such, for money, which stimulates the industry of a country, and so contributes to the development of its resources, but the exchange of produce for produce, of capital for capital, which the use of money facilitates. The corn grower exchanges away a portion of his surplus produce for

LECTURE IV.

money; not for the sake of the money, but for the sake of the money's worth, namely, a portion of the produce of the labour of the wine grower, the tailor, or the shoemaker, which the money will enable him to procure at any future period. He gives up the enjoyment of so much food which he has himself produced, for the enjoyment of so much wine, and clothes, and shoes, and money facilitates the transfer. But these products, which are so much capital, must already exist, or no exchange will take place, and consequently no medium of facilitating exchanges would be needed. Money, therefore, will not flow naturally into a country so circumstanced; and the artificial introduction of money would not be attended with results in any degree corresponding to those, which attend upon its natural influx. The only way in which the presence of money can further the growth of wealth is by facilitating exchanges amongst the producers. If, however, there be no produce to exchange, if the appearance of money is made to precede the existence of capital, there will be no field for its operation as an instrument of exchange, and its local value as a commodity, if such be its nature, will be indefinitely depreciated from the forced supply far exceeding the natural demand.

But it may be urged, that paper credit issued upon the security of land, in a country where there is little capital, will enable industry to carry on more extensive operations with that capital. Let us hear what Mr. Ricardo says in reply to a similar suggestion, before a Committee of the House of Lords in 1819. (Report as to the resumption of Cash Payments by the Bank of England, p. 192.)

Mr. Ricardo on credit.

"Do you not know," he was asked, "that when there is a great demand for manufactures, the very credit which that circumstance creates, enables the manufacturer to make a more extended use of his capital in the production of manufactures?" His reply was, "I have no notion of credit being at all effectual in the production of commodities: commodities can only be produced by labour, machinery, and raw materials; and if these are to be employed in one place, they must necessarily be withdrawn from another."

He was further asked, "Is not the capital invested in land, for example, capable of two uses? 1. Is it not productively used as vested in the land? 2. May not money be raised by credit on that land, which may be applied to the purposes of manufactures?"

Answer. "The question supposes two capitals — the land and the instruments employed in manufactures. The money which circulates them forms no part of the productive stock; it determines only by whom it shall be employed."

"But," he was asked, "may not a man get credit from a bank on the security of his capital, which is profitably employed, whether vested in stock or land; and may he not, by means of that credit, purchase or create an additional number of labourers, without dislodging capital from any existing employment in the country?"

This question seems to be directed to the very point at which Law was aiming. Mr. Ricardo's answer was to this effect: "Impossible! an individual can purchase machinery and raw materials with credit: he can never create them. If he purchases, it is always of some one else; and consequently he displaces some one else from the employment of capital."

Capital incapable of two uses.

"Are you of opinion, then, that there can never be in any country two uses of the same capital — one to acquire an annual revenue by the mode in which it is invested, and the other to acquire a capital or credit, which may also be profitably employed by the person

LECTURE IV. who acquires it, and which will be so wherever there is an increased demand for commodities?"

Answer. "Capital can only be acquired by saving. It is impossible that one capital can be employed by two persons at the same time, or for two objects. The greatest advantage will be sought and obtained at all times by the employer of capital: that is, capital will always be directed towards that one employment, which is most advantageous."

Credit, then, according to the above view, is but the means of transferring the use of capital from one to another person, or from one to another employment. Circulating credit, for instance, in the form of notes payable on demand, enables specie to be transferred from an unproductive employment as a medium of exchange, to a productive employment as an article of commerce. For instance, when a person opens an account with a banker, he deposits a certain amount of capital with the banker, who in his turn lends his credit to the depositor.

Use of circulating credit.

Let us suppose the capital to be the commodity of gold or silver, in the form of money. The depositor would have contented himself with using this capital unproductively, simply as an instrument of exchange, to procure for himself, from time to time, its equivalents; the banker, on the other hand, will employ it as a commodity, in discounting bills, &c. The depositor will, meanwhile, employ the credit of the banker, the use of which is transferred to him in exchange for the use of his capital, as an instrument of exchange.

Will it therefore be correct to say that the capital of the depositor is now employed for two uses? Namely, by the banker as a commodity, and by the depositor, through the banker's credit, as an instrument of exchange?

If we admit for the moment a double use, it will be seen that these two uses are not in the same sense productive uses. The banker uses his depositor's capital as a commodity, productively; the depositor uses the banker's credit, as an instrument of exchange, unproductively. Had the depositor retained his capital in the form of money, and used it as an instrument of exchange, he would have been using it unproductively, just as he now uses the banker's credit. By depositing it with the banker, he enables it to be used by the banker productively, and contents himself with using the banker's credit unproductively. Consequently a bank of credit enables a part of the capital of the country, which would have been employed unproductively as money, to be employed productively as a commodity; but it does not enable capital to be employed in two ways productively: it enables more capital to be employed productively, because in combination with the credit of the banker a comparatively small reserve of capital, whatever be the amount which experience determines to be sufficient to answer occasional demands, will fulfil all the purposes of a circulating medium of exchange.

Now when gold or silver is employed as an instrument of exchange, it is employed in a different way from that in which it is generally employed as a commodity: in the former case it is employed in small quantities; in the latter in masses. And so it happens that the credit of the banker, which has been lent to the depositor of capital, is employed very seldom indeed in one mass, but for the most part in portions. Hence a large portion of the credit of the banker performs no monetary function, it remains in the banker's book, set down to the depositor's account. And Mr. Norman in his Letter on Money, addressed in 1841 to the present Chancellor of the Exchequer (Mr. Charles Wood) says that the aggregate minimum of deposit accounts existing at any given time, hardly falls short of from sixty to seventy-five per cent. Now it is

Mr. Norman's Letter on Money.

LECTURE IV.

evident, that the amount of capital corresponding to these accounts, if retained by the depositor in his own chest, would have not been used at all; whereas it will now be employed by the banker productively, as an article of commerce. Again, of the remaining 40 or 25 per cent of credit, of which the depositor is making use from time to time as an instrument of exchange by means of orders upon his banker, a considerable portion discharges the function of money by being transferred from the account of one banker to that of another, and so through the medium of a set-off between different bankers, the use even of credit is further economised. To what extent this economy of credit can be carried on, may be inferred from the return, in the Second Report of the Committee of Banks of Issue, of the extent of business transacted in the Clearing House in London in 1839, from which it appears that 970,000,000*l.* passed through that house in a single year, and about one fifteenth of that sum in bank notes, viz., 66,000,000*l.* was all the circulating credit required in settling the balances.

The London Clearing House.

When, however, a person invests his capital in the purchase of land, he hands over a certain amount of capital to the owner of a natural agent, who in his turn transfers to him the ownership of that natural agent. The purchaser of the land, in this case, has parted with, and relinquished all control over his capital. The vendor, on the other hand, has the free disposal of that capital, and may use it at his pleasure. The investment, however, as it is termed, of capital in the purchase of the land misleads many persons to suppose that the capital is as it were encased in a shell, and that the capital is as it were deposited in the land, instead of its having been exchanged away for it. They consequently imagine that the capital, which has really been parted with in exchange for the land, is still under the control of the purchaser, just as if it were stored up in a chest, and therefore that it may at any time be used productively, if occasion should require. But if the owner of the land should wish to use the capital, which he has invested in the land, under any other form than that of the natural agent, he must obtain it from some other person in exchange for his land, just as the owner of so much capital deposited in the hands of his banker, if he wishes to employ that capital productively, must obtain it back from the banker at the sacrifice of his credit at the bank, or he must exchange that credit with a third person for capital; but he cannot use his capital in two forms; he cannot at the same time employ it both as fixed, and as circulating capital.

Banks of circulation.

Now a bank of circulation, resting on deposits of capital, may use its credit, as money, unproductively, and its capital, as a commodity, productively. It may on the one hand issue notes, on the other discount bills. In the former case, it borrows money on its credit without paying interest; in the latter, it lends money with interest, on the credit of others. It thus uses the capital of those who use its credit; but it uses that capital only once, instead of its customers using it, namely, when it lends it at interest. But it may be said that the depositors may use the credit of the bank productively by lending it at interest. Not so. No one pays interest for the use of credit, but for the use of the capital, of which that credit enables him to command the employment. Interest is defrayed from the net profits of capital. If A. pays 10 per cent interest to B. for the use of his credit with C., a banker, it is the same as if A. paid it to C. for the use of the capital which B. has deposited with him. If again A. transfers B.'s credit with his banker C. to D., in exchange for D.'s capital, A. transfers the use of B.'s capital deposited with C. to D., and

LECTURE IV.

D. having exchanged with A., for the moment, capital for credit, will ultimately realise the credit by demanding back B.'s capital from C. It is this capital, of which the use was transferred by B. when he lent his credit with his banker. The credit which he lent, was but the medium of the ultimate transfer.

Banks of discount.

A bank of circulation resting upon land, or upon shares in a commercial undertaking, is a bank resting not on capital, but on credit. A bank, on the other hand, founded on deposits of money, may act in the double capacity of a bank of issue and a bank of discount. It may issue notes in exchange for deposits of money, which notes are, in fact, merely acknowledgments of such deposits, and promises to repay them; and again, it may use those deposits in discounting the promissory notes of merchants. But let us suppose for a moment a bank of issue to be grafted not upon deposits of money, but upon the security of land. The bank issues notes payable on demand in money, upon the security of its land: in other words, instead of so much circulating capital, it sets afloat so much circulating credit on the security of so much fixed capital. But supposing difficulties to arise, and circulating capital of a certain amount to be required for a time in the place of circulating credit, from what sources will it be forthcoming? The security of the land is but the mortgage of eventual, not realised capital; but realised capital is required for circulation to set labour in operation, and when the credit of the land cannot purchase raw materials, the land itself cannot create them, or be a substitute for them. It has been already observed that Law had studied the operations of the Banks of Amsterdam and England—the former a bank of deposit, the latter of circulation—and he contemplated the combining the advantages of the

Banks of deposit

two in one establishment. It may be as well to keep in mind the distinction between a bank of deposit, in its proper signification, and a bank of circulation. In the former, as at Amsterdam, are deposited values, as silver, for instance, or gold, and in return a certificate of the value deposited is issued, payable on demand, and this certificate is put into circulation, and passes current as bank-money. The advantage of such a system consists in the convenience of employing paper certificates, or notes, instead of metal; and at a time when the weight and quality of metal coin was continually subjected to arbitrary alterations, such certificates being convertible into a given quantity of metal of a given purity, had a more certain value, and would thus be preferred as a common measure. A bank of circulation, on the other hand, has a more extensive field of operation: it examines the promissory notes of individual merchants; and, where it considers the solvency of the merchant may be relied upon, it discounts his note, lending on its security the notes of the bank, which circulate as money. Its business therefore consists in giving circulation to the unrecognised credit of the merchant, by lending him its own established credit. In order, however, to do this with safety, it must have a fund first of all set apart, sufficient to make good any losses which it may incur from discounting securities, which prove ultimately worthless; secondly, it must keep a reserve of bullion or coin, as its own notes are convertible into specie on demand, and their credit will only be maintained by the demand being immediately complied with. The issues of a bank of deposit do not then increase the quantity of the circulating medium, but merely substitute a paper for a metallic currency; but the issues of a bank of circulation, on the other hand, do augment the circulating medium, because after setting aside the necessary reserve to meet the average

LECTURE IV.

demand for specie, it lends the remainder of its specie, in addition to its notes, for the purposes of commerce. The disadvantage indeed which those countries are exposed to which have only banks of deposit is, that a large portion of their capital remains unproductive, whereas those which have banks of circulation use all their capital productively, except that portion which is kept in reserve to meet the occasional demand for specie. It must never be forgotten that the capital of a country which is employed as money, is not employed as an instrument of production, but simply as an instrument to facilitate the exchange of other capital.

We may now proceed to follow Law through the various stages of his financial enterprise at Paris. Having in vain submitted various schemes for a National Bank to the Council of Finance, he at last obtained permission to establish (2d May, 1716) a private bank, the capital of which should consist of six millions of livres, divided into 1200 shares of 5000 livres each. At this time the public debt had been reduced by a succession of ordinances from 600 millions of various securities, to 250 millions of (Billets d'Etat) State Notes. The shares of the bank were purchaseable with State Notes, to the amount of three fourths of their value; the remaining fourth was required to be paid in silver. The author of the "Notice Historique sur Law," in the Collection of Economistes Financières du 18 siècle, justly calls attention to this fact, as showing that the interests of the bank were, from its origin, bound up with those of the State. It is believed that Law had privately divulged to the Regent Orleans the ultimate scope of his plans, which were only to be disclosed to the public with the result. The bank discounted mercantile bills, undertook to keep the accounts of merchants by transfers in its books, and issued notes pay-

Notice Historique sur Law.

able on demand, in bank specie, that is, in livres of a fixed weight and fineness of metal.

LECTURE IV.

Success of Law's Bank.

The success of the bank was, as might have been expected, immediate. The existing high rate of discount in France, and the perpetual variations in the value of the metallic currency, had created almost a necessity for some such institution. The Regent, from the first, accorded his protection to it. The government set the example of employing its notes; it gave and received them in all payments. The bearers of them, finding the greatest facility in having them cashed at the bank, began to feel confidence in them, and to communicate it to others. Their being payable in bank specie, of a settled weight and fineness, gave them a stability of value, which the circulating medium had never possessed in France since the reign of Philip le Bel. A stipulation for payment, in notes of the bank, now became an equivalent to a stipulation for payment in livres of the same weight and fineness as those of the 2nd May, 1716. The public could not but avail themselves gladly of a settled common measure, and hastened to deposit their silver money in the bank, that they might obtain the use of its paper. During the first year of its establishment, the extension of the circulation of bank paper was left to the operation of ordinary influences. Their effect, however, was not sufficiently complete to satisfy the wishes of Law and the Regent. The circulation of the notes was, as yet, confined to Paris and a few large towns. It was desirable to make them circulate generally in the country. An ordinance was consequently issued on 10th April, 1717, that all official persons connected with the public revenue, should accept payment in the notes of the bank, and further, should cash all such notes on demand. From this moment all remittances between Paris and the country were made in bank notes; as it

LECTURE IV.

was unnecessary to send specie backwards and forwards, and bank notes were more easy of transport. The money from the country now found its way into the coffers of the bank, and Law beheld his project begin to be realised, of a bank of circulation having, for its reserve, all the metallic money of the country. With a capital of six millions, the bank, at last, according to M. Thiers, had succeeded in issuing from 50 to 60 millions of notes, without its credit being in any way shaken; but reasonable doubts may, I think, be entertained of the issues of Law's Private Bank having ever reached so large a sum.

The effect on the circulation.

Now, had there been 50 or 60 millions of capital in France remaining unemployed, for want of a stable circulating medium, to enable it to be transferred from the hands, in which it was lying idle, to the hands which would employ it productively, then, indeed, the credit of the notes of the bank might have supplied the means of transfer with great advantage to the state. Or again, if there had been a large quantity of specie in France, employed as money in facilitating the exchanges of capital, the substitution of bank notes as a medium of exchange would have released a portion of specie from its unproductive occupation as money, in the home market, and, at the same time, caused it to be employed productively, as a commodity, in the foreign market. The process by which the latter result would be brought about would be as follows. The issue of a given quantity of paper money would, at once, raise the money prices of commodities, the circulating medium would become in proportion depreciated, and specie, if it formed a portion of the circulation, would share in the depreciation. As soon as that depreciation had reached a certain level, as soon as a given amount of specie would purchase in France a less quantity of certain commodities, common to France and England, than in England; specie would be sent from the dear to the cheap market, with advantage to France, and it would be employed productively, in the foreign market, as a commodity, until such time as its exportation had so reduced the amount of the circulating medium in France, that money prices had sunk once more to that level, which made it profitable for the merchant to reimport specie. This will always be accomplished more speedily, according as the industry of a country is employed in the most advantageous manner; for this circumstance will further a more rapid accumulation of capital, which, in its turn, will tend to re-adjust the old proportion between the circulating medium and the various elements of capital in the country, and so reduce money prices. The very exportation of specie, under the circumstances just specified, will contribute to cause a more rapid accumulation of capital; for, in return for it, foreign commodities will be imported; and though what is termed, technically, the balance of trade, will be against a country exporting specie, yet she will be evidently carrying on an advantageous trade, by exporting her surplus specie in return for commodities which may be employed in the extension of some branch of industry, and will thereby accelerate the growth of her capital.

Law's idea of a National Bank.

Law, in his grand conception of a national bank, proposed that it should have the entire management of the public revenue; that it should replace the various companies which had hitherto farmed the public taxes, and which were in the habit of making enormous profits, not merely by the surplus which they actually received above the amount of their contracts with the state, but also by the high interest which they required for all advances which they made to the government; that it should negotiate all state loans, and make all payments in behalf of the state; all

LECTURE IV.

which it might accomplish at a diminished charge to the state by means of its issues of paper money. In addition, the bank was to have the exclusive enjoyment of all the privileged branches of commerce, and thus was to unite the business of a merchant and a banker with the most important functions of the public exchequer. Its capital was to be divided into shares, and the shareholders were to participate in the profits. By combining the double character of banker and merchant, it would be enabled to offer its notes to those who wished for circulating capital, and its stock to those who wished to invest their capital.

Unable to obtain the sanction of the government to the entire scheme, Law had succeeded, as we have seen, in establishing the first part of the machinery, namely, the bank, and its operations had been most prosperous. A favourable opportunity now presented itself of combining with it the business of a privileged mercantile company, of which he did not hesitate to avail himself. Shortly before the death of Louis XIV. a charter of exclusive commerce with the recently discovered country of Louisiana had been granted to Antoine Crozat; but his undertaking had not prospered, and he was anxious to relinquish his privilege.

Antoine Crozat's patent.

Law was admitted by letters patent, of August 1717, to succeed Crozat, and was authorised to form a company, to be entitled La Compagnie d'Occident, to which the king granted the sovereignty over the whole of Louisiana and the Illinois, an exclusive commerce with that portion of North America for 25 years, and the monopoly of the beaver trade of Canada.

La Compagnie d'Occident.

The capital of the company was fixed at 100 millions of livres, and it was divided into 200,000 shares of 500 livres each, payable in full, according to Dutot, one of the cashiers of the Company of the Indies, in (billets d'état) state notes; but according to M. Thiers, in his article "Law," in the Encyclopédie

Progressive, in the same proportions as the shares of the bank. Dutot's account may, I think, be preferred. The income of the company would thus amount to four millions of livres, when all the shares were subscribed for, being the interest payable from the state upon 100 millions of state notes, which four millions would represent the amount of capital really available for commercial enterprise. The billets d'état were at this time at a discount of from 66 to 72 per cent. The state, by this arrangement, transferred to a portion of its creditors the revenue from the lands and commerce of Louisiana; yet the holders of state notes did not readily avail themselves of the opportunity of exchanging them for shares in the company, though Law at once invested the whole of the state notes, which the bank possessed, in the stock of the company. Henceforward, then, a portion of the capital of the bank would be invested in the lands of Louisiana, and in the commercial transactions of the company.

It will be obvious that no new capital, in the proper sense of the word, would be created by the issue of shares by the company; it would merely determine in what manner a certain amount of capital represented by 100 millions of state notes should be employed. If those 100 millions were equal to a real capital of 25 millions of French livres, the notes being at a discount of three fourths their nominal value, the shares of the company would only represent that amount of real capital. Until, therefore, the colonial and commercial operations of the company had succeeded in creating new capital, the remainder of the nominal capital of the company was so much fictitious capital, and its use could not in any way act as a stimulus to production. In order, therefore, to affect public opinion in their favour, Law determined upon attaching a real revenue as soon as possible to them; and with this object the company took a lease of the tobacco duties from the

Its actual capital.

LECTURE IV.

government, which caused a slight rise in the market value of their shares.

The prosperity of the bank in the mean time was on the increase, and the Regent determined at last to take it into the hands of the government. By an ordinance of December 4, 1718, in which it was announced that the Regent had repaid the shareholders their capital of six millions in specie, it was declared a royal bank. The soundness of the principles upon which Law had hitherto conducted the transactions of the bank, can hardly be considered to have been sufficiently tested. It had certainly existed for two years and a half without its credit having been shaken; but its paper had been forced into and kept in circulation by the influence of the government, and its experience could scarcely be held to have solved the question, as to what amount of reserve in specie would support a given circulation of bank notes. The Regent, however, had perceived that the bank, by issuing its notes, had drawn into its coffers a large amount of specie; he therefore determined upon trying the experiment for the benefit of the state upon a much more extensive scale, and as there was now a general confidence in paper money, he determined not to hamper the state with the liability, which had been imposed upon Law's bank, of paying its notes on demand in silver coin of a given weight and fineness. Accordingly, the royal bank issued notes payable either in bank specie, as before, or in current silver coin. The two propositions, which Law had always boldly enunciated, were now to be tested practically: 1st, that money was the source of wealth; 2nd, that it rested with the government to maintain a just equilibrium between the supply of and demand for money, so that it should be never too dear or too cheap; for whilst the royal bank, which an ordinance could at any time empower to issue notes, could sup-

Royal Bank.

LECTURE IV

ply money to any amount, the shares of the Company of the West would furnish the government with the necessary machinery for maintaining the circulating medium at its just level.

Issues of Law's Bank.

It has been already observed, that it seems doubtful whether the issues of Law's bank, not the royal bank, ever amounted to sixty millions. Its nominal capital consisted of six millions, of which three fourths were billets d'état (which were at a discount of three-fourths their nominal value), and one fourth silver. It thus had a reserve in specie of one and a half millions, which subsequent experience has shown to be barely sufficient to maintain a circulation of six millions. M. Thiers may, however, be correct in saying that it had issued in the course of two and a half years notes to the amount of sixty millions; but of these a very large number must in the mean time have been cancelled, as they found their way back. For to increase the convenience of employing them, the public were allowed to endorse them over to one another till they were presented for payment at the bank, when they were invariably withdrawn from circulation and new notes issued in their place. The average circulation of the notes may perhaps be estimated at about twelve millions at the most, and for this reason. Six months after the establishment of the royal bank, an ordinance informs us that seventy-one millions of bank notes had been issued, *twelve millions payable in bank silver*, as if this was the amount of the former circulation, and fifty-nine millions in current silver coin. It would seem as if this plan had been adopted to lull to sleep any suspicicn in the public mind as to the notes of the royal bank payable in silver coin no longer representing the same certain fixed value which the notes of Law's bank had done: and the plan had succeeded if the words of the ordi-

LECTURE IV.

nance were not a mockery, which stated, that as the notes of the new standard were preferred by the public to those of the old standard, the issue of them would be raised to 100 millions.

New coinage.

It may be as well to state that during the period when the bank had been in Law's hands, the state had issued a new coinage, the weight of which was reduced one third, the mark of silver being now divided into 60, instead of 40 livres. So that notes of the royal bank, payable in livres of the current silver coinage, were really a third less valuable than those payable in the old bank silver. Coincident with the increased issue of notes, the government passed several regulations to enforce the use of them, instead of metal money, and guaranteed that they should not be exposed at any time to the same depreciation as the silver money. Law now considered the moment to have arrived when the bank could be successfully engrafted on to the "Company of the West." In order then to raise the price of the company's shares, Law determined *to rig the market*, as it is now technically termed. He bought 200 shares on account at par, and paid a deposit of two fifths, when they were at two-fifths discount, and undertook to forfeit his deposit, if he did not complete the purchase; and meanwhile mysterious rumours were adroitly circulated of the brilliant prospects of the company. The attention of speculators was attracted to the shares by Law's purchase, and within less than a fortnight's time, the shares had actually reached par. In a short time it was announced that the merchants of St. Malo had abandoned their exclusive privilege of trading to the East Indies to the Company of the West, which in the mean time had acquired the rights of the Company of Senegal, which had a monopoly of the African trade. The Company of the West had thus acquired the combined monopoly of the trade to Asia, Africa, and America, and it assumed the name of the Company of the Indies. Fifty thousand new shares of 500 livres were now issued, representing a capital of twenty-five millions, which could only be subscribed for by shareholders of four times the value in the Company of the West. On these a deposit of ten per cent was to be paid by the subscribers, who were allowed twenty months to pay up the remainder of the principal. This transaction cannot but remind us of the present system of the established railroad companies issuing new shares, to which the holders of old shares are alone entitled. These skilful combinations caused the new shares to be eagerly sought for; they were termed "Filles," Daughters, and their Mothers, the shares of the Company of the West, rose in value at the same time. Law's original manœuvre was put in execution towards the end of April. Before the end of July the shares in both companies bore a premium of 100 per cent.

The Company of the Indies.

Filles.

Law pushed on his success. He obtained for the company at the end of July a lease of the mint for nine years, for the sum of fifty millions, to be paid within fifteen months. It became necessary, thereupon, to issue new shares in order to raise this sum Fifty thousand shares, a nominal capital of twenty five millions, were consequently created on the same system with the Daughters, to be called "Petites Filles," or Grand-daughters; and they were to be issued at a premium of 100 per cent, which the earlier shares now bore; by which means fifty millions, the desired sum, would be raised. It was at the same time announced, that after January, 1720, a dividend of 12 per cent would be paid to the shareholders of the Company of the Indies. No person was to be entitled to subscribe to the new shares unless he held five of the old shares. The Grand-daughters became even more popular with the speculators than

Petites Filles.

LECTURE IV.

the Daughters, and by the month of August, 1719, the original shares of the Company of the West, which were bought in 1717 for 500 livres in state notes, equivalent to 150 or 160 livres in money, were selling in the market for 5000 livres.

Law's final measure.

Law was now prepared to make his last grand move. By an ordinance of the 27th of August, it was announced that a lease of what were termed the "fermes générales," the five great branches of the custom duties, which it had been hitherto usual for the state to lease out to contractors, and which had been farmed by an opposition company, headed by the Brothers Paris, (termed L'Anti-Système, as Law's was known by the name of Le Système,) was granted to the Company of the Indies, and that it had likewise offered to lend the state 1500 millions at 3 per cent, to enable it to pay off the public debt, and discharge its most burdensome liabilities. The state at present was paying four per cent interest; and this proposal would at once save it fifteen millions annually. A second ordinance followed in a few days, directing the public creditor to pay his government securities into the treasury, which would deliver in exchange orders upon the cashier of the Company of the Indies, payable either in specie or stock of the company. To meet the alternative of so large a demand, Law calculated, first of all, on the assistance of the bank to provide money; secondly, upon an issue of 300,000 new shares to provide stock. These new shares, of the same nominal value of 500 livres as the old shares, were not to be issued under a less premium than the others bore, which were now selling for 5000 livres. By this means they would realise 1500 millions, the sum required. A deposit of 10 per cent was required from the subscribers, and ten months were allowed for the payment of the principal. The public creditor, who now was forced

Undertakes to pay off the public debt.

to accept these shares in lieu of his state notes, was forced to accept a share representing a capital in the books of the company of 500 livres, at the market price of 5000 livres; so that he would be really exchanging a government security for 200 livres for the company's security for 20 livres of annual revenue, the state and the company both paying four per cent interest. Law, in the mean time, issued the new shares in three equal portions of 100,000, and within the space of twenty days the whole quantity was subscribed for. They were termed *cinq-cents*, five hundreds, from the amount of the deposit per share. They attained a premium of more than 50 per cent within a few days; and to prevent all chance of the first call coming too soon upon the subscribers, and so causing a fall in the price of the shares, the interval of payment was extended to three months. Speculation was rife in the mean while before the first three months expired, and by the end of November the shares were quoted at from 18 to 20,000 livres, and they maintained this monstrous premium till the 15th of December, about which time the first call became due.

Issue of Cinq-cents.

In the mean time the bank had issued 640 millions of notes, and by the commencement of the next year it had increased its issues to upwards of one thousand millions. The public creditors, who were certainly entitled by an ordinance of Sep. 26th to purchase the new shares, for which the treasury receipts or state notes (billets d'état) were exchangeable, had now the choice of two alternatives — either to pay the premium on the shares, or to decline them, and content themselves with notes of the bank.

Issues of Royal Bank.

At the end of November, 1719, the market price of the whole of the shares of the Company of the Indies, which were issued to represent a capital of 300 millions (Compagnie d'Occident, 100 millions, Filles, 25 millions,

Petites Filles, 25 millions, Cinq-cents, 150 millions), had reached the enormous amount of 12,000 millions. It was high time for the speculators, who understood their game, to withdraw themselves from the concern. In all great bubble transactions three classes of persons will invariably be found to be engaged. The large mass will consist of rash speculators, who pursue an unskilful system, and simple-minded persons, who do not reflect, but act as they see others acting: the remainder is made up of shrewd speculators, who are fully alive to the risks of the undertaking, and who form a comparatively small body. When this last class, on the present occasion, found the shares of the Company of the Indies quoted at 20,000 livres, about the end of November, knowing the enormous amount of fictitious capital in the market, and that a call upon the shareholders was approaching, they thought it high time to convert their fictitious capital into some better kind of security. For an entire fortnight the high premium was maintained by skilful management, during which they disencumbered themselves of their shares. As the call drew near, other persons, from inability to meet it, brought their shares into the market. As the supply now outstripped the demand, a depreciation of the shares ensued. The mass of the shareholders took alarm: buyers were only to be found in the ranks of the unskilful speculators; the foundations of the edifice of credit were shaken; it began to crumble to pieces.

Fall of shares

Difficulty of Law's system.

At the opening of the new year, Law had at last to grapple with the great difficulty of his system; namely, he had to keep up the price of the shares and the notes of the bank at one and the same time. The shareholders, for instance, hastened to convert their shares into bank notes, only for the purpose of exchanging the notes at the bank for money. But the bank had issued upwards of one thousand millions of notes; and though the convenience of bank paper for the negotiations of the share market had caused specie to flow into the coffers of the bank for the last three months of 1719, yet its reserve of specie was quite unequal to the present emergency. The only resource was to proscribe the use of gold or silver money, excepting for small payments, and to maintain the circulation of the notes by state regulations. A series of ordinances with this object succeeded each other, and ultimately, after various enactments, to reduce, if possible, the *value* of all property, particularly of precious stones, by prohibiting their *use*, as if value and utility were coincident, the precious metals, as they are termed, were demonetised — gold not being allowed to circulate as money at all, and silver only in coins of the actual value of pieces of ten and five sous, in the present day, equal to about twopence and one penny respectively of English money.

Precious metals demonetised.

Law's fundamental idea had meanwhile been carried into final execution by an ordinance, which fixed the value of the shares at 9000 livres, and established an office for the mutual conversion of shares into bank notes, and bank notes into shares. By the agency of this new machinery, he calculated upon preventing any redundancy or deficiency of the circulating medium. He conceived that the bank now formed a sort of reservoir for money, and that through the medium of the shares of the Company of the Indies the supply could be kept at a just level. If the circulation of bank notes became redundant, provision was made for their being exchanged for the stock of the company: if it should become deficient, the stock of the company would find its way to the bank, and be converted into bank notes. And as the use of metallic money was abolished, there was supposed to be no other standard of value but the notes of the bank.

Laws' fundamental idea.

LECTURE VI.

The working of the machinery did not, however, fulfil the expectations of the projector. The holders of the company's stock continued to flock to the bank to exchange it for bank notes, which entailed an increased issue of the notes.

Within two months after the final development of the system, upwards of 1600 additional millions of bank notes were put into circulation, being more than double the supposed average amount of the metallic money of the whole country. So that at the beginning of May, 1721, there had been issued by the bank, notes of the nominal value of 2,696,400,000 livres.

Stock of the Company.

The whole stock of the Company of the Indies, at this time, including a few additional shares, which had in the interval been created, represented a nominal capital of 312 millions, the interest of which, at 4 per cent, would be 12 millions 480,000 livres. But the company had in the course of its transactions guaranteed a dividend of 200 livres per share, equivalent to 40 per cent upon its original capital. Dutot, the cashier of the company, represents that its revenues were fully equal to make good the undertaking, and supplies a table of them in his "Reflexions sur le Commerce et les Finances." If such were really the case, the shares of the company might in due course of time have recovered their character in the market, after the alarm of the public had subsided, though they would have been subjected to a very great depreciation, had not the bank increased its issues to keep up their price.

Dutot's opinion of its solvency.

The inevitable effect, however, of so much paper money being launched into circulation was, that the money price of all articles was more than trebled, which proved the fallacy of the system as to its capability of duly regulating the circulation. Had the business, indeed, of the bank not been mixed up with the affairs of the company, and had the shares of the company been left to find their level, the shareholders would have been much distressed, and, in the majority of cases, utterly ruined; but the connection of the bank with the company led to the operations of the former being made subsidiary to the assistance of the latter; and thus the general public, who had not speculated in shares, became greatly inconvenienced by the rise of money prices, and those classes who had to depend for support upon their labour, would be almost ruined by it. The Regent, acting upon the advice of D'Argenson, his former minister of finance, whom he had recalled to his councils, and contrary to the expostulations of Law, issued an ordinance reducing gradually the value of the shares of the company from 9000 to 5000 livres, and that of the notes of the bank to one half of their current value. Law had the discredit of being the author of this measure.

The rise of money prices.

The public, who had hitherto been completely in the dark as to the cause and meaning of the rise of prices, understood as little of the real purport of the last measure. They were not aware that they had been already robbed of two thirds of their capital, when they were forced to accept state notes, which would only command a third of the commodities, which silver of the same nominal value, as the notes, would have commanded previous to their issue. They now imagined that the state had by its decree robbed them of half the value of their notes; whereas, although the nominal value of the notes would have been reduced one half, money prices would soon have sunk proportionately. The outcry was in consequence universal, and the Regent had the feebleness to revoke the ordinance.

Feebleness of the Regent Orleans.

I think the term feebleness may be justly applied to the conduct of the Regent, for as M. Thiers observes, "if the ordinance was injudicious, its revocation was more so." A declaration that the shares of the com-

LECTURE IV.

pany and the notes of the bank should be again of the value which their title announced, was really nugatory; because no person could be again persuaded of the fact, and consequently, they could not recover their former place in public estimation. It was but the repetition of a legal falsehood, and without relieving those who were already ruined by it, it entailed ruin upon those who would be obliged once more to receive the notes at their original nominal value. The results showed that public confidence in a circulation based upon an inadequate amount of capital, when once shaken, cannot be restored by artificial means. The prepossession in favour of the bank note, which had naturally grown up from its original convertibility on demand into silver money of a given weight and fineness, was gone; and in spite of the revocation of the ordinance of the 21st of May, its market value fell within a short time to ninety per cent discount. The shares of the company were for a short time sustained by purchases on the part of the bank, but ultimately participated in the common depreciation. It is unnecessary to trace the various steps by which at last a return to a metallic currency was effected.

Depreciation of bank notes.

The investigation of the working of Law's system has been entered upon for a double purpose, partly to show from the history of events, how erroneous were the prevalent notions of his day as to the nature of value, and partly to exhibit the dangerous results to which such erroneous notions may lead. Law had confounded money with wealth; credit with capital. Instead of regarding money and credit as merely media of transferring capital from one hand to another, and so indirectly stimulating productive industry, by enabling it to be set more readily in motion, he considered them to be as directly operative as capital itself, and thus he was led to suppose that a well devised system of credit might enable a country

Money confounded with wealth.

to make two uses of the same capital. Such, it is conceived, was the fundamental principle involved in his scheme of a national bank issuing notes on the security of the land of the country, and such, it is conceived, was the fundamental idea on which he constructed his system in France, of a national bank issuing notes on the security of the shares of the Company of the Indies.

LECTURE V.

LECTURE V.

Systems of taxation in France and England.

THE distinctive peculiarities of the systems of taxation, which prevailed in France and England respectively, will in some measure account for the different tendencies of speculative inquiry in the two countries on questions connected with national wealth. In France, a considerable portion of the taxes were direct, in England, on the other hand, they were chiefly indirect; in France, they were imposed at the arbitrary discretion of the king's council, in England, they could not be levied without the consent of the representatives of the Commons, and an instance occurs, as early as in the reign of Henry VII., of a general subsidy having been refused. (Roper's Life of Sir Thomas More.) Accordingly, we find the investigations of the earliest writers in France more immediately directed to the circumstances which regulate the distribution of wealth, as they perceived that the burdens of taxation were distributed most unequally: whereas, in England, where the taxes were mainly levied indirectly upon articles of consumption, and so bore a definite proportion to the means of each contributor, as measured by his consumption of such articles, the determination of the laws which regulate the production of wealth, seems to have been a subject of more immediate interest. Thus the earliest French writers, in the collection of the works of the most distinguished economists of the French and English schools, now publishing in

Économistes Financiers.

Paris, are classed under the head of "E'conomistes Financiers," including Le Maréchal Vauban, Le Sieur de Boisguillebert, John Law of Lauriston, as a naturalised French subject, Jean François Melon, Law's secretary, and M. Dutot, the cashier of the Company of the Indies. The three last names have already been alluded to in the preceding Lecture.

Traditions of the feudal system in France.

The traditions of the Feudal System were not entirely extinguished in France until the revolution of 1789. Amongst these was the legal inequality of the Tiers Etat, which comprised all the productive classes of the nation, and its subjection to a system of direct taxation, from which the nobles and the clergy were both exempt. The Taille, for instance, the Capitation tax, the Vingtièmes, and a host of petty imposts, bore almost exclusively upon profits, and rents contributed little or nothing to the state. Of course there might be some exceptions; but this would be the general rule. The tendency of such a system was clearly to check the accumulation of capital, and so to limit the means of setting productive industry to work, the inevitable result of which would be a retardation of prosperity, and most probably an actual impoverishment of the country.

Vauban.

Vauban was convinced by a variety of facts, which a course of statistical inquiries had brought under his notice, that the continuance of the existing system, such as he found it, would be most ruinous to France, and he therefore proposed to substitute, in the place of the Taille and other taxes, a Dîme Royale, the king's tenth, similar to the clergy's tenth, to be levied in kind on the annual gross produce of the land, and in money on the annual gross income from personal property and other sources.

Projet d'une Dîme Royale.

It is not necessary to examine the details of his plan, which he termed "Projet d'une Dîme Royale," as to its applicability to further the end which he had in view.

Steuart's Political Economy.

Sir James Steuart, in the 4th volume of his Principles of Political Economy, has assigned a chapter to its examination, and points out a variety

LECTURE V.

of objections to it. There can be no doubt that had Louis XIV., to whom the Maréchal presented a copy of his work, entertained a favourable view of the principles advocated in it, many modifications would have been found necessary in executing the scheme. But the work did not secure for its author the consideration to which he was entitled. It was published by him in 1707, without his name, and its sale was immediately prohibited by an order of the king's council; and, if we are to believe the memoirs of the Duc de St. Simon, the illustrious author, to whom both his sovereign and his country were in other respects so deeply indebted, met with so ungracious a reception from the king, that he withdrew in grief and disappointment to his château, where he died shortly afterwards. His work, however, with all its defects, is still valuable, from the information which it supplies in regard to the condition of the industrious classes in France, towards the conclusion of the reign of Louis XIV., and the general embarrassment then pervading every rank of society.

Reign of Louis XIV.

"From the researches," Vauban writes in his preface, "which I have been enabled to make during several years since I have given attention to the subject, I have observed, that of late about one-tenth part of the people is reduced to beggary, and actually begs subsistence; that of the nine other parts, there are not five which are able to assist the first part, because they are themselves almost reduced to the same unfortunate condition. Of the remaining four parts, three are in any thing but easy circumstances, and are hampered with debts and lawsuits; and the tenth division, in which I include the military, the legal and clerical professions, all the hereditary nobility, the nobility of distinction, all the civil and military officials, the merchants, and the tradesmen of property, does not comprise more than 100,000 fami-

General misery in France.

lies; and I think I shall be within the mark in saying, that there are not ten thousand of these, great or small, whose circumstances are in every respect easy; and of this latter body, the majority, in some way or other, with the exception of a few merchants, receive payments from the Crown."

Sieur de Boisguillebert

Almost contemporaneously with the interdict against the sale of Vauban's work, the resentment of the ministers of Louis XIV. was directed against the Sieur de Boisguillebert, one of the chief magistrates of Normandy, as the author of a work entitled "Factum de la France." The practical object of this treatise was to recommend the adoption of certain modifications in the mode of levying the taille, and the substitution of a capitation tax of one tenth, payable in money upon real and personal property, in lieu of the indirect taxes usually farmed out to contractors. This alteration, it was contended, would secure a large increase in the revenues of the Crown, whilst the demands upon the funds of the subject would at the same time be much reduced. With these changes it was proposed to combine the abolition of all duties upon the transport of commodities from one province of the kingdom to another, as well as upon the exportation of them, and the reduction of the duties upon foreign imports. "Wealth," he writes, "consists in the continual exchange of the surplus which one individual possesses for the surplus which another possesses; for the moment that the means of effecting this exchange are wanting, a country becomes distressed in the midst of abundance. Now such will be the result whenever the just proportions of commodities are destroyed, and whenever one party to the transaction cannot effect an exchange, except at a loss, in respect of the cost of production; in which case commerce is suspended and distress ensues, for as the opulence of a state

LECTURE V.

consists in the maintenance of all the various departments of labour, and as they reciprocally depend upon one another for support, the depression of one branch of industry acts injuriously upon all the others." (Chap. X.) Such De Boisguillebert contended had been the result of the heavy taxes levied upon agricultural produce. They had raised the market price so high that the consumption of wheat, wine, &c., was checked by it, and the growers were obliged to abandon their produce to the tax-gatherer; and as the cessation of consumption entailed as a necessary consequence the cessation of production, with every diminution of production there was a corresponding diminution of national wealth. "How can the peasant of Picardy or Normandy afford to drink the wine of Anjou or the Orleanais, when he has to pay twenty or twenty-four sous for what the wine-grower sells for a single sou? And how can the wine-grower continue to cultivate the vine, when the single sou, which he receives for his produce, will not defray the expense of cultivation? One effect of levying indirect taxes upon the consumption of domestic produce is to dry up the sources of the direct taxes; and whilst a great portion of the indirect taxes is lost to the Crown from the expenses of collecting them, they have checked cultivation to that extent, that the Crown has lost six times as much by the diminution in the direct taxes on produce (la taille), as it has gained by the indirect taxes on consumption."

Taxes on agricultural produce.

We find that at this time a growing disposition existed in France to attribute the distress of the country to a deficiency of money. This notion De Boisguillebert combats as full of absurdity, pointing out, that although a country like Peru, whose only produce was silver, and where silver was used not as a measure of exchangeable value, but as the only article of exchange, the people would die of famine, if they had no silver, since they would have no commodity to exchange for food and clothing; yet in a country like France, where it is used only as a medium of exchange, other articles, such as a promissory note, or even the word of a merchant, might perform the same function. De Boisguillebert had a clear appreciation of the distinction in the separate employments of silver, as money, and as a commodity, and that when it was employed as money it was not employed productively, and the reverse, when employed as a commodity. "Silver is anything but an element of wealth in a country which does not produce it: it is the medium by which commerce is carried on, and the guarantee of the future enjoyment of a commodity, which is not at once handed over on the part of one of the parties to the exchange, and it discharges this function in common with such a host of other articles, such as verbal promises, paper, parchment, and commodities themselves, that the use of it is dispensed with, for the most part, in transactions where some had supposed it to be indispensable. Nay, it is never required except where no confidence is placed in the verbal or written undertaking of one of the parties. It is immaterial whether there is much or little of it in a country, for the purposes of its opulence; that is, its enjoyment not merely of the necessaries, but the luxuries of life. One thing only is indispensable: whether prices are high or low, everything must be in proportion: otherwise, without proportion, there will be no commerce, and then no wealth, or rather great distress, as experienced at present in France. A person who possessed 1000 francs of annual revenue in the reign of Francis I., was as wealthy, and passed his life as comfortably and luxuriously, as one who now enjoys 15,000 francs of revenue, because the same measure of wheat then only cost 20 sous, which now costs 15 or 16 francs, and the price of shoes was at that time

LECTURE V.

only five sous. The labourer, however, who sold his wheat for 20 sous, and the shoemaker who sold his shoes for five sous, found the transaction answer, because the just proportions were maintained. But if in the present day, wheat were selling for 15 francs, the shoemaker would starve if he could only sell his shoes for five sous: as in like manner the labourer would be stripped of everything, if he had to sell his wheat at 20 sous, and to pay four francs for his shoes." (Ch. IV.)

Entertaining such views, De Boisguillebert, had he lived, would have been found amongst the opponents of Law's scheme, the success of which in reviving the prosperity of France, depended on the soundness of Law's doctrine that the presence of money was the cause, not the effect, of wealth. De Boisguillebert, however, had not advanced in the analysis of the intrinsic value of money, beyond the position, in which Locke had left the subject. "The vendor of a commodity," he says, "rarely, if ever, trafficking with the possessor of the particular commodity which he wishes to procure in exchange for his own, and not being able to obtain it except by the intervention of a numerous body of vendors and purchasers, there was a necessity for a guarantee on the part of the first purchaser, that the wishes of the vendor should be ultimately satisfied. The services of silver have thus become necessary, by a certain agreement and general consent of mankind, that in every country, except under very extraordinary circumstances, the bearer of a given quantity of silver should be secured the enjoyment of that proportion of the commodity which he wishes for, which will compensate him for having parted with his own commodity, with the same certainty as if the original transaction had been one of barter." (Ch. IV.)

De Boisguillebert's notion of value.

Factum de la France.

The work from which I have quoted, "*Factum de la France*," which caused its author to be exiled from the seat of his magistracy, was but a practical exposition of views already set forth in 1697 by the publication of the "*Détail de la France,*" which, however, had not attracted much attention. The same enlightened principles pervade both treatises; and although, as De Boisguillebert's biographer, M. Daire, observes, his glance can not be said to have at once embraced all the numerous and complex phenomena of production, yet the lessons which he gave to his contemporaries are not unworthy of our regard in the present day. It certainly had not escaped him, that a moderate tariff of custom duties was calculated to secure a larger revenue than an exorbitant scale. Of this fact he gives a curious illustration in ch. xv. of the "Detail." Having alluded to the ruin which the farmers of the French customs had formerly experienced in consequence of Henri IV.'s retaliating measures on Philip the Third of Spain for having raised the duties enormously on exports and imports, he states that such heavy duties were imposed in France on the exportation of French brandy to England, that the farmer of the customs in one of the maritime towns of France received in his first year no returns upon brandy. On inquiry, he found that the English despatched small boats to the coast, and that the exports of brandy were lowered at night over the cliffs by bodies of smugglers; so that in fact no duty at all was paid upon it. He therefore determined to exact only half the duty to which he was entitled, which not merely brought him a very considerable profit upon his contract, but by reviving the legitimate trade of the town, restored it to its ancient prosperity.

Détail de la France.

Moderate custom duties.

Law's "Considérations sur le Numéraire et le Commerce" would come next in order of time; but as that work has been discussed in the last Lecture, we may pass on to the "Essai Politique sur le Commerce," of Jean François Melon, who had been secretary to Law

Jean François Melon.

LECTURE V.

until the downfal of the system in 1720, and subsequently secretary to the Regent Orleans. This work was published in 1734, and the fame which it procured for its author presents a curious contrast to the disgrace which had attended De Boisguillebert's labours.

Melon's view of commerce.

Melon's work recommended itself to the prejudices of the age in which he lived, by advocating the principles of the mercantile system; and as his exposition of the system was clear and lucid, its doctrines were made intelligible to the minds of many persons who had hitherto supported it, without understanding its theory. Commerce, according to Melon's view, was the *exchange of a superfluity for a necessary*. Hence, liberty of commerce was held, by him, to consist in a licence to merchants not to export and import freely all kinds of merchandise, but only those commodities, which would procure for every citizen the means of exchanging his superfluities for the necessaries which he might require.

" There are regulations for all manufactures; there are fixed measures and weights; there are marks and seals, which control the workmen, and obviate the fraudulent cupidity of the merchant. All this is established for the sake of the consumer; so that, in order to ascertain whether or not new regulations are opposed to liberty of commerce, we must not inquire whether the merchants or the workmen are harassed by them; it is not for their sake that they are made. We must examine whether the proprietor of the raw material has a better vent, and whether the consumers have a cheaper and more certain supply. If these two conditions are fulfilled, then the merchant and the workman cannot be too much favoured, nor have too many facilities for their undertakings." (Chap. XV.)

De Boisguillebert's definition of commerce.

Now De Boisguillebert had virtually, though not in terms, defined commerce to be *the mutual exchange of superfluities*. It will be perceived that, according as the one or the other of these definitions is adopted, the advantages of commerce will appear to be one-sided, or reciprocal, and we thus find that whilst the bitterest jealousy of trade has prevailed between states which have held to the mercantile theory, a reciprocal liberty of commerce has been fostered in countries, where statesmen have been trained up in the opposite school of ideas.

Condillac's view.

"It is false," wrote Condillac, in 1776, "that in exchanges an equal value is given for an equal value. On the contrary, each of the parties to the bargain always gives a less for a greater value." On the other hand, Mr. Huskisson, in 1810, declared, that "the exchange of equivalents is the foundation of all commerce, from the simple barter of the untutored Indian, to the most complicated and extensive operations of the London merchant." In comparing statements, apparently so contradictory, we must be careful not to be misled by the ambiguous word value. In the language of the mercantile system, the word *value* comprises what Adam Smith distinguishes as utility or value in use, which he keeps separate from the idea of exchangeable value. Adam Smith would admit, that, in commerce, a person generally exchanges away an article relatively less useful to himself for one relatively more useful; but such qualities do not determine the respective values of the two articles. The greater or less utility of a commodity may furnish a motive for the exchange, but will not decide the proportion in which one commodity will exchange for another. Those proportions must be decided by some other consideration than the capacity of commodities to satisfy our wants, namely, by some relation which they bear to a common standard, and it is that relation which expresses their value.

Mr. Huskisson's opinion.

Alterations of the coinage.

The notion of the value of money being purely conventional had paved the way for the repeated

LECTURE V. exercise of the prerogative of the Crown, in augmenting and diminishing the value of money at its pleasure. Money was said to be augmented in value, when a given weight of silver was coined into a greater number of pieces of a given denomination, the value of the coin being held to be augmented as its weight was diminished. Melon maintained that the augmentation in the value of the coin was always advantageous to the Crown, and to the people, in their mutual relation of debtors, inasmuch as the revenues of the Crown would be collected, and the charges would be defrayed with greater ease to all parties, in proportion to the greater abundance of money. This doctrine, with its various corollaries, could not but challenge opposition, and it gave occasion to Dutot, the cashier of the Company of the Indies, to publish a refutation of it in a series of letters, which appeared ultimately in their complete form, in 1738, in a work entitled "Réflexions Politiques sur le Commerce et les Finances." This treatise contained the ablest exposition of the principles of currency hitherto attempted; and although the author's relations with Law somewhat biassed his judgment, in examining the operations of credit, yet the sound and lucid doctrines which he propounded, in discussing the operations of money, relieved the question from much of the embarrassment, in which Melon's work had involved it. Dutot's book was, in its turn, ably criticised by Paris-Duverney, one of Law's most vigorous opponents, whose intimate connexion with the measures of finance adopted by the French Government upon the failure of Law's system, had subjected him to some unfavourable reflexions in the course of Dutot's work, ("Examen des Réflexions Politiques sur les Finances, par Paris-Duverney.")

Dutot.

Paris-Duverney.

Forbonnais.

The addition of the name of Forbonnais will complete the list of Financial Economists. His work, however, entitled "Recherches et Considérations sur les Finances de France," is not so much a treatise upon finance, as an historical review of the three great economical experiments, which had hitherto been tried in France, namely, the agricultural system of Sully, the manufactural and commercial system of Colbert, and the financial system of Law.

The partisans of the mercantile system had, for the most part, supported Law's financial measures; so that the failure of Law's scheme could not but weaken the hold which Colbertism had over men's opinions. We should, consequently, not be surprised at seeing the standard of revolt openly raised against the mercantile system, by a philosophical mind, which had studied the phenomena of agricultural industry, and had conceived its importance, as the productive instrument of national wealth, to be paramount. M. Quesnay, the originator of a new order of ideas, was chief physician to Louis XV. of France, and was enabled, by his position, to secure for his opinions the ready attention of the Court, as well as of the chief members of the King's Government. His views were made public, for the first time, in 1756, in the French Encyclopédie, under the articles "Fermiers" and "Grains," and their publication formed the commencement of a new era in the mode of treating such subjects.

M. Quesnay's novel theory.

Up to this time, indeed, the opponents of the mercantile system had carried on a kind of "Guerilla," one writer assailing its views of money, another its principles of exchanges, a third, its doctrine of profits; but no system of combined operations against it had as yet been organised. Its outposts had certainly been stormed and carried, but the citadel had not been as yet assailed. Quesnay, however, having, at a glance, discovered the key of the enemy's position, determined to subject *the nature of wealth* itself to a

Analysis of wealth.

LECTURE V.

fresh analysis, knowing that if he could but succeed in showing, that the end, which the mercantile system sought to accomplish, was not the true end to which all combinations of industry should be directed, the means, which were, of course, subordinate to that end, would at once be discredited.

Quesnay assumed, as the basis of his system, that "the earth was the sole source of wealth, and agriculture that which multiplied it." Labour, applied to land, he held, was the only labour that produced something more than the wages of the labourer, i. e. more than the equivalents of the expense of production, and it was exclusively the surplus produce of the land, that formed the fund out of which the wages of all other kinds of labour were defrayed. The first kind of labour was thus the sole kind employed *productively*, in extracting from the earth new materials, upon which the other kinds of labour might be subsequently employed, in modifying their form, and adapting them to the different uses of mankind. Society thus at once divided itself into two great classes —the productive class, consisting of the cultivators of the soil, and the stipendiary class, subsisting entirely on the produce of the former class, of which it receives a portion in exchange for its services.

Productive labour.

In course of time, however, as the produce of the land was found to be more than sufficient to support these two classes, the cultivator, in many cases, devolved the task of cultivation, and a portion of the produce, to another party, reserving to himself the remainder of the produce in the character of proprietor. Such is the theoretical outline which Turgot has traced in his "Reflexions sur la Formation et la Distribution des Richesses," and such the practical division which Quesnay assumed in his "Tableau Economique." To use his own words, "La Nation est réduite à trois classes de citoyens: la classe pro-

Turgot sur les Richesses.

ductive, la classe des propriétaires, et la classe sterile." According to this division, the whole revenue of the land belongs to the proprietary class, who have for their own enjoyment the *net produce*, which remains over and above, after the advances of the cultivator have been repaid. The cultivator's advances consist in the food, &c. which he has himself consumed, and the wages which he has paid for the services of the unproductive class, which has likewise furnished him with his farming implements, &c.

LECTURE V.

Quesnay's Tableau E'conomique.

The gross revenue of the land will thus be the measure of the annual reproduction of wealth. "In economical language," writes the Abbé Baudeau, "the word 'reproduction' signifies the entire aggregate of food and raw materials, of which the one part will be consumed rapidly, by living beings, the other will be used slowly, after having been more or less modified in form." (Introduction à la Philosophie Economique, chap. i. s. 4.)

L'Abbé Baudeau.

It is obvious, that the conclusions of the school of Quesnay are involved at once in their definition of wealth. The proposition "La terre est l'unique source de richesses," implies that wealth consists exclusively in the raw produce of the soil: hence, of course, no labour except that employed in agriculture could be productive of wealth. In this sense the labour of the artisan was termed unproductive; for Quesnay, admitting that the artisan produced forms, and that his labour added value to the raw material, denied that he produced really wealth. "I do not deny," he says in his second dialogue, "Sur les Travaux des Artisans," "that there is an addition of wealth to the primary materials of the works fashioned by artisans, since labour augments in effect the value of the primary material. But we must distinguish between an addition of wealth by combination, from a production of wealth: that is, between an augmen-

Wealth the raw produce of the soil.

LECTURE V.

tation of it, by the combination of raw materials with a certain expenditure in the consumption of articles which were in existence before this augmentation, and a generation or creation of wealth, which forms a renewal and real increase of it (renaissante)." The supposed production of wealth by the artisan would thus be in truth nothing more than the preservation of wealth, by encasing it as it were in new forms.

The labour of the artisan unproductive.

Quesnay, however, in terming the labour of the artisan unproductive and barren, did not deny to the arts utility, inasmuch as by the forms which they imparted to matter, they adapted it to the comfort and preservation of human life; but, according to his view, they did not create value, the essential characteristic of an article of wealth, but only utility, inasmuch as by the new forms which they produced they created a new use, but the value of their work was made up of the value of the new materials employed, and the commodities consumed by the artisan in the course of his occupation. If, he continued, the labour of artisans were productive of wealth, the greater the number employed upon any work, the higher would be its exchangeable value, and the greater the addition to the national stock of wealth; but it is generally admitted that the greater the economy of labour and other expenditure in the arts, the greater is the advantage resulting to the state from a diminution in the price of the commodities. "This drinking-glass," he writes, in the dialogue above referred to, "only cost one penny: the raw material of which it is made cost a farthing: the labour of a glass-blower has quadrupled the value of this material. We have here a production of wealth equivalent to treble the original amount: it would therefore be advantageous, according to your view, to discover a mode of making a similar glass, which would employ the labour of two workmen for a year: and still better, if it were to employ the labour of four workmen for a year: consequently, you would say that it would be very disadvantageous if a machine were to be invented which would make, without cost, or with very little cost, beautiful lace and splendid pictures. In reality, the invention of printing gave occasion for very serious discussions upon the diminution of the labour of copiers; nevertheless, after a careful examination, printing was fully adopted. You must thus, my good friend, reconcile your ideas, if you can, with these contradictions; otherwise the object of the pretended production of wealth, by the labour of artisans, does not seem worthy of consideration."

Tableau Économique.

Now Quesnay had said in his "Tableau Economique" that it was by the sale of the productions of the soil, at first hand, that the value of the annual reproduction of the wealth of a nation was known; and, in his 18th maxim, "Telle est la valeur venale, tel est le revenue: abondance, et non valeur, n'est pas richesse. Disette et cherté est misère. Abondance et cherté est opulence." And again, "Qu'on ne croie pas que le bon marché des denrées est profitable au menu peuple, car le bas prix des denrées fait baisser le salaire des gens du peuple, diminue leur aisance, leur procure moins de travail et d'occupations lucratives, et anéantit le revenue de la nation."

Value according to Quesnay's view.

Quesnay seems thus to employ the word value, in regard to agricultural produce, in a different sense from that in which he uses it with respect to manufactures. In regard to the latter, their selling value, according to Quesnay's own views, represented precisely the cost of their production. An increase, therefore, in their value, in this sense, would only imply an increase in their cost; and this would evidently entail, not the production, but the consumption of wealth: but when it was admitted, in the course of the argument, that the labour of the artisan augmented in effect the value of the raw material, the exchangeable value must have been meant; inasmuch as, in the first place, the raw material is expressly distinguished from the commodities required for the subsistence of the workmen; and, secondly, it would have been a mockery for the speaker, in the dialogue, who represents Quesnay, to avow that he did not deny that the labour of the artisan increased the cost of production. The fallacy of the entire argument seems to consist in the ambiguous use of the word "value," which he does not merely employ in the twofold sense just enumerated of exchangeable value and cost of production; but at one time he uses the term *collectively*, at another *distributively*. Thus, he says, those who do not distinguish between the real and the fictitious augmentation of wealth, believe that the production of wealth, which results from the labour of the artisan, consists in the augmentation of the exchangeable value of his work, which is inconsistent. Now, it would be quite possible for the exchangeable value of the work of the artisan class to be augmented without the cost of its production being augmented, if the *quantity* of that work were only to be augmented, in which case its exchangeable value, *collectively*, might be increased, though the exchangeable value of each portion of the work, i. e., its exchangeable value *distributively*, might remain unchanged, or even be diminished: so that there would not of necessity be any contradiction in supposing the mass of manufactured produce to be increased, and its collective value augmented, yet the price of each separate article and its cost of production to be diminished. Quesnay was aware, in all probability, that the argument which he employed, was rhetorical, as, after making his opponent retort it unskilfully upon him in reference to agricultural labour, he charges him with wishing to escape from the difficulty by changing his ground, and thereupon he himself proceeds to another topic.

Commerce.

In a similar manner the labour of the merchant was not admitted by Quesnay to be in any way productive: commerce, he maintained, was but the exchange of value for equal value (le commerce n'est qu'un échange de valeur pour valeur égale), and that relatively to these values there was neither gain nor loss to the parties. "As for me," he says, "I have always seen in commerce nothing more than the exchange of value for equal value without production, although this may be profitable from circumstances, to one or other of the parties, and even to them both. In fact, one may always presume that it is profitable to both parties; for, on the one side and on the other, they procure the enjoyment of wealth, which they could not obtain, except by an exchange; but invariably there is an exchange of one kind of wealth of a certain value for another kind of wealth of an equal value, and consequently, no real augmentation of wealth."

"The productions, which I want to sell and the artisan wants to buy, exist, before I can sell them, or the artisan can buy them. Thus, our commerce, in the sale and purchase of these productions, does not give them birth. It is not, therefore, productive of the things which I want to sell, and which the artisan wants to buy."

Again, "as it is the interest of the purchaser to buy at as low a price as possible, and of the vendor to sell at as high a price as possible, and both are compelled to make a sacrifice of interest, there are other conditions, independent of the will of the vendor or purchaser, which determine the price of merchandise; their commerce, therefore, is not productive of the wealth, or the exchangeable value of the productions, which they exchange with each other, since both

LECTURE V.

the merchandise and the silver have their price settled before the exchange."

This theory of commerce at once exploded the whole tariff-apparatus of the mercantile system. If commerce was nothing but an exchange of equivalents, the balance of trade was an airy phantom, and it would be no more disadvantageous to buy manufactured goods than raw materials. Otherwise, how could the commerce of two countries be maintained if the gain was all on one side? and if it were really disadvantageous for a country to buy manufactured goods from foreigners, how could it be expected that foreigners should consent to receive her manufactures in exchange for their own raw materials?

Annual increment of national wealth.

"Of the gross produce of the land, the annual reproduction of wealth, a large portion is at once required to make good the advances of the cultivator. The surplus represents the annual increment of national wealth, and it constitutes the disposable capital of a country, just as the proprietors constitute the disposable class for the general purposes of the state, other than those of production." Hence sprung Quesnay's suggestion of repealing all the existing taxes, and imposing in their stead a single tax (impôt unique), which should be levied at once upon the net produce of the land. He contended that all taxes, however indirectly imposed, must ultimately be defrayed out of this net produce. If they were paid by the productive class, they would form a portion of their outgoings, which would have to be replaced out of the gross produce of the land: if they were paid by the unproductive class, as the latter body earned its subsistence by working for the productive class, the funds from which the tax must be defrayed, would again have to be furnished by the productive class out of the gross produce of the land, and in both cases the amount of net produce would be

Impôt Unique.

LECTURE V.

A single tax upon the net produce.

equally reduced. By levying, therefore, a single tax at once upon the net produce, much of the expenses of collection under the existing system of diffused taxation would be saved. On Quesnay's theory of wealth and productive labour, the advantages of a single direct tax, in a mere financial point of view, were self-evident, inasmuch as the revenues of the state would be augmented by the saving of expenditure without the burden of taxation being increased: in addition, however, such a tax was less objectionable in its operation than indirect taxes, inasmuch as it did not check the growth of national wealth to the same extent. Indirect taxes, for instance, operate as obstacles to consumption; but the consumption of an article is what stimulates its reproduction, "Tel est le debit, telle est la reproduction." All obstacles, therefore, to the consumption of agricultural produce, such as heavy transport duties, restrictions upon exportation to foreign countries, &c., were so many discouragements to agricultural industry, and every such discouragement tended to reduce the quantity of net produce. Again, every obstacle thrown in the way of the manufacturer and merchant increased their expenditure, and consequently the cost of their work or merchandise; but the increase cost of their work had to be defrayed from the net produce of the land: the greater therefore the saving in the expenditure required for procuring a given quantity of manufactures or merchandise, the greater would be the residue of net produce. It could not, therefore, be for the interest of the proprietor of the land to throw impediments in the way of the industry of the manufacturer or merchant, as they would react upon himself, nor could it be for the interest of the manufacturer or merchant to restrict the production of the agriculturist, for with every increase in the gross revenue of the land there

LECTURE V.

would be an increase in the fund for the payment of the services of the unproductive class, and a corresponding increase in the demand for their work. "Qu'on maintienne," says Quesnay in his 25th maxim, "l'entière liberté du commerce; car la police du commerce intérieur et extérieur la plus sure, la plus exacte, la plus profitable à la nation et à l'état, consiste dans la pleine liberté de la concurrence."

Liberty of commerce.

Although the spirit of Quesnay's system was so liberal and generous in its results, it cannot be denied that his definition of wealth and productive industry was only less narrow, than that which we meet with amongst the supporters of the mercantile system. De Boisguillebert entertained juster views when he said that wealth consisted in an abundance of commodities suitable for consumption, and that opulence was nothing else than a great consumption of such commodities.

De Boisguillebert.

Mr. Macculloch.

Mr. Macculloch, in the introductory discourse prefixed to his edition of the "Wealth of Nations," after reviewing the leading features of Quesnay's system, observes, "that in assuming agriculture to be the only source of wealth, because the matter of which all commodities are composed must be originally derived from the earth, M. Quesnay and his followers mistook altogether the nature of production, and really supposed wealth to consist of matter; whereas, in its natural state, matter is very rarely possessed of immediate and direct utility, and is always destitute of value. It is only by means of the labour which must be laid out in appropriating matter, and in fitting and preparing it for our use, that it acquires exchangeable value, and becomes wealth. Human industry does not produce wealth by making any additions to the matter of our globe, this being a quantity susceptible neither of augmentation nor diminution. Its real and only effect is to produce wealth by giving utility to matter already in existence; and it has been repeatedly demonstrated, that the labour employed in manufactures and commerce is just as productive of utility, and consequently of wealth, as the labour employed in agriculture. Neither is the cultivation of the soil, as M. Quesnay supposed, the only species of industry which yields a surplus produce after the expenses of production are deducted. When agriculture is most productive, i. e. when none but the most fertile soils are cultivated, no rent, or *produit net*, is obtained from the land, and it is only after recourse has been had to poorer soils, and when, consequently, the productive powers of the labour and capital begin to diminish, that rent begins to appear; so that, instead of its being a consequence of the superior productiveness of agricultural industry, rent is really a consequence of its becoming less productive than others."

This is rather a startling mode of stating the fact, that in every country there is some land under cultivation which returns no *produit net*, but merely repays the outlay of labour and capital in the form of wages and profits, and that agricultural industry is not universally *productive*, in Quesnay's sense of the word, but in some cases is as *stipendiary* as the labour of the manufacturer and the merchant, and must be content with earning bare subsistence.

One of the most questionable positions which M. Quesnay maintained was, that low prices were prejudicial to the lower orders. "Qu'on ne croie pas que le bon marché des denrées est profitable au menu peuple; car le bas prix des denrées fait baisser le salaire des gens du peuple, diminue leur aisance, leur procure moins de travail et d'occupations lucratives, et anéantit le revenu de la nation." Quesnay's theory of prices.

Now both facts and the reason of the thing are opposed to this statement. Mr. Malthus, in his "Principles of Political Economy," has shown, from various periods of English history, that the bullion price of Mr. Malthus.

labour does not rise and fall with the bullion price of corn; but, on the contrary, that the bullion price of labour has risen, whilst the bullion price of corn was falling. As far as the reason of the thing is concerned, there is no necessary connexion between the price of labour and the price of raw produce: they may both rise and both fall together in common with all other commodities, if money becomes more plentiful or more scarce; but this will be merely a nominal rise and fall, and cannot affect the condition of the labourer; but raw produce may fall whilst wages rise in price, if only the supply of raw produce be greater than the demand for it, and the demand for labourers be greater than the supply of them; and raw produce may rise in price in consequence of an increased demand for it, yet the labour market may be overstocked with labourers, and wages continue low.

M. de Gournay.

By the side of M. Quesnay, though under an independent banner, we find M. de Gournay, the Intendant-general of Commerce, combating the restrictions of the mercantile system, and by his station and reputation for talent contributing greatly to the dissemination of more enlarged and comprehensive views with respect to commerce. With him, according to many writers, originated the saying, "laissez faire, laissez aller," leave *labour* to itself, leave *produce* to itself; though its origin is by others attributed to a merchant of the name of Legendre, on occasion of his being consulted by Colbert as to his proposed tariff. Neither Quesnay nor M. de Gournay contemplated the formation of a school; but the system of Quesnay, which became distinguished by the name of "La

La Physiocratie.

Physiocratie," awakened curiosity by the novelty of its theory, and arrested attention by the scientific mode in which its doctrines were stated; so that in a short time Quesnay numbered a large body of admirers and disciples, who were distinguished by the name of "Les Economistes." Amongst these the most illustrious for their writings were Le Marquis de Mirabeau, Dupont de Nemours, Mercier de la Rivière, l'Abbé Baudeau, and Le Trosne. The works of the last four, in conjunction with Quesnay's own publications, make up the list of "Physiocrats" in the collection now publishing in Paris. Turgot must be considered as the statesman of this school, although he was not a blind disciple of the system. His work upon the formation and distribution of wealth has been already alluded to. It is the clearest and most attractive of all the treatises based on the principles of the Physiocrats, and it comes nearest to the work of Adam Smith in its exposition of the general principles of the science of national wealth.

Les E'conomistes.

Turgot.

M. Necker was the most distinguished adversary of the Economists in France. They had at once raised a most important practical question, as to the removal of the existing restrictions upon the trade in corn. Colbert had prohibited the exportation of grain with a view of securing for the manufacturers an abundant supply at low prices. His policy, as was to be expected, had entailed consequences most prejudicial to agriculture. Dupont and Necker were before long engaged in a controversy on the subject; but the most vigorous supporters of the mercantile system in opposition to the doctrines of the French Economist School were to be found amongst the ranks of the Italian economists: amongst these the Abbé Galiani stands pre-eminent, whose celebrated dialogues "Sur le Commerce des Grains," which he wrote in Paris when secretary of the Neapolitan embassy, drew Mercier de la Rivière into the controversy. In Italy itself, Beccaria raised his voice against the doctrines of the Physiocrats in his lectures on political economy delivered before the university of Milan in 1768 and 1769; but the most complete exposition of the funda-

M. Necker

Dupont de Nemours.

Abbé Galiani.

Beccaria.

LECTURE V.

PietroVerri.

mental error of their system in maintaining the exclusive productiveness of agricultural labour appeared in 1771, when Pietro Verri published his "Meditazioni sulla Economia Politica."

"Reproduction," he writes, "is just as much attributable to labour employed on manufactures as to agricultural labour. All the phenomena of the world which are produced by the hand of man, or rather by the universal operation of natural laws, gives us the idea, not of an actual creation, but only of a modification of matter. To combine and to separate are the only elements which the human mind can discover in analysing the idea of reproduction, and it is as much a reproduction of value or wealth, if the earth, the air, or the water in the fields is converted into grain, as if with the aid of the hand of man the glutinous secretion of an insect is transmuted into velvet, or certain little bits of metal are organised so as to produce a sound. Whole cities, and entire states, are supported by nothing else but the produce of this most fertile unproductive class, whose reproduction comprises the value of the raw materials, the consumption proportionate to the hands employed, and a further share which goes to enrich the person who has embarked in the undertaking, and prosecuted it with successful talent."

Reproduction of value.

Again, "the reproduction of value is shown by that amount of price which the wares or manufactured goods bear above the original value of the raw materials, and the cost of the commodities consumed during the process of fabrication." Again, "the price of all commodities depends upon the combination of the two elements of demand and scarcity."

These are very different opinions from those entertained by the Physiocrats. We must not, however, suppose that either Beccaria or Verri were partisans of the mercantile system. They had sufficient acuteness to detect the falseness of Quesnay's principles, whilst they recognised the truth of many of his conclusions. Thus Verri maintained that "liberty of commerce in respect of grain could never, under any circumstances, be prejudicial either to the subsistence or the abundance of a nation;" that "the balance of trade, as it is called, is not sure evidence of a prosperous commerce," for the real question is, whether more or less annual reproduction has taken place in consequence of the commerce. "No one can be a vendor without being a purchaser. A nation composed of vendors alone would be a chimera; it would be an effect without a cause."

Bandini.

We must not, however, in turning over this page of our inquiry, which the system of the French economists occupies, omit to notice the writings of Bandini, whom the Italians regard as the precursor of Quesnay in the leading principles of his system. His "Discorso Economico," was written as early as 1737, though according to his biographer, it was not published till 1775. Its object was to call the attention of the Grand Duke Francis to the condition of the district of the Siennese Maremma, comprising about two fifths of Tuscany, which was little better than a pestilential swamp, and of which the cultivation had been almost totally abandoned. He contended that, under the combined operation of heavy indirect duties, and restrictions on the commerce of grain, it was impossible for the cultivator to make head against his expenses. "If," he says, "the consumption is not proportioned to the quantity of produce, the latter loses estimation, and its price falls. This fall in price entails a loss upon cultivation, which leads to the ruin of the country people, to poverty, to the distress of the towns, and, finally, to scarcity."

LECTURE V.

"Nature," he elsewhere says, "has given to the earth a fertility proportioned to the wants of its inhabitants. Providence, too, has filled the world with ample supplies; but, in order to keep up intercourse between men and between countries, he has so disposed them in his wisdom that no one should possess all that is designed for him.

"From the earliest period of the world neither has grain been gathered by shepherds, nor wool produced by the earth to clothe the labourer; but, by the shepherd and the labourer innocently exchanging their mutual surplus, all have found themselves adequately fed and adequately clothed. One district produces wine in superabundance, but is deficient in grain: another, though most fertile in grain, has not a climate adapted to ripen the grape so as to make wine. Providence has provided these two countries with grain and with wine, respectively, without any other obligation than that each should hand over its surplus to the other.

Artificial obstacles to exchanges.

"But if one country, swerving from this beneficent law, in order to augment unjustly the value of the superfluity which it parts with, loads it with a duty or raises difficulties in the way of commerce, as for the most part resulted upon the breaking up of the Roman empire, both countries will soon begin to be distressed from a scarcity of grain and of wine. Inasmuch as wine, for example, being raised in price by the duty imposed upon it, will require more measures of grain than before to compensate for the expenditure upon it; the natural equilibrium between the respective surpluses being destroyed, the surplus of grain will balance a less quantity of wine: hence the poor man, who was before just able to procure for himself a supply of wine during the year, in exchange for the surplus of his grain, will be obliged to drink water during several months, and to consume a less quantity of wine. In this manner, the consumption being diminished, a glut of wine will ensue: it will lose its value in the market, and it will no longer answer for the labourer to cultivate the vine, much less to plant it."

Quesnay himself could not have pleaded the cause of the cultivators of the soil in more expressive language. Bandini, having incidentally stated that agricultural labour, when not discouraged from exerting its full powers, will be found not merely to pay its expenses, but to secure a double or even a quadruple return, proposes the repeal of the established duties on the transport and consumption of agricultural produce, and that a direct tax should at once be levied upon rent. "It appears to me," he writes, "that a tenth, or a certain per centage, ought to be paid on account of all arable lands, and pastures, and ground-rents (terratici), but not by the labourers, nor the shepherds, nor the farmers (coloni), but by the proprietors of the land, and that it ought to be doubled upon all who do not effectively discharge their duty, as inhabitants, without any exemption founded upon privilege or naturalization." For this apparent sacrifice, he contended, that the proprietors would be fully indemnified by the increased rental from new lands being brought into cultivation, and by the reduction of indirect taxes.

Direct tax upon rent.

It is impossible to deny to Bandini the credit which his compatriots have claimed for him; and under the enlightened administration of the Grand Duke Pietro Leopoldo, the principles which he had advocated, were found to lead in their application to the happiest results. The population of the Maremma multiplied: it rapidly acquired, by the exercise of a free commerce of raw produce and other commodities, the

Practical effects of Bandini's work.

LECTURE V. means of increasing the fertility of the soil, as well as of improving the character of its products. It thus became more industrious, more wealthy, and more happy. "Such," observes Count Pecchio, in his history of Political Economy in Italy, "were the effects of a good book upon a good Prince."

LECTURE VI.

LECTURE VI.

A DISTINGUISHED writer has observed, in reference to the great importance of appropriate definitions of the fundamental terms of political economy, that the comparative merits of the system of the economists of the school of M. Quesnay, which was discussed in the previous lecture, and that of Adam Smith, depend upon their different definitions of wealth and of productive labour. If the definitions which the economists have given of them be the most useful and correct, the system, which is founded upon them, is the correct one. If, on the other hand, the wider meaning assigned to these terms by Dr. Smith be more appropriate, then his system must be considered as superior both in utility and correctness.

Importance of definitions.

In this passage it would seem to be assumed, that in political economy, equally as in geometry, no correct definition of a term can be devised which shall not imply everything which belongs to the term, or, in other words, that the meaning of the term and the nature of the thing shall be one and the same. We must not, therefore, be surprised at the almost entire absence of definitions in Adam Smith's "Inquiry into the Nature and Causes of the Wealth of Nations," since his object was rather to explain the true character of the facts which the terms in ordinary use denoted, and he, no doubt, felt convinced that a more precise nomenclature would follow, as a necessary consequence of a more accurate tone of thought on such subjects.

Writers, antecedent to Adam Smith, who undertook expressly to treat of political economy, included,

LECTURE VI.

under that term, a much wider range of subjects than those to which, by the unassuming title of his work, he professed to confine his investigations. The great end of the political science is the happiness of the community, and its field of view embraces all the great variety of means which tend to further that end. But political economy, by its very name, implies a more limited department, whether we regard it as a specific branch of the political science, which the poverty of our language does not allow us to distinguish by a specific name, or merely as the science of managing the affairs of a household, applied to the corresponding portion of the concerns of a community.

Political economy distinct from the political science.

Adam Smith's view of political economy.

In Adam Smith's view, "Political economy, considered as a branch of the science of a statesman or legislator, proposes two distinct objects: first, to provide a plentiful revenue or subsistence for the people, or more properly, to enable them to provide such a revenue or subsistence for themselves; and, secondly, to supply the state or commonwealth with a revenue sufficient for the public services. It proposes to enrich both the people and the sovereign."

An inquiry, therefore, into the nature and causes of the wealth of nations would, according to the above statement, be identical with an investigation of the fundamental principles of the science of political economy; and to this more limited field the English, as distinguished from the Continental school of writers, have adhered since the publication of Adam Smith's work. The great founder of what has been termed the industrial system, as distinguished from the mercantile and agricultural systems, showed his usual discernment in selecting a title for his work, which should express its subject matter, rather than denote the nature of the science of which he was about to give a novel exposition.

LECTURE VI.

The circumstance, that political economy had hitherto been confounded with the science of government, had been calculated to mislead writers as to the proper province of their inquiry, and we thus find some of the most distinguished leaders of the French economist school, such as Mercier de la Rivière and the Abbé Baudeau readily diverging into the exclusive domain of politics, and at last discussing questions affecting the distribution of power, rather than the distribution of wealth. Such results could not but excite a jealousy on the part of statesmen, and a prejudice on the part of the public against political economists, as theoretical innovators in state matters; more particularly as writers who considered themselves employed on a science whose subject was the welfare of communities, felt it to be their duty to recommend the adoption of particular measures, as calculated to promote a certain distribution of wealth, according, as they conceived, to the best interests of society. From such objections political economy has been at last set free by the judicious limitation which Adam Smith adopted in excluding the element of government from his inquiries, and so confining his discussions to that sufficiently large class of means, which are embraced under the term wealth, and the command of which contributes, in a material form, to the welfare of communities. The functions of the political economist were thus kept quite separate from those of the statesman, and made justly subordinate to them; the former being employed upon the investigation of one set of causes and effects, the latter upon the operation of those effects in their turn, in common with many others, as causes of further effects. The business of the statesman thus commences where the political economist concludes his labours; and it falls within the province of the former, exclusively, to decide to what extent the conclusions of the latter

Deviations of earlier writers.

Functions of the political economist.

should be acted upon. Many persons, not being aware of the comparatively narrow sphere which the political economist of the school of Adam Smith is content to occupy, and that he does not intrude his advice, but merely supplies certain general principles for the use of the statesman, leaving it to his discretion to determine whether or not the occasion is suitable for their application, have objected to his confining his attention to wealth, as falling short of his duty. This objection might have some plausibility, if the political economist of the present day, who confined his attention to wealth, asserted his subject to be of the paramount importance which the economist of olden time claimed for his studies, when he professed the happiness of mankind to be the object of them. There have doubtless been incautious writers, who have brought discredit on political economy, by seeming to recommend measures solely on account of their being productive of wealth; but if this error be avoided, the objection above alluded to will not be well founded, and may be safely disregarded.

"The annual labour of every nation is the fund which originally supplies it with all the necessaries and conveniences of life, which it annually consumes, and which consists always either in the immediate produce of that labour, or in what is purchased with that produce from other nations." Such are the opening words of the introduction to the "Wealth of Nations," in which it will be observed that Adam Smith, by implication, assumes the subject matter of his treatise to be identical with the national stock of the necessaries and conveniences of life, and defines such stock *really* to be the produce, either immediate or mediate, of the annual labour of a nation.

Subject of Adam Smith's work.

Again, at the commencement of Chapter V. he writes, "Every man is rich or poor according to the degree in which he can afford to enjoy the necessaries, conveniences, and amusements of human life." We behold here the torch burning more brightly as it approaches us, which Antonio Serra kindled, and which has been handed on along the chain of writers which we have traced, and of which De Boisguillebert was the last link.

Serra's earlier statement.

Antonio Serra had been the first to point to the arts of industry, which provided mankind with the necessaries, conveniences, and delights of life, as the efficient causes of wealth, which one country might equally with another set in operation. De Boisguillebert had likewise said that wealth was nothing else than the power of procuring for oneself the comfortable maintenance of life, by the enjoyment of superfluities as well as necessaries; that money was only a means to secure this end: so that a country might be rich without much money, and the possessor of money, on the other hand, might be much distressed, if he could not exchange it away for the necessaries and conveniences of life.

Adam Smith, however, was not content to hand on the torch merely unextinguished. He imparted new fire to it, and, as it were, kindled it afresh by defining wealth to be the produce of human labour.

Locke's Essay on Civil Government.

Locke, indeed, in his Essay on Civil Government, referred to in the Third Lecture, in explaining how "the property of labour had been able to overbalance the community of land," had shown that it is "labour indeed that puts *the difference of value* on everything," or, as he elsewhere expresses himself, that "the improvement of labour makes the far greater part of the value:" but, as Mr. M'Culloch aptly observes, Locke does not seem to have been fully aware of the importance of the principle which he had elucidated, nor did he deduce from it any notable practical conclusion: on the contrary, in

LECTURE VI.

his tract on "Raising the Value of Money," published two years later, he laid it down broadly that all taxes, howsoever imposed, must ultimately fall upon the land; which was a conclusion quite in accordance with the principles of the Physiocrats, but totally inconsistent with the doctrine that "labour is the creative instrument of value."

Galiani's Trattato della Moneta.

The same kind of consideration seems to be due to a passage in the Abbé Galiani's "Trattato della Moneta," to which M. Say, in the Preliminary Discourse to his Traité d'Economie Politique, calls attention, as being to a certain extent an anticipation of Dr. Smith's doctrine. "Whilst speaking of labour, I may remark, that not merely in the case of pure works of art, such as pictures, sculptures, engravings, &c., but also in many substances, such as minerals, rocks, wild plants, &c., their value is due exclusively to labour. The quantity of matter in these substances does not contribute to their value further than by increasing or diminishing the labour." Yet Galiani in the same work says, that, whatever one person gains, some other person loses; which is a proposition evidently at variance with the obvious conclusion, that if labour creates wealth, a person may acquire wealth himself without depriving a neighbour of it.

The originality of the Abbé Galiani's view may perhaps be questioned, as he seems to have been acquainted with Locke's writings; but we might go as far back as to Sir W. Petty, whose work on Taxes and Contributions has been elsewhere quoted, if it were the scattered spark, and not the kindled flame that we sought for. It is not, however, the incidental discernment of a truth, but the clear appreciation of the principles on which it rests, and of the conclusions to which it leads, that constitutes a discovery. Servetus and Cæsalpinus rightly discerned the passage of the blood through the heart; but the disco-

What constitutes a discovery.

very of the circulation of the blood was peculiarly the work of Harvey. Cæsalpinus, to use the expressive language of Professor Monti of Pavia, touched it, handled it, and was on the very point of raising the veil and discovering it; but whilst the great discovery sparkled around him on every side, it mocked him, and eluded his grasp. So it was with the precursors of Adam Smith. They had perceived that the labour of man was productive of wealth. Galiani all but raised the veil, and discovered the consequences to which the principle led: it was reserved, however, for Adam Smith to make known how the circulation of wealth in great states originated and was maintained.

Labour in its rudest form seems to have been barely capable of providing support for all the members of a community; but amongst civilised nations, "the produce of the whole labour of society is so great, that all are often abundantly supplied, and a workman, even of the lowest and poorest order, if he is frugal and industrious, may enjoy a greater share of the necessaries and comforts of life than it is possible for any savage to acquire." This has been chiefly effected by the division of labour, which enables labour to be applied with greater skill and judgment; and the result is the greater productiveness of it. In illustration of this fact Adam Smith selects the trade of a pinmaker, and shows how the important business of making a pin is divided into about eighteen distinct operations, which, in some manufactories, are each performed by distinct hands: the result of which is, that the same number of persons, who, if they wrought separately and independently, and without the skill which continued practice alone brings with it, could not have made more than 200 pins in all probability, now make, in consequence of a proper

The division of labour.

LECTURE VI.

division and combination of their different occupations, upwards of 48,000 pins in a day.

Multiplication of productions.

"It is the great multiplication of the productions of all the different arts, in consequence of the division of labour, which occasions in a well-governed society that universal opulence, which extends itself to the lowest ranks of the people. Every workman has a great quantity of his own work to dispose of beyond what he himself has occasion for; and every other workman being exactly in the same situation, he is enabled to exchange a great quantity of his own goods for a great quantity, or what comes to the same thing, for the price of a great quantity of theirs. He supplies them abundantly with what they have occasion for, and they accommodate him as amply with what he has occasion for, and a general plenty diffuses itself through all the different ranks of society."

"When the division of labour has thus been once thoroughly established, it is but a very small part of a man's wants which the produce of his own labour can supply. He supplies the far greater part of them by exchanging that surplus part of the produce of his own labour, which is over and above his own consumption, for such parts of the produce of other men's labour as he has occasion for. Every man thus lives by exchanging, or becomes in some measure a merchant, and the society itself grows to be what is properly a commercial society." Having then traced out in what manner money has come to be the great medium of commerce, Dr. Smith proceeds to examine the rules which men observe in exchanging their produce. These rules determine what may be called the relative or exchangeable value of goods. Now the exchangeable value is distinct from the value in use or utility of an object, and things which have the greatest value in use, such as water, have frequently little or no value in exchange; and on the contrary,

Exchangeable value.

those which have the greatest value in exchange, such as the diamond, have frequently little or no value in use. What then are the principles which regulate the exchangeable value of commodities?

Definition of value.

In a civilised community, a man's own labour can supply him with a very small portion of the necessaries and conveniences of life; he must derive the greater part of them from the labour of other people, and he will thus be rich or poor according to the quantity of that labour which he can command, or which he can afford to purchase. "*The value of any commodity*, therefore, to the person who possesses it, and who means not to use or consume it himself, but to exchange it for other commodities, *is equal to the quantity of labour which it enables him to purchase or command.* Labour, therefore, is the real measure of the exchangeable value of all commodities.

Real price.

"*The real price* of every thing, what every thing really costs to the man who wants to acquire it, *is the toil and trouble of acquiring it.* What every thing is *really worth* to the man who has acquired it, and who wants to dispose of it, or exchange it for something else, *is the toil and trouble which it can save to himself*, and which it can impose upon other people. What is bought with money or with goods is purchased by labour as much as what we acquire by the toil of our own body. That money or those goods, indeed, save us this toil. *They contain the value of a certain quantity of labour, which we exchange for what is supposed at the time to contain the value of an equal quantity.* Labour was the first price, the original purchase-money that was paid for all things. It was not by gold or by silver, but by labour, that all the wealth of the world was originally purchased; and its value, to those who possess it, and who want to exchange it for some new productions, is precisely equal

LECTURE VI.

to the quantity of labour, which it can enable them to purchase or command."

Such is the foundation upon which the system of Dr. Smith was built up, and such the rule which determines the exchangeable value of goods in a simple and rude state of society: but as society advances, the real price of a commodity is no longer determined by the amount of labour immediately employed in its production. Before any exchanges can be made, an accumulation of produce, beyond what is required by the producer for his own consumption, must have taken place. This surplus he may either exchange away, as we have already seen, for the produce of other men's labour, by the consumption of which he will increase his own enjoyment of life, or he may employ it to supply himself with additional materials and tools for his work, and so increase the productive power of his own labour. In exchanging then the subsequent produce of his labour, he will seek an equivalent for the produce or stock which he has applied to improve the productiveness of his labour, and this equivalent is termed the profits of his stock, being in reality the indirect return to the labour originally expended in the production or acquisition of the stock. It thus happens that "in the price of almost all commodities the profits of stock form a component part distinct from the wages of labour, and in this state of things the whole produce does not belong to the labourer, but must be shared by him with the owner of the stock, wherever they are distinct persons." There are certain things, however, the quantity of which cannot be augmented, and amongst these is land. When the whole of the land of any country has become private property, a new element of price springs up. Hitherto it has been supposed that the application of labour rests solely with the will of the labourer and the owner of stock; but

The profits of stock.

when land is no longer open to fortuitous occupancy, but has all been appropriated, the person who seeks to employ his labour, or his stock, or both upon land, must acquire the power of doing so; and for this power he must give to the owner of the land a portion of his produce; and this constitutes the rent of land, and forms an element of the cost of production. Rent, according to this view, would seem to be the indirect wages of the labour originally employed in the appropriation of the land; but Dr. Smith refers its origin to the selfishness of human nature, from which the owners of the soil are not exempt, "who love to reap where they never sowed, and demand a rent even for its natural produce." Rent would thus be merely the consequence of a monopoly.

Rent of land.

Now this seems to be both incorrect and likewise inconsistent with what had been previously laid down respecting exchangeable value. It is incorrect, because there is always some appropriated land which will not yield rent, which the owner must cultivate in the joint capacity of labourer and capitalist, and which he cannot let to another person to cultivate, because there is no surplus after wages and profits are defrayed, and therefore no value for which he can obtain rent. It is also inconsistent with the definition of exchangeable value, as the creature of human labour, and the representative of labour. Thus, if A.'s land is twice as fertile as B.'s farm, A. will obtain the same amount of produce at the expense of half the labour and capital which B. employs. Whilst the whole of B.'s return will just compensate his outlay, A. will have a considerable surplus, which has resulted from the superiority of the natural powers of the soil. The use of those natural powers will thus save to any cultivator a certain expenditure of labour and capital: those natural powers will thus possess exchangeable value, and the price of them

Objections to Adam Smith's view of rent.

is what is properly termed the rent of the land. Doubtless, as soils of superior fertility are limited in quantity, this circumstance gives to rent the appearance of originating in a monopoly, but the price of the productive power of such lands is determined by totally different considerations from those which a monopoly gives rise to.

Thus, whilst the produce of B.'s farm will fetch 100*l*. in the market, such being the necessary return for the labour and capital expended in raising it, the produce of A.'s land will be worth just as much, because the acquisition of it will save the expenditure of an equal amount of labour and capital. The value, therefore, of the produce of A.'s farm is determined by considerations altogether independent of the payment of rent: rent, indeed, is paid, inasmuch as the sale of the produce secures more than the ordinary rate of profit, and it is paid on account of the superior quality of the soil.

Natural price.

Hence, when Dr. Smith says that the natural price of commodities, meaning thereby the price which is sufficient to pay the rent of land, the wages of the labour, and the profits of the stock employed, varies with the natural rate of its component parts, of wages, profits, and rent, he appears to have confounded variations in the proportions in which produce is shared amongst the producers, with variations in the proportions in which produce is exchanged; but the latter proportions can only be affected by changes in the circumstances under which some of the commodities are produced, and which will derange their mutual relations. Variations in rent cannot cause prices to fluctuate; for rent, properly speaking, is not an element of price, and variations in the rate of wages and profit, where the proportion of fixed capital is unchanged, affect all commodities in the same degree, so that their relations, in respect of such variations would remain undisturbed, and their exchangeable value not be altered.

Productive labour.

The economists had limited the term *productive labour* to labour employed upon land, inasmuch as such labour alone realised an amount of net produce. Adam Smith extended the application of the term to all labour from which value results. "There is one sort of labour," he writes, "which adds to the value of the subject upon which it is bestowed; there is another which has no such effect. The former, as it produces a value, may be called productive, the latter, unproductive labour. Thus the labour of a manufacturer adds generally to the value of the materials, which he works upon, that of his own maintenance, and of his master's profit. The labour of a menial servant, on the contrary, adds to the value of nothing. Though the manufacturer has his wages advanced to him by his master, he in reality costs him no expense, the value of those wages being generally restored, together with a profit, in the improved value of the subject upon which his labour is bestowed. But the maintenance of a menial servant never is restored. A man grows rich by employing a multitude of manufacturers: he grows poor by maintaining a multitude of menial servants. The labour of the latter, however, has its value, and deserves its reward as well as that of the former. But the labour of the manufacturer fixes and realises itself in some particular subject, or vendible commodity, which lasts for some time, at least after that labour is past. It is, as it were, a certain quantity of labour stocked and stored up, to be employed, if necessary, upon some other occasion. That subject, or what is the same thing, the price of that subject, can afterwards, if necessary, put in motion a quantity of labour equal to that which had originally produced it. The labour of the menial servant, on the contrary, does not fix or realise itself in any particular subject, or vendible commodity. His services generally perish in the very instant of their performance, and seldom leave any trace or value behind them, for which an equal quantity of service could afterwards be procured."

"This mode of applying the term *productive labour* to that labour which is directly productive of wealth, however wealth may be defined, is obviously," as Mr. Malthus observes, "of the greatest use in explaining the causes of the increase of wealth. The only essential objection to it, is that it seems to underrate the importance of all other kinds of labour, at least the term *unproductive labour* used by Adam Smith to express all other kinds of labour, has been frequently so interpreted, and has formed, in consequence, the great objection to the classification."

Unproductive labour.

One of the greatest embarrassments to the political economist arises from the necessary employment of terms, which have already an established acceptation in common use. On the one hand, if he employs them in their ordinary sense, the reader may, perhaps, be perplexed by the vagueness of their meaning, and if he extends or limits the scientific sense of them, his language becomes continually subject to misinterpretation. On the other hand, as he must frequently make innovations in the use of terms, for the sake of precision and consistency in so doing he runs the additional risk of misleading himself. Thus, when Adam Smith, at the opening of his treatise, laid it down, that "the annual labour of every nation is the fund which originally supplies it with all the necessaries and conveniences of life which it annually consumes, and which consist always either in the immediate produce of that labour, or in what is purchased with that produce from other nations," he is evidently speaking of the whole annual labour of a nation, and not of a part of it; and by so doing, he affixes at once to the term *labour*, a meaning which is inconsistent with the subsequent application of the epithet "*unproductive*" to it, under any circumstances. His division, therefore, of labour into productive and unproductive, seems at once to be objectionable, as being at variance with the scientific sense of the word "labour," which he had previously adopted. The popular meaning of the word would allow us to speak even of the labour of consumption, and, as he who does not produce, by the law of our nature consumes, unproductive labour, in the popular sense of the word, seems "ex necessitate rei" to be identical with consumption. For instance the boy, who blows bubbles, consumes soap and water; the cook, who fries fish, consumes coals and butter; the servant, who cleans boots and clothes, consumes blacking and brushes. In a word, are we not entitled to regard domestic servants, if it is convenient to do so, as instruments of consumption, in the use of which an opulent proprietor indulges himself to further his enjoyment, just as he might employ a boy to blow bubbles for his amusement? But Adam Smith says, "their labour has its value, and deserves its reward." If this be so, this reward apparently consists of food, and clothing, and lodging; in a word, of a multitude of products or commodities, the value of which will correspond to the value of their labour. On this supposition there is an exchange of equivalents between the parties, although the product of their labour is not readily appreciable. On the other hand, if there is no product resulting from their labour, there can be no element of value on their side, and consequently no exchange of values, and that which Adam Smith calls a reward, is a conditional gift: and that which seems to be an exchange of values, is, in fact, nothing but a distribution of wealth.

Domestic servants.

Mr. Malthus, considering the principle of the divi-

LECTURE VI.

Personal services.

sion adopted by Adam Smith to be most important in elucidating the growth of national wealth, proposes that the term personal services should be substituted for unproductive labour. "Labour, then," he says, "may be distinguished into two kinds, productive labour, and personal services, meaning by productive labour, that labour which is so directly productive of material wealth, as to be capable of estimation in the quantity or value of the object produced, which object is capable of being transferred without the presence of the producer; and meaning by personal services, that kind of labour or industry, which however highly useful and important some of it may be, and however much it may conduce indirectly to the production and security of material wealth, does not realise itself on any object which can be valued and transferred without the presence of the person performing such service, and cannot therefore be made to enter into an estimate of national wealth.

"This, though differing in name, is essentially the doctrine of Adam Smith."

Distinction between Adam Smith and Mr. Malthus.

Admitting fully the advantage of adopting the suggestion of Mr. Malthus, I cannot so readily acquiesce in his view, that his proposed division of labour is identical with that of Adam Smith. According to Mr. Malthus, all sorts of labour are productive; but some are directly, others indirectly so. But indirectly productive labour is a very different thing from unproductive labour, as it is, in fact, a species of productive labour; whereas, in Adam Smith's system, unproductive labour is a species of labour altogether distinct from productive labour. Thus, Adam Smith writes, "the labour of some of the most respectable orders in society is, like that of menial servants, unproductive of any value, and does not fix or realise itself in any permanent subject, or vendible commodity, which endures after that labour is past, and for which an equal quantity of labour could afterwards be procured. The sovereign, for example, with all the officers both of justice and war who serve under him, the whole army and navy, are unproductive labourers. They are the servants of the public, and are maintained by a part of the annual produce of the industry of other people. Their service, how honourable, how useful, or how necessary soever, produces nothing for which an equal quantity of service can afterwards be procured. The protection, security, and defence of the commonwealth, the effect of their labour this year, will not purchase its protection, security, and defence for the year to come. In the same class must be ranked some both of the gravest and most important, and some of the most frivolous professions; churchmen, lawyers, physicians, men of letters of all kind; players, buffoons, musicians, opera-singers, opera-dancers, &c. The labour of the meanest of these has a certain value, regulated by the very same principles which regulate that of every other part of labour; and that of the noblest and most useful produces nothing which could afterwards purchase or procure an equal quantity of labour. Like the declamation of the actor, the harangue of the orator, or the tune of the musician, the work of all of them perishes in the very instant of production."

This appears to be one of the most objectionable passages in the whole of Dr. Smith's work. We see evidently the leaven of the "net produce" of the French Economist School working in the writer's mind, and though he could not acquiesce in the narrow definition of production which M. Quesnay had adopted he was unwilling to reject altogether the principle implied in it, namely, that there was *a difference in kind* between certain sorts of labour. M. Quesnay drew the line at once at that limit where labour ceased to be employed directly upon land, and ad-

M. Quesnay's view.

LECTURE VI. mitted *differences of degree* in the productiveness of labour within this limit. Adam Smith advanced the limit to the point where the results of labour ceased to be realised in what he terms "a vendible commodity," and beyond that limit he conceived a difference of kind to commence. Distinctions of this sort, it is obvious, are perfectly arbitrary, and resolve themselves into questions of convenience, provided they do not give rise to inconsistencies in the nomenclature; if the latter provision be not observed, they may at once be justly objected to.

Mr. Senior's statement.

One of the most philosophical statements on this branch of our subject is to be found in Mr. Senior's article on Political Economy in the Encyclopædia Metropolitana.

"It appears to us," he writes, "that the distinctions that have been attempted to be drawn between productive and unproductive labourers, or between the producers of material or immaterial products, or between commodities or services, rest on differences existing not in the things themselves, but in the modes in which they attract our attention. In those cases in which our attention is principally called, not to the act of occasioning the alteration, but to the result of that act, to the thing (as) altered, economists have termed the person who occasioned that alteration a productive labourer, or the producer of a commodity or material product. Where, on the other hand, our attention is principally called not to the thing (as) altered, but to the act of occasioning the alteration, economists have termed the person occasioning the alteration an unproductive labourer, and his exertions, services, or immaterial products. A shoemaker alters leather, and thread, and wax, into a pair of shoes. A shoe-black alters a dirty pair of shoes into a clean pair. In the first case our attention is called principally to the things as altered. The shoemaker, therefore, is said to make or produce shoes. In the case of the shoe-black, our attention is called principally to the act as performed. He is not said to make or produce the commodity, clean shoes, but to perform the service of cleaning them. In each case, there is of course an act and a result; but in the one case our attention is called principally to the act; in the other, to the result."

It might have been perhaps more correct to have represented the shoe-black as altering blacking and dirty shoes into clean shoes. If the shoe-black is a private servant, he is simply an instrument of his master to assist him in the consumption of blacking, which consumption takes place, not when it is applied to the boot, for a clean boot is of more value than a dirty boot, but when the boot is soiled afresh. The master, therefore, really consumes the blacking, and the servant assists him. On the other hand, the shoe-black may keep a stall, as is frequently seen in the streets of Paris, and his services may be at the command of the public: in this case, he is a trader, and supplies clean shoes in exchange for dirty shoes and money.

M. Arago, in his Eloge Historique of James Watt, read before the Academy of Sciences, on Dec. 8th, 1834, relates the following anecdote:—

Newcomen's Steam-engine.

The first machine of Newcomen (constructed in 1765) required the most unremitting attention on the part of the person whose business it was to close and open incessantly certain cocks (robinets), by which at one moment the steam was admitted into the cylinder, at another, a jet of cold water entered to condense it. It happened on a particular occasion that whilst a boy named Humphrey Potter was thus employed, his comrades, who were at play, excited him so much by their cries, that he found himself at last unable to resist the temptation to join them. But the task im-

LECTURE VI.

posed upon him was one which he could not venture to abandon for a single minute. The excitement of the moment, however, kindled in him a spark of genius, and suggested to him certain relations between the parts of the machine, which he had before not observed. Of the two cocks, one required to be opened at the moment when the balance-rod, which Newcomen first introduced, completed its descending oscillation, and to be closed at the conclusion of its ascending oscillation. The operations of the second cock were just the reverse. There was thus a necessary dependence between the movements of the balance-rod and the opening and shutting of the two cocks, and it occurred to Potter that the balance-rod might be made to communicate the necessary motion to the other parts of the machine. He at once attached cords from the handles of the cocks to certain parts of the balance-rod, and found that the tightening and loosening of these cords, with every ascending and descending oscillation, would produce the same effect that he hitherto produced with his hand. For the first time the Steam-engine worked by itself, without any further care than that of feeding the furnace with coals. More complicated constructions were soon adopted to replace the simple contrivance of the child; but the origin of them all was owing to the mere longings of a boy to join his play-fellows.

Continuous links in the chain of production.

According to Adam Smith's division, this boy would be classed under the head of unproductive labourers; yet without his co-operation in opening and shutting the cocks, the power of the Steam-engine in its infancy could not have been exerted to keep in motion the machinery, by means of which the labour of the spinner or the weaver became immediately productive. The first link of a chain-cable is just as instrumental as the last link in holding a ship by its anchor;

and so each individual, who forms a link in the great chain of operations of human labour, however far remote his place may be from that of the person out of whose hands the product issues, in its finished state of preparation for the consumer, as he has in his place contributed a share to that general result, seems justly entitled to be considered a productive labourer equally with the last workman.

Having shown that value in exchange was the creature of human labour, Adam Smith proceeds to point out the distinction between the real and the nominal prices of commodities. The value of money being determined by the same considerations which affect all other value, the nominal or money price of commodities may fluctuate with variations in the value of money, whilst their real price, measured by the amount of labour or labour's worth, which is required for their production, will be undisturbed. The distinction between the real and the nominal price of commodities may thus be of material importance, because the same nominal price may at different times correspond to very different real prices. At the same time and place, indeed, the real and nominal prices of all commodities will be in proportion to each other; so that the nominal price is generally regarded with more attention than the real price; but if contracts are extended over a considerable period of time, as in the case of land let out upon long leases, a corn rent would be likely to represent a more constant value than a money rent.

Whenever an article is sold for its real cost, under which term the ordinary rate of profits is comprised, in addition to what may be called the prime cost, it is sold, according to Adam Smith's phraseology, for its natural price. But the actual price at which any commodity is commonly sold is called its market price, which may exceed, or fall short of, or corre-

Natural and Market price.

LECTURE VI.

spond to the natural price. This market price depends on the proportion which the supply bears to the effectual demand; but it has a tendency to settle in the same level with the natural price, wherever the production of a commodity admits of free competition. Particular accidents, or natural causes may keep up the market price for a long time above the natural price; but the market price can seldom continue long below the natural price, for in such a case the market price will not afford the ordinary rate of profit. But the profit of the capitalist is the proper fund for his subsistence; he cannot, therefore, continue to produce unless he is enabled to subsist. When there is perfect liberty, fresh stock, as Adam Smith terms it, or as we might say, fresh capital will flow towards that particular investment, the produce of which maintains a higher price in the market than its natural price, until by the competition of an increased number of vendors, the quantity brought to market is sufficient to supply the effectual demand at the natural price of the commodity; and, on the other hand, if the market price becomes depressed below the natural price, labour, or capital, or land, will be withdrawn from the particular employment until its produce is no more than sufficient to supply the effectual demand.

Component elements of price.

The terms *labour*, or *capital*, or *land*, have been used in this last sentence, inasmuch as Adam Smith, resolving price into the component parts of rent, and profit, and wages, seems to consider that a diminution in the price of a commodity may in one case affect rent, in another profit, in another wages, and that according as it affects one or other of these component parts, the landlord, or the capitalist, or the labourer, will withdraw from the particular employment, and so reduce the supply of the commodity. Such, however, does not seem to be a correct view of the case. The worst machine will evidently be forced out of employment first; but the worst machine simply repays the real cost of production; that is, it replaces the amount of capital actually expended in purchasing the raw material and the labour of the workman *plus* the subsistence of the capitalist. A fall of price, therefore, below the level of the natural price at once disables the capitalist from subsisting upon the produce of the worst machine in use. He ceases, in consequence, to invest capital in its employment, because the profits of such investment would be below average profits. It is thus by immediately influencing profits that a diminution of price brings about a diminution of supply.

Effect of diminished prices.

The withdrawal of capital, however, from any particular branch of industry in its turn affects the rent of all the machines employed in it. The competition of the capitalists for the hire of the machines which previously earned rent, decreases with the fall of profits, and the worst machine that previously earned for its owner a rent, finds no longer any bidder for it, inasmuch as under the alteration of circumstances its actual produce will now only secure a subsistence for the workman and the capitalist. A diminution of price, therefore, below the natural price of an article at any given time, if it continues for a long period, will affect the rent of the machines employed in the production of the article. Labour and capital are transferable to other employments, and they will be transferred, until they secure for the labourer and capitalist a return of average wages and profits; but a machine can seldom be adapted to produce more than one particular commodity. Land is, perhaps, the great exception to this rule, and in this respect nature asserts her great superiority over art.

We have seen in the course of our inquiry that the

LECTURE VI.

Profits of manufacturers.

partisans of the mercantile system entertained the most exaggerated notions of the value of the results of labour when employed in manufactures. Melon, in his Essai Politique sur le Commerce, Chap. X., in advocating the policy of prohibiting the exportation of raw materials, and the importation of manufactured goods, observes, "certain raw materials augment prodigiously (in value) under the hand of the workman: a pound of flax, converted into linen, doubles and trebles its price, and if converted into fine lace, multiplies it more than a hundred fold." On the other hand, the economist school maintained, to use the words of M. Turgot in his "Mémoire sur les Importations," that the owner of land possessed alone a real revenue (c'est que le propriétaire de fonds est le seul qui ait un véritable revenue), which consisted of the net produce, this net produce being, according to the Abbé Baudeau, the surplus of the gross produce, or its value, after the expenses of cultivation have been deducted. According to their classification of all other branches of labour, not immediately employed upon land, under the head of Sterile, the manufacturer earned only wages, inasmuch as the cultivator of the soil advanced to him the raw material or capital. The expenses of cultivation, on the other hand, were twofold, being made up of the wages of the cultivator, and the interest upon the capital which he advanced, which the Abbé in his reply to M. Necker's book upon the corn trade, considers might fairly be calculated at 10 per cent, under the various circumstances of waste, as well as of risk. The surplus produce went to the landlord, who in some cases had shared in advancing capital, for which after the necessary interest had been deducted, the remainder would constitute the net produce.

"The produce of the land," writes Mercier de la Rivière, divides itself into gross produce and net produce. As in general, produce can only be obtained by means of previous expenditure, it appears first of all as gross produce, that is, a mass, more or less great, of products, charged with replacing the value of the expenditure to which they have given rise: when these expenses have been replaced out of this mass, the surplus which remains is net produce: it is so much gain to the community, because it is by itself, and in every respect an increase of wealth to the community ("il est tout gain pour la société, parcequ'il est par lui-même, et à tous égards, un accroissement de richesses pour la société). L'Ordre Naturel des Sociétés Politiques," ch. ii. The economists thus assigned to agriculture in their system an analogous position to that which manufactures occupied in the mercantile system.

Net produce.

One of the most important divisions of Adam Smith's work contains an indirect refutation of the doctrine of both these schools. His tenth chapter is dedicated to the investigation of the causes of the apparent inequalities of wages and profits in different employments, in which he shows that these differences arise partly from natural circumstances in the employments themselves, partly from artificial regulations, founded on particular views of state policy. Natural circumstances, however, affect the rate of profits less than the rate of wages. The risk or security with which an investment is attended, seems to be the only natural circumstance, that causes any real difference of importance in the rate of profit. There are often great apparent differences in the profits of different trade, but wages are frequently concealed under the garb of profits. For instance, the great apparent profit of an apothecary is really to a very great extent, but the reasonable wages of his labour, and the price which he charges for his drugs, is mainly the recompence of his skill, which, if it be valued, and its price deducted from the seemingly great profits

Inequalities of wages and of profits.

of his capital, there will remain but the ordinary profits of capital. On the other hand, natural circumstances affect very much the apparent wages of labour: the disagreeableness of the occupation, the necessity of severe exertion, the risk of life, the inconstancy of employment, will cause the rate of wages to be peculiarly high; but high wages are in these cases not so much the recompence of ordinary labour, as the compensation for surmounting certain extraordinary difficulties in the undertaking. Many of the artificial regulations of state policy to which A. Smith calls attention, have been abolished in our own country since his work was written. Of this kind were the restrictions of apprenticeship, and the exclusive privileges of corporations, which, as they restrained competition, tended to keep up the rate of profits and wages in certain branches of industry. On the other hand, the multiplication of charitable foundations for the education of indigent people to the learned professions, has tended rather to produce an unnatural supply of teachers, and so to reduce the price of their labour, by increasing competition. The operation of this cause does not seem likely to diminish in influence; but, as A. Smith observes, this inequality is, upon the whole, perhaps, rather advantageous than hurtful to the public. It may sometimes degrade the profession of a public teacher; but the cheapness of literary education is surely an advantage which greatly overbalances this trifling inconvenience. The obstructions which have been raised in almost every state against the free circulation of labour, occasion in some cases very inconvenient inequalities in the rate of wages. In our own country, indeed, the transfer of labour from one employment to another is now set free by the repeal of the statute of apprenticeship, in 1814, by 54 Geo. III., c. 96.; but the free circulation of labour from place to place is still par-

Regulations of State policy.

Free circulation of labour.

tially, and, perhaps, unduly impeded. It is true, that the obstruction which Corporation Laws gave to the free circulation of the labour of artisans and manufacturers is for the most part removed; but our peculiar Law of Settlement obstructs very considerably the circulation of the ruder kinds of labour, and tends to keep down the wages of it. The propriety, however, of modifying the existing law has been admitted, and the attention of the legislature is at present directed to it.

Law of settlement.

Adam Smith having, in his first book, analysed the productive powers of labour, and traced the effects of improvements in them upon the real price of raw produce, and likewise of manufactures, proceeds in his second book to analyse the nature of capital, and to point out the different effects resulting from the different employments of it. Capital, according to his view, is that part of the national stock or accumulated produce of labour, which is employed so as to yield a revenue. In the rude state, each individual derives his revenue from his labour only; but, as soon as the produce of his labour supplies more than is needed for his immediate consumption, he begins to accumulate a stock of produce.

Nature of capital.

"But when he possesses stock sufficient to maintain him for months or years, he naturally endeavours to derive a revenue from the greater part of it, reserving only so much for his immediate consumption as may maintain him till his revenue begins to come in. His whole stock, therefore, is distinguished into two parts. That part which he expects is to afford him this revenue, is called his capital. The other is that which supplies his immediate consumption, and which consists either, first, in that portion of his whole stock which was originally reserved for this purpose; or, secondly, in his revenue,

LECTURE VI.

from whatever sources derived, as it gradually comes in; or, thirdly, in such things as have been purchased by either of these in former years, and which are not yet entirely consumed; such as a stock of clothes, household furniture, and the like. In one or other, or all of these three articles, consists the stock which men commonly reserve for their own immediate consumption."

Perplexity of Adam Smith's statement.

This passage furnishes, amongst many others, an apt illustration of the logical perplexity of many of Adam Smith's statements. Either his powers of abstraction were not equal to cope with the mass of facts which had come under his observation, or he did not think it prudent to tax the attention of his readers too rigorously. Otherwise we can hardly account for his classing under the head of stock, which is so much produce already accumulated, "revenue as it gradually comes in," and "supplies his immediate consumption." Adam Smith was doubtless correct in considering the annual consumption of almost every owner of stock to be supplied partly from the reserved produce of the labour of former years, i. e. his stock; partly from the incoming produce of the labour of the present year, i. e. his revenue: but the classing of the incoming revenue serving for immediate consumption under the head of stock, seems to be at variance with the previous division of produce, upon which the definition of stock itself is based. Revenue, as it gradually comes in, is incoming produce; stock is accumulated produce: that portion of produce which is consumed as it comes in, is never accumulated; it therefore cannot form, correctly speaking, a part of a man's stock, which is the aggregate surplus of revenue which has not been immediately consumed. The propriety, likewise, of confining the term capital to that portion of a man's stock which is actually employed in increasing the productiveness of labour, has likewise been questioned, with good reason; but at present we may pass on to the further division which Adam Smith adopts, of circulating and fixed capital. "Capital," he writes, "may be employed in raising, manufacturing, or purchasing goods, and selling them again with a profit. Capital thus employed yields no revenue or profit to its employer whilst it remains in his possession or continues in the same shape. The goods of the merchant yield him no revenue or profit till he sells them for money, and the money yields him as little till it is again exchanged for goods. His capital is continually going from him in one shape and returning to him in another, and it is only by means of *circulation* or *successive exchanges* that it can yield him any profit. Such capitals, therefore, may very properly be called *circulating capital.*"

Circulating and fixed capital.

Or capital "may be employed in the improvement of land, in the purchase of useful machines, and instruments of trade, or in such like things as yield a revenue or profit *without changing masters* or circulating any further. Such capitals, therefore, may very properly be called *fixed capitals.*"

This division of capital is convenient for many purposes. It is also of real importance that the capitalist should be aware, in determining upon the mode of employing his capital, that fixed capital requires the co-operation of a certain amount of capital in circulation, in order that it should yield a revenue: that all fixed capital requires to be continually supported by circulating capital; and that the proportions in which circulating and fixed capital must be combined, vary in different occupations.

Mr. Ricardo's use of the terms circulating and fixed.

Mr. Ricardo has adopted a different use of the terms *circulating* and *fixed,* in which he has been followed by Mr. Mill and Mr. M'Culloch. "Ac-

LECTURE VI.

cording as capital is rapidly perishable," writes Mr. Ricardo, "and requires to be frequently reproduced, or is of slow consumption, it is classed under the head of circulating or of fixed capital" (Ch. I. Sect. 4.). "A brewer, whose buildings and machinery are valuable and durable, is said to employ a large portion of fixed capital: on the contrary, a shoemaker, whose capital is chiefly employed in the payment of wages, which are expended on food and clothing, commodities more perishable than buildings and machinery, is said to employ a large portion of his capital as circulating capital." This division of capital is based upon totally different considerations from those which Adam Smith had in view; and the members of the two divisions will not always coincide: as, for instance, gold and silver money, which is classed by A. Smith under the division of circulating capital, will come, as it is amongst the most durable articles, under Mr. Ricardo's division of fixed capital. Mr. Ricardo, in analysing the effects on the relative value of commodities resulting from the employment of perishable or durable capital in different proportions, perceived that variations in the rate of wages, or the rate of profits, will evidently affect the cost of production very differently, according as the use of perishable or durable capital preponderates in any branch of manufacture. The food of the labourer being perishable, as compared with the tools with which his labour is assisted, the former requires to be reproduced at once after each operation; whereas the latter may be reproduced at intervals, and not till after several operations. In order, therefore, that the capital of the manufacturer may be preserved, as the cost of an article in which perishable capital of 100*l.* value, and durable capital of 20*l.* have been employed, will have been much greater than where durable capital of the value of

Proportions affect the cost of production.

100*l*. and perishable capital of the value of 20*l*. have been employed, a far greater return of expenditure must be at once obtained in the former than the latter case, or the manufacturer will not be able to continue to produce the commodity. Consequently the remunerating price of commodities, in the production of which human labour is chiefly employed, will be much higher than the remunerating price of commodities in the production of which self-acting machinery is mainly instrumental, although equal capitals are employed in both cases.

Manufactures and commerce productive.

Adam Smith, on the other hand, was investigating the different ways in which capital might be employed so as to yield a revenue or profit to the employer. One great object of his work was to show that labour employed in manufactures and commerce was entitled to be called productive, equally as labour employed in agriculture, inasmuch as value resulted from its employment; and with this object he divides capital into circulating and fixed capital, and shows how, in the one case, a person makes a profit by continually changing the shape of its investment, in the other by keeping it invested under one and the same form.

Inconvenience of Adam Smith's division.

There is one inconvenience in Adam Smith's employment of the terms, circulating and fixed, which may be noted in contrasting them with Mr. Ricardo's nomenclature. The money of an individual is part of his circulating capital, and he can only derive a revenue from it by parting with it; but the money of a society has more of the character of fixed capital, as a greater revenue accrues to a society, from its use as an instrument for facilitating exchanges at home, than from exchanging it as an article of commerce with foreign countries. For instance, the first division of articles, in which capital is fixed, according to Adam Smith, consists of "all useful machines and instruments of trade, which facilitate and abridge

LECTURE VI. labour." Now money is most useful to a nation as an instrument for facilitating exchanges, and abridging the tedious operations of barter; and as by such exchanges the production of national revenue is indirectly stimulated, and the result is an augmentation of produce, it seems, in its character of money, to be rather a portion of the fixed capital of a country; more particularly as the waste of it requires to be made good from the circulating capital. Adam Smith seems to have overlooked this *productive* use of money.

Again; of the four parts of which the circulating capital of an individual is composed, according to Adam Smith, e. g. money, provisions, materials, and finished work, the three latter form part of the gross revenue of a nation; but the money of a society makes no part of the revenue of the society whilst employed as money. On the contrary, the expense of keeping up the national stock of money must be deducted from the revenue of a nation. Money, therefore, seems to have all the characteristics of fixed capital, in reference to a nation; and every saving in the expense of supporting it is an addition to the revenue. Dr. Smith, however, was unwilling to disturb his classification, and contented himself with admitting, that that part of the circulating capital of a society which consists in money, bears a very great resemblance to fixed capital, so far as the revenue of the society is affected, and thereupon proceeds with his investigation of money as a particular branch of the general stock of a society, as if it were a part of its fixed capital.

In the case of an individual, it is his circulating capital which furnishes the materials and the wages of labour, and puts industry in motion. "Every saving, therefore, in the expense of maintaining the fixed capital, which does not diminish the productive powers of labour, must increase the fund which puts industry into motion, and consequently the annual produce of land and labour, the real revenue of every society.

A paper circulating medium.

"The substitution of paper in the room of gold and silver money, replaces a very expensive instrument of commerce, with one much less costly, and *sometimes equally convenient.* Circulation comes to be carried on by a new wheel, which it costs less both to erect and to maintain than the old one."

Adam Smith then proceeds to explain the principles which should govern the operations of banks of circulation, and leaves very little to be desired, excepting a less digressive style of discussion. It is to be regretted that he did not combine together the various portions of his work, in which he treats of monetary questions, such as the digression which he introduces into Book I. chap. xi., concerning the variations in the value of silver; the chapter on metallic and paper money, Book II. chap. ii., to which our attention has been already directed; a digression concerning banks of deposit, particularly concerning that of Amsterdam, introduced in Book IV. chap. iii.; and a discussion upon the advantages of a moderate seignorage upon the coinage, engrafted on an Account of the Methuen Treaty, in Book IV. chap. vi. These various disquisitions supplied by far the richest mine, both of facts and sound principles, which, up to the time of their publication, had been laid open to the student of finance, and they will well repay a careful examination in the present day.

The French Economists.

The French Economists, in considering all the labour of a society, that was not employed in agriculture, to be unproductive, and that the various classes of manufacturers and merchants merely reproduced, annually, the funds which the agriculturists provided for their subsistence, held that the

LECTURE VI. wealth of a mercantile or manufacturing society could never be in the slightest degree augmented by its industry, unless it annually deprived itself of the enjoyment of a portion of the funds destined for its subsistence. Whereas the labour of an agricultural society annually afforded a net produce over and above the funds required for its subsistence, and thus its revenue and wealth was continually augmented by its industry, without the necessity of its submitting to any privation. Adam Smith, on the other hand, contended that in all cases, parsimony, and not industry, is the immediate cause of the increase of capital. Industry, indeed, provides the subject which parsimony accumulates. But whatever industry might acquire, if parsimony did not save and store up, the capital would never be greater.

Parsimony. "Parsimony," he writes, "by increasing the fund which is destined for the maintenance of productive hands, tends to increase the number of those hands, whose labour adds to the value of the subject upon which it is bestowed. It tends, therefore, to increase the exchangeable value of the annual produce of the land and labour of the country. It puts into motion an additional quantity of industry, which gives an additional value to the annual produce."

A similar, and equally correct view, has been adopted by the author of the article on Political Economy, in the "Encyclopædia Metropolitana." "The most laborious population," he writes, "inhabiting the most fertile territory, if they devoted all their labour to the production of immediate results, and consumed its produce as it arose, would soon find their utmost exertions insufficient to produce even the mere necessaries of existence."

Mr. Senior, accordingly, sets up a third productive principle by the side of labour, and the agency of nature, and to this principle he proposes to give the

LECTURE VI.

name of *abstinence,* which he defines to be the conduct of a person, who either abstains from the unproductive use of what he can command, or designedly prefers the production of remote, to that of immediate, results.

Abstinence.

A still greater divergency from the doctrines of the economists was to be expected on the part of the author of the "Wealth of Nations," on the subject of taxes, and respecting the ultimate incidence of taxation. They had contended that the fund from which all taxes were finally paid, was the net produce of the land. On the other hand, Adam Smith maintained, that as the private revenue of individuals arose from three different sources, rent, profit, and wages, every tax must finally be paid from some one or other of those three different sorts of revenue, or from all of them indifferently. He fully admitted with the economists that taxes were, in many cases, not finally paid from the particular source of revenue upon which they were intended to fall; but his analysis of the ultimate incidence of taxation is necessarily incomplete, from the defects in his theory of rent, and also from the circumstance that he has, for the most part, considered taxes as partially imposed, in which case their ultimate incidence may be very different from what would be the result when they are generally imposed. The most valuable portion of his discussion upon the sources of the public revenue of a society, is to be found in the maxims which he lays down with regard to taxation in general. Although the primary importance of the principle, which his first maxim inculcates, namely, the equality of taxation, has been impugned, it has been generally admitted, that if the conditions of certainty in the amount, convenience in the mode and time of payment, and the absence of waste and vexatiousness in the collection, which form the

Incidence of taxes.

Necessary conditions of taxation.

LECTURE VI.

substance of the last three maxims, are not combined in a tax, the prejudice that will result to private interests from its imposal, will outweigh all the advantages that can possibly accrue to the public service.

The sketch which has been attempted in the present Lecture of Dr. Smith's great work, is necessarily incomplete; but the main features of it have, it is hoped, been faithfully delineated, and the most important steps which he made in advancing the science, been pointed out sufficiently in detail. Subsequent writers have contributed to complete the analysis of the causes of the production of wealth, whose works will be referred to in their proper place.

LECTURE VII.

LECTURE VII.

THE doctrines of Adam Smith, as set forth in his "Inquiry into the Causes of the Wealth of Nations" recommended themselves at once to the acceptance of his contemporaries, and obtained a ready reception among economists in all countries, in respect of the groundwork of the science. The labour of man was henceforth recognised as the primary productive agent; exchangeable value was referred to its true source, and the functions of capital, in its ancillary relation to labour, were more clearly appreciated. In a word, the phenomena of the production of wealth were satisfactorily explained; but the circumstances which determine its distribution, demanded a further and fuller investigation than Adam Smith had bestowed upon them, whose views in this branch of the subject, were not so happy and exempt from question, as in the earlier analysis.

"The annual labour of every nation is the fund which originally supplies it with all the necessaries and conveniences of life which it annually consumes." Such were the opening words of the "Wealth of Nations," and the truth of the statement cannot be impugned. It has, however, formed the groundwork of a common error, according to which, an augmentation of national wealth accompanies every multiplication of the number of labourers, or, in other words, the productive power of a state bears an invariable proportion to its population.

Relation of produce to population.

LECTURE VII.

Such an opinion had even received countenance from Adam Smith, when he laid it down in treating of the wages of labour (B. I. c. viii.), that "the most decisive mark of the prosperity of any country is the increase of the number of its inhabitants." Such also had been the general notion of antiquity, as we may gather from its laws and its philosophy. Still further, with the exception indeed of a few states, we find in the ages which connect antiquity with the modern order of ideas, national encouragements universally held out to stimulate a more rapid increase of numbers. Ἄνδρες γὰρ πόλεις καὶ οὐ τείχη, are the well known words of Demosthenes, and the historian of the Peloponnesian war places the same sentiment in the mouth of the greatest of Athenian statesmen.

Notions of antiquity.

The privileges which were awarded under the Spartan system to the fathers of three and four children respectively (Aristot. Pol. II. c. 6.) had their counterpart in Western Europe, at a subsequent period, in the ordinances of the "Lex Papia Poppæa (anno 762), which established the jus trium liberorum in the capital, the jus quatuor liberorum in Italy itself, and the jus quinque liberorum throughout the provinces of the Roman empire. The ex emptions which this law awarded to fathers of families, were still further enlarged by the emperors Arcadius and Honorius, and that which had hitherto been a privilege dependent upon an imperial grant, became ultimately a matter of general right. Cod. viii. tit. 59. c. 1.: "Nemo posthac a nobis jus liberorum petat; quod simul hac lege omnibus concedimus." It is true that Justinian subsequently modified the harshness of the law as far as the civil disabilities inflicted upon celibacy were concerned (Cod. vi. tit. 51. c. 1. de caducis tollendis), but the civil immunities attendant on marriage were maintained, and the spirit which dictated them pervades the legislature of subsequent ages.

Not to diverge too widely from the main object of our inquiry, we must refrain from tracing the operation of this spirit in foreign codes, and may content ourselves with directing our attention to our own statute law, whereby, as by 46 G. III. c. 56, exemptions from taxes were specifically granted to the fathers of more than two children, born in lawful wedlock. This statute, indeed, has been repealed by 56 G. III. c. 66; but it serves to illustrate the spirit of British legislation in the early part of the present century.

Legislation of modern times.

To a similar effect the laws of France and Italy accorded exemptions from military service or pecuniary contributions, not indeed to the industrious and careful father of a family, who had reared up one or two sons physically and morally well qualified to do good service to the state, but to him whose wife had brought forth the greatest number of children, irrespectively of their being weak or strong, well or badly brought up, able to earn their livelihood, or dependent on others for their support. The father, who had trained up two brave and industrious sons, his only offspring, to advance their country's best interests, met with no favour from the legislator, whilst he who had ten idle children loitering at home, and consuming what others had toiled to produce, was treated with the greatest consideration. Such was the legacy which Rome in her degeneracy had bequeathed to succeeding ages.

The idea which gave birth to such institutions, identified the population with the power of a country. It may be beyond dispute, that a powerful country will be a well peopled country; but it would be to confound a necessary condition with a cause, if it should be imagined that the power of a country is

Popular error.

LECTURE VII.

augmented *pari passu* with its population. Yet no aphorisms were so unquestioned, as those which affirmed this fact.

Re-examination of the subject.

Events, however, occurred in the latter part of the last century, which arrested the attention of observant minds, and led to a re-examination of the data, upon which the received opinions on this subject had been founded. The British colonies in North America were the scene of phenomena altogether at variance with the experience of the Old World. The "Wealth of Nations" was published in 1776, and in the 8th chapter of that work, the author observes, "that in Great Britain and most other European countries, the inhabitants are not supposed to double in less than 500 years. In the British colonies in North America, it has been found that they double in 20 or 25 years. Nor in the present times is the increase principally owing to the continual importation of new inhabitants, but to the great multiplication of the species. Those who live to an old age, it is said, frequently see there from 50 to 100, and sometimes many more descendants." It thus appeared that under other circumstances than those which existed in the Old World, the advance of population was so much accelerated, as to baffle all the received rules of calculation. The term of doubling, which in Europe was supposed to correspond to a period co-extensive with the Magnus Annus of Egyptian Astronomy, being found in America to be shorter even than that usually assigned to a single generation of mankind.

Contrast between the two hemispheres.

About the same time that these facts were awakening surprise by the strong contrast which the conditions of human life presented in the two hemispheres, an event occurred in Europe which threatened to shake to pieces the established foundations of society, and gave an unlooked-for importance to cer-

LECTURE VII.

The French Revolution.

tain questions connected with the distribution of wealth.

It can hardly be disputed that the revolution of 1789 was an attempt on the part of the French people to find a political remedy for great social evils; although it cannot be denied, that there were simultaneously great political evils, that called for political remedies. But it was the social misery of the French people that rendered such a revolution possible, and the experiment was made by men who had faith in the efficacy of political institutions to influence the material as well, as the moral welfare of a population.

That most mysterious yet most important social problem, "Why are the conditions of life so unequal?" was now submitted to a rigorous investigation. Why are the means of subsistence so unequally distributed? Why is there so much misery amongst mankind? These and such like questions were now mooted on all sides, and the boldest essays were made to solve them by actual experiment. It was natural for minds that referred the social evils of the ancient régime to political causes, to seek for a remedy in the operation of opposite institutions, and thus we find the remnant of feudal privileges and feudal obligations swept bodily away, and replaced by a system of equal political rights, whilst the free disposal of property as well as the rights of primogeniture were abolished, and an equal parcelling of estates substituted for the ancient feudal entirety. These were the chief permanent measures, but a host of temporary expedients were adopted as occasion seemed to call for them, in contradiction to the experience of past ages. To meet the demands of the consumers, a *maximum* of prices was established in 1793, which was attended with the inevitable result of an enhancement of prices. A paper currency was forced into circulation by arbitrary enactments only to become depreciated. All indirect taxes were suppressed, and forced contributions were levied upon property. Still there was no diminution in the number of the destitute; on the contrary, society daily became more and more steeped in pauperism, whilst the disappointment of the philosophers who had suggested the measures, was only equalled by the dismay of the statesmen who had approved the execution of them.

Godwin's Political justice.

The solution, then, of this great social question, "Why is there so much destitution and misery amongst mankind?" seemed to be as remote as ever, when a work appeared in this country, in which views of a similar kind to those which French writers had made popular, upon the causes of social evil, were boldly and energetically advocated. Mr. Godwin's treatise upon Political Justice, to which allusion is here made, was first published in 1793. The scope of this work may be explained sufficiently for the present purpose in the words of the author. "May it not happen," he writes, "that the grand moral evils that exist in the world, the calamities by which we are so grievously oppressed, are to be traced to its defects (i. e. the defects of government) as their source, and that their removal is only to be expected from its correction?" Monarchical institutions were, according to this writer, the primary cause of existing social evils, whilst the great secondary cause was to be found in the established administration of property.

Established administration of property.

"Accumulated property," he writes, "treads the powers of thought in the dust, extinguishes the sparks of genius, and reduces the great mass of mankind to be immersed in sordid cares, besides depriving the rich of the more salubrious and effectual motives to activity. If superfluity were banished, the necessity for the greater part of the manual industry of mankind would be superseded, and the rest, being amicably shared among the active and vigorous members of the community, would be burdensome to none." The extravagant doctrines of Plato's "Polity" are reproduced by Mr. Godwin, with an apparent fervour of conviction in the certainty of his conclusions, unlike the misgiving, which other advocates of the perfectibility of the human race could not but entertain. "There is one other circumstance," he elsewhere writes, p. 460, "which, though inferior to those above enumerated, deserves to be mentioned. This is population. It has been calculated that the average cultivation of Europe might be improved, so as to maintain five times her present number of inhabitants. There is a principle in human society, by which population is perpetually kept down to the level of the means of subsistence. Thus, among the wandering tribes of America and Asia, we never find through the lapse of ages that population has so increased as to render necessary the cultivation of the earth. Thus, among the civilised nations of Europe, by means of territorial monopoly, the sources of subsistence are kept within a certain limit; and if the population became overstocked, the lower ranks of the inhabitants would be still more incapable of procuring for themselves the necessaries of life. There are, no doubt, extraordinary concurrences of circumstances, by means of which changes are occasionally introduced in this respect; but in ordinary cases the standard of population is held, in a manner, stationary for centuries. *Thus the established administration of property may be considered as strangling a considerable portion of our children in their cradle.* Whatever may be the value of the life of man, or rather, whatever would be his capability of happiness in a free and equal state of society, the system we are here opposing, may be considered as arresting upon the threshold of existence four fifths of that value and that happiness." This was a startling position for a writer to take up in England,

Population.

Faulty distribution of property.

LECTURE VII.

at a time when the political horizon across the Channel was lighted up with the glare of the French Revolution.

Mr. Godwin seems, as already observed, to have had no doubts, that the equalisation of conditions would furnish a panacea for all existing social evils. On the other hand, one of the most distinguished leaders of the new order of ideas in France, whose gifted intellect, however, could not save him from being swept away by the furious tide of the revolution — I allude

Condorcet.

to Condorcet, could not resist some misgiving as to there being a limit to the amelioration of man's condition. In his "Esquisse d'un Tableau Historique des Progrès de l'Esprit Humain," having intimated the probability of such improvements in the various modes of applying man's labour as to secure much greater returns for a greatly diminished expenditure, so that not only would the same extent of soil support more individuals, but each individual would be less laboriously and more productively employed, he continues, p. 362, "But in this advance of industry and comfort (bien-être), from which there will result a more advantageous proportion between the wants of man and his means of satisfying them, each generation will be called to a greater share of enjoyment, and, by consequence of the physical constitution of the human species, to a proportionate increase in its numbers. Must there not, then, arrive a period when these laws, equally necessary, will counteract each other, when the augmentation of numbers surpassing that of the means of subsistence, there will necessarily result either a continuous diminution of comfort and population — a movement really retrograde, or at least

His theory of an oscillation.

a kind of oscillation between good and evil? In societies arrived at this stage, will not this oscillation be a continually operating cause of periodical misery, as it were? Will it not mark the boundary where further amelioration becomes impossible, and where there is set a term to the perfectibility of the human race, which it may attain in the infinite lapse of ages, but can never hope to pass?"

Perfectibility of the human race.

These, and such like, were the speculations in which the ardent spirit of inquiry indulged itself towards the conclusion of the last century, and, backed as they were by the formidable experiments of the French nation, they assumed an importance which, in the present calm state of thought on such subjects, it is difficult for us to appreciate.

Mr. Godwin's Essay on Avarice and Profusion.

An essay of Mr. Godwin's, published in the "Enquirer," on the subject of avarice and profusion, called forth a writer of a totally opposite school of thought. Whilst Mr. Godwin attributed the evils of society to the imperfection of political institutions and the vices of government, and regarded the passions of man as the results of the prevailing administration of property, his opponent declared that the great obstacles to social progress were to be found in those very passions inherent in man's nature, which he was too little disposed to control, and that the improvement of the individual must be a condition precedent to the improvement of society.

Mr. Malthus. Essay upon the Principles of Population.

The first edition of the Essay upon the Principles of Population made its appearance in the concluding year of the 18th century. Its author, Mr. Malthus, struck at the same time with the acknowledged disorder of European society, and with the subversive tendency of the doctrines advanced in explanation of them by the advocates of political remedies, had recourse to a careful study of facts, and extended his inquiry over the entire range of clime and country, that modern enterprise had laid open to the investigation of modern science. It was an incontestable fact, as had been established more than once by the experience of North America, that under certain cir-

LECTURE VII.

cumstances the human race had doubled its numbers in twenty-five years: it was equally beyond dispute that the rate of increase amidst the various nations of Europe was inconceivably slower; so much so, that the species might almost be supposed to be subject to different physiological influences in the two hemispheres. To refer these variations to political causes was, on the surface of things, unsatisfactory. When Adam Smith pointed out the strong contrast between Europe and North America, the British colonies were subject to the laws of the mother country, and were ruled with a somewhat more arbitrary sceptre than the parent state: on the other hand, the population of the United Provinces as well as that of the Swiss Confederation, when compared with the subjects either of the representative of the Roman Emperors, or the descendant of the Grand Monarque, exhibited a rate of increase in no way proportionate to the respective peculiarities of their political institutions. Some other solution seemed then to be required than that which Mr. Godwin and other writers had suggested.

Variations in the increment of population.

No hypothetical calculations were on this occasion needed in order to shape the problem. The question lay within a very narrow compass. What are the obstacles which prevent the law of population, as ascertained by the experience of the British Colonies in North America, from being universal? How has it come to pass that within the same period of twenty-five years England has only received an increase of one-sixth of its numbers? Common sense at once suggested the reply: that either a given number of children had not been born, or a given number had been hurried on from the cradle to the tomb in the intervening period. In the former case, man, in the exercise of his freewill and responsibility, had refrained from giving them origin: in the latter, nature, in obedience to certain mysterious laws, had withheld sustenance from them: in the former case, moral causes would have saved the species from the operation of those physical correctives, to which in the latter case it would have been subjected in common with the inferior orders of created life. It was of the highest importance to ascertain which of the explanations was supported by experience, as the former would imply the maintenance of a people in the most mature condition which human nature is susceptible of; the latter might be consistent with a very low standard of mental and physical development.

Experience of the New World.

Mr. Malthus having ascertained, as it were, by two observations, that the human race had doubled itself twice over within the space of fifty years, in a country where there was an unlimited extent of virgin soil open for settlement, assumed the North American Colonies to furnish the type of that condition of things, which would universally prevail unless disturbing causes intervened. Hence he inferred that the human race would invariably multiply in geometrical progression within periods of time, the extent of which would be determined by the greater or less interference of artificial obstacles.

Increase of population geometrical.

Argument à priori.

We might arrive at the same conclusion from abstract considerations. If a living product possesses a power of reproduction equal to the productive power of that which gave it origin, a mass of products must ultimately result, if the power of reproduction be freely exercised, which will constitute an ascending geometrical series: if the reproductive power be less than the productive power, however freely it be exercised, the species will ultimately become extinct: if it be greater, it will multiply indefinitely. Of course in a calculation of this kind it is assumed that the productive power of individuals is uniform, the exceptional cases of defect being compensated by exceptional cases of excess.

LECTURE VII.

Population of Sweden.

The population of Sweden, according to Mr. Godwin, had only doubled itself in the course of a whole century. It was impossible, in contrasting this phenomenon with that which North America presented, to overlook the different character of the two countries: the one rich in certain mineral treasures, but with a surface little adapted to support either vegetable or animal life; the other teeming with the produce of both the temperate and torrid zones, and capable of supplying food and clothing to millions of human beings as yet unborn. Was this a mere coincidence, or was there some necessary connection between the relations of population and produce? Mr. Malthus appealed to experience to decide the question. If it should appear as a fact that food and population obeyed one and the same law; that in Sweden an entire century had elapsed before the means of subsistence had undergone a twofold increase, whilst in the Western Hemisphere the same result had taken place in a quarter of a century, it would be reasonable to infer, that there was some necessary connection between the supply of food and the advance of population, between the means of support and the numbers to be supported.

Experience of the Old World.

To the Old World, therefore, Mr. Malthus determined to look for the rule as to the increase of the means of subsistence, if, by any means, it might throw light upon the relative retardation of the increase of the human species. That the produce of land might be doubled in some given period, e. g., twenty-five years, he admitted to be perfectly possible, but that it should be quadrupled after the lapse of a second period of equal length, he maintained to be contrary to our experience of the known qualities of land. "The very utmost," he writes, "that we can conceive is, that the increase in the second twenty-five years might equal the present produce. Let us then take this for our rule, though certainly far beyond the truth, and allow that, by great exertion, the whole produce of the island might be increased every twenty-five years by a quantity of subsistence equal to what it at present produces. The most enthusiastic speculator cannot suppose a greater increase than this. In a few centuries, it would make every acre of land like a garden.

Increase of produce arithmetical.

"Yet this ratio of increase is evidently arithmetical. It may be fairly said, therefore, that the means of subsistence increase in an arithmetical ratio."

It may be as well, in order to prevent ambiguity, lest any of my readers should not be familiar with mathematical terms, to explain the distinction between arithmetical and geometrical progression.

Relations of progression.

A series of numbers or quantities is said to be in arithmetical progression, when they successively exceed or fall short of one another by a certain constant number or quantity; in other words, increase or decrease, by a common difference; e. g. 1. 3. 5. 7. 9. On the other hand, quantities are said to be in geometrical progression, when each succeeding term is respectively a certain multiple or quotient of the preceding term; that is, when the series increases or decreases by a common multiplier or divisor; e. g. 1. 2. 4. 8. 16.

Now it is evident, that the terms of an ascending geometrical series, whose common multiple is 2, will very soon outstrip the terms of an arithmetical series, whose common difference is 2, and that the sum of the former will far exceed the sum of the latter; for instance, the sum of 5 terms of the simple geometrical series above cited will be 31, whilst that of the corresponding arithmetical series will be only 15.

It being therefore assumed that population is capable of increasing in a geometrical ratio, whilst the supply of food can only be augmented in an arithme-

LECTURE VII.

Supply of food controls the growth of population.

tical ratio, population will absolutely *tend* to outstrip food; but as a fact, it is found that the supply of food controls the growth of population; so that in a given period the increase of population will be represented by a geometrical series, consisting of fewer terms than the arithmetical series which represents the increase of the supply of food. For example, the sum of an arithmetical series of five terms, 1. 2. 3. 4. 5., equal to 15, will correspond to the sum of a geometrical series of four terms, 1. 2. 4. 8., equal to 15. Unless this correspondence of the results be secured, it is clear that the condition of the population will retrograde, as its numbers increase, inasmuch as the share of food of each individual will be diminished in proportion to the excess in the aggregate number of individuals.

As long as all the soil of the best quality in a country has not been brought into cultivation, it is evident that the terms of the arithmetical series which represent the increase of the supply of food, may succeed one another at shorter intervals of time, than will be the case in countries, where the most fertile districts have all been long occupied. In the former case, labour alone is required to set in operation the productive powers of the soil; in the latter, capital, or accumulated produce, must be combined with labour; in the former case a double amount of labour alone will secure a proportionate return: not so, however, in the latter case; for a double amount of return can only be secured by a certain sacrifice of capital, which is so much continually deducted from the accumulated stock; the alternative being that of allowing the land to remain fallow, and thereby the process of production to be interrupted.

"No limits," writes Mr. Malthus, p. 26, "whatever are placed to the productions of the earth. They may increase for ever, and be greater than any assignable quantity; yet still the power of population being a power of a superior order, the increase of the human species can only be kept commensurate to the increase of the means of subsistence, by the constant operation of the strong law of necessity acting as a check upon the greater power.

Alternative.

Such is the alternative where it is impossible to shorten the intervals at which the terms of the arithmetical series representing the supply of food succeed each other: in such a case, the intervals which separate the terms of the geometrical series, representing the numbers of the population, are lengthened by the increased activity of destructive elements. For instance, the interval of twenty-five years, which prevailed in N. America, corresponds, with respect to the increase of population, to the interval of 100 years in Sweden. The period of doubling has thus a fourfold extension in the latter country. How is this brought about?

"We will suppose," writes Mr. Malthus, p. 29, "the means of subsistence in any country just equal to the easy support of the inhabitants. The constant effort towards population, which is found to act, even in the most vicious societies, increases the number of people before the means of subsistence are increased. The food, therefore, which before supported seven millions, must now be divided between seven and a half or eight millions. The poor, consequently, must live much worse, and many of them be reduced to severe distress. The number of labourers, also, being above the proportion of the work in the market, the price of labour must tend towards a decrease, while the price of provisions would, at the same time, tend to rise. The labourer, therefore, must work harder to earn the same as he did before. During this season of distress, the discouragements to marriage, and the difficulty of rearing a family, are so great, that population is at a stand. In the mean time the

LECTURE VII. cheapness of labour, the plenty of labourers, and the necessity of an increased industry amongst them, encourage cultivators to employ more labour upon their land; to turn up fresh soil, and to manure and improve, more completely, what is already in tillage; till, ultimately, the means of subsistence become in the same proportion to the population as at the period from which we set out. The situation of the labourer being then again tolerably comfortable, the restraints to population are, in some degree, loosened, and the same retrograde and progressive movements with respect to happiness are repeated.

Oscillations. "This sort of oscillation will not be remarked by superficial observers; and it may be difficult even for the most penetrating mind to calculate its periods: yet, that in all old states, some such vibration does exist, though, from various transverse causes, in a much less marked, and in a much more irregular manner, than I have described it, no reflecting man, who considers the subject deeply, can well doubt."

M. Quetelet. In illustration of Mr. Malthus' position, we may refer to a table which M. Quetelet has given in his "Essai de Physique Sociale," l. I., ch. ii., § 14.; "Influence des Années," which has reference to the Netherlands. (*See* page 211.)

The year 1817, it will be observed, presents a greater number of deaths, both in the towns and in the country, than the preceding years, whilst the births and marriages, on the contrary, diminished. This year, as well as that of 1816, were years of great dearth. Again, in 1826, the price of bread rose in

Belgium. Belgium, and there ensued an increased mortality, combined with a very considerable diminution of marriages and births, whilst in 1821, and 1824, which had been years of plenty, we may observe that both the mortality was diminished, and the

LECTURE VII.

Years.	Births.		Deaths.		Marriages.
	Towns.	Country.	Towns.	Country.	
1815	59,737	135,625	49,007	88,592	48,854
1816	58,095	138,507	47,327	88,796	40,801
1817	55,207	122,348	55,240	97,368	33,881
1818	55,665	128,041	49,169	91,247	39,218
1819	61,788	143,504	49,738	98,659	42,401
1820	61,263	133,685	50,681	94,496	43,258
1821	65,356	145,003	49,706	88,414	44,796
1822	67,794	151,747	52,078	95,475	46,949
1823	65,318	148,299	48,815	91,877	45,424
1824	67,030	151,636	47,662	87,253	44,665
1825	68,078	153,813	50,689	95,449	47,097
1826	67,919	153,970	58,749	110,155	48,054
Total	753,250	1,706,178	608,861	1,127,781	525,398
Average	62770	142,182	50,739	93,981	43,783

number of marriages and births was much augmented in the following years, 1822, and 1825.

Coincidence with Condorcet's theory.

This is precisely the kind of oscillation, the occurrence of which M. Condorcet, in the passage already quoted, could not but admit to be theoretically inevitable. That history does not furnish us with repeated instances of the same kind, may be readily accounted for from the circumstance that the annals of the past are a record rather of political than social movements, which have influenced the fortunes of the rulers of communities more than the communities themselves. M. Condorcet, indeed, held that the period at which such an oscillation might possibly be experienced was so remote, that for the purposes of his argument it might be safely disregarded; but a careful observation of facts warns us against admitting such a delusive hypothesis. On the contrary, in the absence of preventive obstacles, such oscillations must repeatedly occur; but a wise

LECTURE VII.

forethought may contribute to extend the intervals between such oscillations; and such a result is one of the most unerring tests of an advancing civilisation.

Mr. Malthus, then, assuming the tendency of population to be positive and constant, proceeded to classify the obstacles to its free development, according as they operated by reducing the proportion of births, or by increasing the proportion of deaths, distinguishing the former by the name of *preventive*, the latter by that of *positive* checks. M. Rossi, the distinguished Professor of Political Economy in the College Royal of France in 1836-7, observes, that the latter of these terms has not been happily chosen, and suggests the word "repressive" as conveying a more definite meaning. I have myself on a previous occasion ventured to make a similar remark, and to suggest the term "diminutive," at that time being unacquainted with M. Rossi's criticism. I must, however, admit, that neither of the proposed substitutes are altogether free from ambiguity; and the original objection may perhaps be considered more verbal than substantial.

Classification of the checks on population.

The cause of the retarded progress of population in the principal states of modern Europe, as Mr. Malthus considered, was clearly not traceable to the degeneracy of the race, in respect of its powers of reproduction, but to the operation of a twofold obstacle, e. g. "the foresight of the difficulties attending the rearing of a family acts as a preventive check, whilst the actual distresses of some of the lower classes by which they are disabled from giving the proper food and attention to their children, acts as a positive check." The greater or less degree in which these checks will respectively operate, must depend upon the predominance of the middle class of society, amongst whom considerations as to the difficulties of providing the increased amount of comforts, which a

Preventive and positive checks.

family will require, will have greater weight than amongst the lower classes, who are disposed to trust to the chance of events for the requisite supply of the necessaries of life.

But we cannot close our eyes against the fact that this restraint, which certainly does operate more strongly amongst those whose own exertions, or the exertions of whose predecessors, have secured for them the enjoyment of something more than the mere necessaries of life, may entail a recourse to vicious substitutes; and thus it would appear probable, that the superior power of population cannot anyhow be checked, without producing misery or vice. But whilst misery is a necessary consequence of population outstripping subsistence, vice is not an inevitable attendant on population being restrained within the limits of subsistence. The occasions when a positive check comes into force are invariably marked by similar calamities to those which now (1847) desolate Ireland; whereas the opportunities for the exercise of a preventive check may be furnished by prudent self-control; so that it is possible for a community to advance in moral and material welfare under the restraint which social institutions should encourage, but it will remain stationary, or even retrograde, before the evils which individual recklessness gives rise to.

Alternative of misery or vice not necessary.

One great object of Mr. Malthus' work was to warn statesmen of the shoals towards which the course of previous legislation was rapidly setting the vessel of the state. Of the necessity of his task we have the best evidence in the remarkable unpopularity which it entailed upon the author; for the harshness of tone, and the occasional exaggeration of statement in his work, which might reasonably be attributed to its controversial character, cannot of themselves account for the extraordinary outcry which assailed him from

Object of Mr. Malthus' work.

LECTURE VII.

every quarter. The great truth which he wished to impress upon society was this; that the natural instinct of the human race more than supplied a sufficient stimulus to the increase of population, and that the legislator, who should furnish either directly or indirectly any artificial incentive, was entailing physical evil or vice upon the coming generation.

Case of Ireland.

Let us, for example's sake, observe the results of an indirect stimulus having been supplied by the legislature in the case of Ireland. The following data are available from the returns furnished by the collectors of the hearth-money: —

Years.	Population.
1754	2,372,634
1767	2,544,276
1777	2,690,556

From which it appears that during the interval of the 10 years, subsequent to 1767, the increase had been 146,280, and during the preceding 13 years, the increase had been 171,642; a rate tolerable constant for 23 years.

In 1784, by 23 and 24 Geo. III. c. 19., bounties were granted by the legislature on the exportation of corn, in order to stimulate by artificial means the conversion of pasture lands into tillage, the Agistment Act having been passed in 1764: and whereas in 1773, the average export of corn had not exceeded 66,248 barrels, the effects of the Bounty Act, within five years after it came into operation, was to raise the quantity to 648,894 barrels (A. D. 1789). About the same time, and with a similar object, the practice was introduced of granting partnership leases to groups of labourers, very often 20 or more. Mr. Wakefield, in his account of Ireland, in describing the condition of Galway under the system of partnership leases, says: "These

Partnership leases.

people divide the land, and give portions to their children, which consist of one fourth or one fifth of what they call a man's share; that is, of the land which originally belonged to one man in the lease. A certain portion of the whole farm or *take*, is appropriated for tillage, and this portion is then divided into lots, perhaps 20 or 30: these lots are again subdivided into fields, which are partitioned into smaller lots, each partner obtaining one or two ridges; but these ridges do not continue in the hands of the same occupier longer than the time they are in tillage. The pasture is held in common, and the elders of the village are the legislators, who establish such regulations as may be judged proper for the community, and settle all disputes that arise among them. Their houses stand close to each other, and form what is here called a village."

Minute subdivision of lands.

Effect upon population of Ireland.

The indirect effect upon the population may be gathered from the altered rate of increase, as shown by the following returns:—

1785	- - - - -	2,845,932
1788	- - - - -	3,900,000
1791	- - - - -	4,206,612

It seems hardly credible, that in the four years following the introduction of the bounty system, the population should have increased one fourth in numbers; yet the returns of the number of houses show a still greater rate of increase:—

1785	—	474,322
1788	—	650,000
1791	—	701,102

Rate of increase equal to that in

Still further, in 1805, the population of Ireland was estimated by Mr. Newenham at 5,395,456; ex-

LECTURE VII.

North America.

hibiting thus a rate of increase during the previous twenty-five years only second to that which the British colonies in North America had furnished, and confirmatory of Mr. Malthus's inference, as to the capability of the human race to double its numbers in about a quarter of a century.

Now, had the food of the Irish population consisted of corn—had the exported grain in this case been the surplus of the annual crop, after a sufficiency had been reserved for seed and the support of the labourer, however inconvenient it might have been to the English consumer to be compelled to buy at so dear a market, for the bounty which the state supplied was so much paid indirectly by the English consumer of Irish corn, still the state might have been secured from being called upon at any subsequent time to feed the Irish corn-growers; but inasmuch as the corn grown by the greater part of the cultivators of the soil in Ireland was grown almost exclusively for the foreign market, the exports of corn were no index of the surplus power of the people so to feed themselves. Grain crops, indeed, were raised in Ireland just as silk or cotton manufactures were produced in Lancashire, as articles of exchange, not of consumption, the food of the cultivator in Ireland consisting of a far cheaper, but far more uncertain article, the potato. Of the extent to which this esculent has been cultivated we have the best information in the returns which have lately been furnished by Mr. Griffiths, and which the Chief Secretary for Ireland referred to in the House of Commons, January 19, 1847:—

Grain not grown for home consumption.

	£
Oats, 4,000,000 acres, at 3*l.* 10*s.* - - -	14,000,000
Wheat, flax, grass crops, 2,000,000 acres, at 7*l.* -	14,000,000
Potatoes, 1,500,000 acres, at 10*l.* - - -	15,000,000
Pasture, meadow, 6,500,000 acres, at 1*l.* 5*s.* -	8,125,000
	£51,125,000

Now, it has been calculated that two thirds of the Irish population live entirely upon potatoes, so that half the entire grain crop of the country is in all probability exported; whereas, had the food of the people been grain, the whole produce of the grain crop would only have sufficed to support two thirds of the existing population, it being calculated that 15,000,000*l.* worth of potatoes will support a population that would consume grain of double the value. Yet Ireland continues to export grain, and the agricultural families constitute about two thirds of the whole population.

Operation of Bounty Act

It would thus seem that the operation of the Bounty Act has been to stimulate unduly the cultivation of corn, *for the purpose of exportation*, not for the purpose of food; and thus that agriculture in Ireland has assumed quite an unnatural character under its influence, and corn-tillage is, as it were, a factitious kind of industry. An undue demand has thus been created for labour, not otherwise self-remunerating, and thus the growth of the agricultural population has been inordinately stimulated. Had not the state held out a bounty, the landlord would not have allowed his pasture lands to be broken up, nor the middleman have invested his capital in clearing and enclosing them, nor would the race of labourers have been unduly encouraged to multiply their numbers by the fatal facility of renting small patches of land for the produce of their grain crop, and been led to trust the support of their families to an inferior kind of food.

Undue demand for labour.

Opponents of Mr. Malthus.

The schools of writers opposed to Mr. Malthus divide themselves into two great classes, both of which seem to consider that the march of population is natural and providential, and should not be interfered with, and that it is within the province of the state to control the operation of positive checks. The earlier school, whose doctrines provoked Mr.

LECTURE VII. Malthus' work, maintained that the existing distribution of wealth was faulty, and that under an improved distribution, there would be always sufficient produce for the support of any number of labourers. The later school, which seem to have originated subsequently to his work, admitted, indeed, the possibility of a surplus population at times, but considered emigration to be the natural remedy under such an emergency.

Both these questions deserve consideration; but as the latter is of more immediate interest, it may claim our attention first.

Emigration. That emigration is one of the modes by which in the natural order of Providence the human race is to fulfil the injunction of "be fruitful and multiply, and replenish the earth, and subdue it," is unquestionable, but that it can ever be regarded as a *remedy* for over-population, may be more than doubted. Its advocates, however, are generally men of benevolent feeling; but they are also men of imaginative minds, who do not consider that the emigrant, who is thrust out by a community under the pressure of population against food, is a man of little or no capital, whose existence depends upon his finding an immediate market for his labour, in a country of strangers, in the expectation of which he is not unfrequently disappointed, and condemned to drag out a lingering existence of mental mortification and bodily suffering in his adopted country, far more painful than all that he would have undergone at home. It has been aptly observed by M. Rossi, that the advocates of emigration resemble physicians, who, when they despair of their patients' recovery, recommend them to try change of climate.

But what is the real fact? Is emigration ever more A palliative of the evil. than a palliative of the evil; or is it not rather one of those dangerous palliatives the employment of which is followed by a recurrence of the symptoms in an aggravated form, because, meanwhile, the true remedy is neglected? Nay, is it not probable, that emigration, by relieving the immediate pressure, will thereby remove for a time the necessity of seeking an appropriate remedy, the application of which will always be irksome? It was shown in a previous course of lectures, that the rate of increase in the case of the population of Ireland seemed to have been accelerated in consequence of the emigration of numerous bodies of labourers, and such a result, we should be led by theory to expect. Either the best workmen emigrate, in which case the productive power of the country in proportion to its population is reduced; or the worthless and idle emigrate, in which case the pressure of population against food is relieved, and that relief at once gives an impulse to the movement of population.

Two classes of emigrants.

Local emigration.

Experience thus seems to negative the supposed positive effect of emigration in readjusting the proportions of population to food. In its operation it seems to be equivalent to a short pestilence; but it is more discriminate for the most part in its victims. Its effect upon the labour market is rather to stimulate the demand for new hands by creating an export trade of old hands. It may, indeed, under certain circumstances, be of temporary use as an industrial safety-valve, to let off the steam, when the action of the engine is checked, but its being let off does not affect the further generation of steam, unless the fire is reduced. Local emigration, if such a term may be used to denote the transfer of labour at home from localities where it is in excess, to localities where the supply is deficient, is undoubtedly of service, as any other commerce, and such transfers of labour may safely be encouraged, as

LECTURE VII.

they further the division of labour, and promote the advancement of a country in productive power.

Colonisation.

On a similar principle the effects of colonisation, as distinguished from emigration, may not be disadvantageous where its direction is judicious. On the contrary, it may be beneficial by opening new markets, from the colonists producing new articles of exchange, and so creating a demand for the produce of the mother country. But it must be remembered that the industry of an infant colony is essentially agricultural, and unless the mother country is prepared to admit without restriction the raw produce of the colony into the home market, colonisation will be as barren in its results as a forced emigration. Under any circumstances, if it be looked to as a direct remedy for what is termed over-population, its advocates will be disappointed, for the evil, which it is customary to refer to over-population, is really to be attributed to a faulty organisation of productive power.

On the other hand, if colonisation be regarded as a system of industrial conquest, by which the waste spots of the earth's surface are to be occupied and cultivated, and by which the commerce of a great race is to be extended, and greater scope given to its productive power, there is no reason to doubt that such results will attend it, where the mother country does not tie up the hands of the colonists. But colonisation, in its most favourable aspect, will in one sense rather act as a stimulus to population, for it will create a demand for labour, and thus it must be cautiously and sparingly pursued, or it may overstimulate population, and the advantage accruing to the mother country be so far proportionately diminished.

Vicious distribution of wealth.

As for that section of Mr. Malthus' opponents, who maintained that a vicious distribution of wealth is entailed by the existing constitution of society, and that a more equal partition is all that is required to secure abundant subsistence for an unlimited increase of numbers, their suggestion is open to similar objections to those, which make emigration nugatory. If it be admitted, for the sake of argument, that it would be possible to organise by political changes a more equal distribution of wealth, so that the existing extreme classes of society should be brought indefinitely near to the middle class, such a state of things would not furnish any new element of resistance to the principle of population: on the contrary, so large a mass of the community becoming for a time exempt from the operation of positive checks, their rate of increase would be accelerated, and thereby more than compensate for any retardation in the growth of the comparatively few families, who composed the former upper class. In addition, the means of indulging in any save almost necessary expenses would no longer exist, as in the present constitution of society, and there would no longer be any reserve fund of food corresponding to that which at present is employed in the maintenance of animals subservient to our comfort or luxury: so that a deficient harvest, which now leads to a dearth, would invariably produce a famine, no class having any superfluous store to bestow upon those who might want the necessaries of life. The correctness of this view is too well established by the events now passing in Ireland, where so large a proportion of the population engaged in agriculture are, upon one and the same level, just above starvation.

Over earnestness of Mr. Malthus.

It must, however, be admitted that Mr. Malthus, with the ardour that a new career of discovery frequently awakens in the human mind, pushed on his argument with a reckless disregard for all other considerations than that of maintaining a just equilibrium between population and subsistence. On the other hand, human benevolence is not sufficiently indiscriminate in its choice of objects, nor sufficiently careful in its selection of means; and it frequently happens that institutions, such, for instance, as foundling hospitals, lead to consequences foreign from the intentions of the founders, and give rise to evils greater than those which they were meant to mitigate. Mr. Malthus, therefore, did good service both to the state and to individuals, when he pointed out the true tendency of many existing practices which had their origin either in the hereditary prejudices of an uninquiring public, or in the unreflecting impulse of individual feeling. He has himself admitted the probability that, having found the bow curved too much one way, he had bent it back too much in another direction, in order to straighten it.

Defect of Mr. Malthus' system.

The real objection, however, to Mr. Malthus' system is not that it is untrue, but that it is incomplete. The history, indeed, of civilisation displays a course of social advancement at variance with the assumption, that the human race tends absolutely to increase faster than the means of subsistence. There are other powerful counteracting tendencies in human nature developed with the occasion for their use. Thus, indeed, man, in the social state, experiences new desires to which he is a stranger when moving in the narrower circle of domestic life. By his own hearth side, surrounded with the objects of his tenderest affection, he thinks not of himself; but the feeling of self-love is at once awakened when he finds himself thrown amidst strangers, with whom he has no sympathies, and from whom he cannot expect co-operation; whose opinions are influenced by appearances, and whose very numbers make distinctions between individuals inevitable.

Distinction of classes.

The grounds of classification, indeed, may vary in different societies; but the distinction of classes is recognised equally beneath the tent of the wandering Arab as in the palaces of European princes: the form, indeed, which it assumes, may differ on the banks of the Thames and of the Ganges, but the principle is of universal application.

New feelings are thus called into play by the distinction of classes — feelings which moderate and counterbalance the strong, natural impulse hitherto predominant; viz., the fear of sinking through improvident self-indulgence, and the hope of rising by prudent self-restraint. These feelings are as much a part of man's nature as the feeling which impels him to continue his race, and their operation is as inevitable as the increase of population itself, though it must be admitted that their action may be neutralised by bad social institutions. When this fact was pressed upon his attention, Mr. Malthus, in his published correspondence with Mr. Senior, in 1829, maintained "that the desire of bettering our condition, *as far as it affects the direct increase of food*, is perfectly feeble, compared with the tendency of population to increase:" but there appears to be some slight confusion of thought in this statement, which is not strictly in point. If Mr. Malthus meant to impugn Mr. Senior's position, that "the desire of bettering our condition is as natural a wish as the desire of marriage," he should have said that the desire of bettering our condition, *as far as it affects the direct increase of population*, is perfectly feeble, compared with the desire of marriage; for no one ever maintained that restraint and self-denial, the offspring of the desire to better one's condition of life, could directly increase food. Their indirect operation, however, may affect the relation which food and population bear to each other in such a degree, as to diminish the pressure of population against food; and so wherever this pressure tends to diminish,

Correspondence with Mr. Senior.

LECTURE VII.

Natural course of society.

society may be considered to be advancing in its *natural* course, Οἷον γὰρ ἕκαστόν ἐστι τῆς γενέσεως τελεσθείσης, ταύτην φαμὲν εἶναι τὴν φύσιν ἑκάστου. Aristot. Pol. l. i. c. i.

Mr. Malthus unhesitatingly maintained that the superior power of population could not be checked without producing either misery or vice. This is an unnecessarily gloomy view of the prospects of society: but M. Rossi has well observed, that it is not in the midst of misery and that stupid indifference, which is frequently the result of it, that we can expect a wise forethought to grow up, which shall lead to future self-restraint. He who has ceased to fear, has ceased to hope; and, with hope and fear, all calculation of consequences departs. The question, however, may be asked, How happens it that we find certain nations have kept steadily advancing in moral and material prosperity, in spite of most severe dearths, which seems at first sight paradoxical?

Effect of social institutions

The explanation is to be sought for, not so much in the political, as in the social institutions of nations. The mass that survives, is a different class from the mass that perishes. We must never forget that nations are not homogeneous compounds, any more than individual men, and that nations may differ very considerably from one another, according as different classes of men predominate in them. Wherever, indeed, the institutions of a community contribute to call into exercise the higher faculties of our nature, we shall there find the class, which is capable of reflecting, and thereby duly controlling the instincts of animal life, continually augmented in numbers, and tending to form the predominant class. It is under these circumstances that one nation in spite of occasional dearths, attains to a high degree of civilisation, whilst another, differently composed, is kept stationary, or even retrogrades. The class whom famine

The middle class.

sweeps off in the former case, is but a small minority: in the latter they are the mass, or a great majority. That political institutions may favour the growth of *the middle class*, which is the distinctive element of modern society, is undeniable; but the measures which Mr. Godwin and similar writers advocated, were not calculated to promote this result.

LECTURE VIII.

LECTURE VIII.

THE last quarter of the eighteenth century supplied a most ample harvest of facts to the new School of Economists, which had adopted the principles of Adam Smith, and pursued the experimental method, which he had introduced. The great social experiments, to which the Political Revolution in France had given rise on the continent of Europe, have been already alluded to. Contemporaneous with those experiments, an industrial revolution was silently operating in England, leading to results, still more remarkable, and more important in their bearings upon economical questions; for the conditions, under which human labour was henceforth to be applied, were thereby undergoing a modification, only second in extent to that, which Attic piety commemorated of old in the Eleusinian mysteries.

Industrial revolution.

Watt and Arkwright.

The great motive power, which the genius of Watt had first disciplined (his earliest patent was taken out in 1769) was applied, about the year 1785, in furtherance of the discoveries of Arkwright, and the combination of the steam-engine with the spinning-frame, as it changed the aspect of production, so it gave rise to a new class of problems, bearing upon the distribution of produce. At the same time the emancipation of so large a portion of the American continent from the dominion of European interests gave a new face to many great questions of commerce. The prosperity of the United States of North America, for instance, inflicted a death-blow upon the ancient theory of the Balance of Trade, whilst the

Balance of trade.

colonial traditions of Europe were annihilated by the mother countries becoming tributary to their former subjects for the raw material of their staple manufactures. The Science of Finance, likewise, received a new impulse, from the extraordinary development which manufacturing industry underwent, and that branch of the system which was more particularly concerned with indirect taxation, was subjected to a most complete revision. The protracted struggle, which England was maintaining against the system of the French Revolution, could not but hasten the march of events. It was impossible to diminish the burden of taxation, as long as this struggle lasted: hence it became of the last importance to augment the means of supporting the burden; and thus the indirect result was a more rapid development of the elements of change.

Science of finance.

Adam Smith had explained, with sufficient precision, those branches of economical inquiry, which were more peculiarly connected with the production of wealth, as far as agriculture and the arts were concerned; but his investigations were not so complete in reference to commerce. On the other hand, as his system was essentially experimental, based upon an examination of facts, the operations of *industry*, properly so called, in distinction from *labour*, had not assumed that importance which entitled them to a special analysis.

Adam Smith's work not complete.

The course of events, however, subsequent to the publication of the "Wealth of Nations," had given prominence to many commercial and industrial questions, which consequently demanded solution at the hands of his successors. Amongst the first and the most distinguished writers of the Continent, who justly appreciated the value of the "Inquiry into the Nature and Causes of the Wealth of Nations," was M. Jean Baptiste Say, "who, not merely," to use

M. Jean Baptiste Say.

LECTURE VIII.

Mr. Ricardo's words, "has done more than all other continental writers taken together, to recommend the principles of that enlightened and beneficial system to the nations of Europe, but who has succeeded in placing the science in a more logical and more instructive order, and has enriched it by several discussions, original, accurate, and profound."

Traité d'Economie Politique.

His earliest work was his "Traité d'Economie Politique, ou Simple Exposition de la Manière dont se forment, se distribuent, et se consomment les Richesses," published in 1803, whilst Napoleon Buonaparte was First Consul.

The science of Political Economy was now, for the first time, formally limited to the legitimate sphere, which Adam Smith had by implication marked out for it, namely, the investigation of the laws which govern the formation, distribution, and consumption of wealth. M. Say, however, extended the meaning of the term wealth, under which head he embraced immaterial as well as material products: in this respect, differing entirely from the English School. He enlarged the signification of the word "utility," defining it to be "cette faculté qu'ont certaines choses de pouvoir satisfaire aux divers besoins des hommes:" and thus, whatever was capable of satisfying the wants of man was, according to M. Say, an article of wealth, as such a capacity was the first foundation of value.

Utility.

Mr. Malthus' Principles of Political Economy.

It is not proposed, on the present occasion, to do more than allude to the discussion of this question, which is to be found in "Mr. Malthus' Principles of Political Economy." Mr. Malthus, who, in several respects, was strongly opposed to M. Say's views, in regard to rent, for instance, considers that this enlarged definition of wealth has led M. Say almost inevitably to contradictions and inconsistencies.

"One motive," he says, "which seems to have in-

LECTURE VIII.

Objections to M. Say's definition of wealth.

duced M. Say to force into his definition of wealth 'les plus nobles vertus et les plus rares talens,' is to enlarge and exalt the domain of Political Economy, which he says has been reproached with occupying itself upon worldly goods, and encouraging a spirit of avarice. But even if such a classification would give the subject more importance, this additional importance would be dearly purchased at the expense of the precision of its conclusions. The question, however, is not whether the results of useful labours may not, very properly, find a place in a Treatise on Political Economy, as they have done in the Inquiry of Adam Smith, but whether the specific term *wealth*, should be so defined, as to make not only its own meaning quite indistinct, but to introduce still greater indistinctness into the terms of the science of morals."

"The fact really is," he continues, "that if we once desert matter in the definition of wealth, there is no subsequent line of demarcation which has any tolerable degree of distinctness, or can be maintained with any tolerable consistency, till we have included such a mass of immaterial objects as utterly to confuse the meaning of the term, and render it impossible to speak with any approach towards precision, either of the wealth of different individuals or different nations.

"If then we wish, with M. Say, to make Political Economy a positive science, founded on experience, and capable of making known its results, we must be particularly careful in defining its principal term, to embrace only those objects, the increase or decrease of which is capable of being estimated, and the line, which it seems most natural and useful to draw, is that which separates material from immaterial objects."

Immaterial products.

It was observed, in the Sixth Lecture, that Adam Smith's classification of labour, under the heads of productive and unproductive labour, was open to grave objections. M. Say, on the other hand, by in-

LECTURE VIII.

cluding immaterial products under the name of riches, enlarged the domain of productive labour indefinitely. Mr. Malthus, considering this indiscriminate sense of the word *productive* to be even more objectionable than the confined sense in which Adam Smith had used it, suggested that it might be desirable to substitute the term *personal services* for unproductive labour. In reference to this, Mr. Senior observes, in the "Encyclopædia Metropolitana," "those who thought the principles of Adam Smith's division convenient, feeling, at the same time, the difficulty of terming unproductive the labour, without which all other labour would be inefficient, invented the term *services*, or immaterial products, to express its results." After investigating the origin of those distinctions, and tracing it up rather to the mode in which the objects are considered, than to the objects themselves, Mr. Senior proposes to retain the distinction between services and commodities as convenient, applying the term *services* to the act of occasioning an alteration in the existing state of things, the term *commodity*, to the thing as altered, and including both commodities and services under the general term *product*.

Personal services.

Mr. Senior's use of the term product.

International commerce.

The most valuable portion of M. Say's labours are to be found in his discussions on international commerce. Adam Smith had observed that it was "the great multiplication of the productions of all the different arts, in consequence of the division of labour, which occasions in a well governed society that universal opulence which extends itself to the lowest ranks of the people." He had likewise pointed out, that "as it is the power of exchanging that gives occasion to the division of labour, so the extent of this division must always be limited by the extent of that power, or, in other words, by the extent of the market. When the market is very small, no person can have any encouragement to dedicate himself entirely to one employment, for want of the power to exchange all that surplus part of the produce of his own labour, which is over and above his own consumption, for such parts of the produce of other men's labour as he has occasion for." The extension of the market would thus seem to be regarded by Adam Smith as a condition precedent to any further subdivision of labour.

Subdivision of labour.

It remained for M. Say to show that every subdivision of labour, causes of itself an enlargement of the market, where it is judiciously carried out. Adam Smith had been the first to point out that the powers of production were rendered most effective by the introduction of a division of labour amongst the producers, which led first to an increase of dexterity; secondly, to a saving of time; thirdly, to an improvement of machinery. M. Say completed Adam Smith's work by showing that no conceivable increase of these powers, provided there be a proportionate increase in the division of labour, can ever lead to a general overloading of the market, inasmuch as each new commodity forms a new equivalent for purchasing some other commodity, and each new product renders the market so much the more extensive.

Commercial outlets.

In the fifteenth chapter of his "Traité de l'E'conomie Politique," M. Say first expounds his views under the title of "Des Débouchés," or, to adopt an English equivalent, "On Commercial Outlets."

"It is usual," he writes, "for persons engaged in the several branches of industry to say that they find a difficulty not in producing, but in selling; that there would always be an abundant supply of goods, if it were easy to find a market for them. When they cannot dispose of their produce readily and advantageously, they say 'money is scarce;' and the great object of their desires is a rapid consumption, which will tend to multiply sales, and keep up prices. But if they are asked what circumstances favour the disposal of their produce, it will be perceived that the mass have only confused ideas on the subject, are bad observers, and still worse interpreters of facts, hold for certain that which is as yet doubtful, desire that which is directly opposed to their interests, and seek to obtain an authoritative sanction to a system of protection, fertile in evil consequences to themselves."

In order then to obtain clear and just ideas upon a subject, which occupies so wide a field when we regard its bearings upon international commerce, it will be desirable to analyse certain facts which are within the compass of each individual's observation.

Every product then possesses a certain utility, i. e. a certain quality of satisfying some desire of man. By virtue of this utility it becomes an object of demand to those who seek the satisfaction of the desire to which it is adapted. If the product costs nothing, each person who desires it will provide himself with a sufficiency; but on any other supposition, those who wish to enjoy it, must either furnish the cost, or its equivalent. Now it is customary to regard money as the equivalent in certain proportions of all commodities. Let this be admitted to be a fact: but the question then suggests itself, by what means does money find its way into the hands of those who wish to purchase any given commodity? Is it not the case that money itself, for we must exclude from consideration the representatives of money, which, under certain conditions of credit, frequently fulfil its functions, consists in a commodity which has itself been procured at a certain cost, i. e. by the sacrifice of a certain quantity of produce given in exchange for it? Before a person is in a condition to purchase a commodity with money, he must have purchased the

Money a commodity.

money itself, and that purchase he must have effected by the sale of his own produce, or of produce that belongs to him. The proprietor of land, if he lets it to the cultivator for a produce rent, sells, on his own account, the portion of produce which accrues to him as the proprietor: if he lets it for a money rent, the farmer sells a portion of produce on his account, and hands over to him its equivalent in money. If the capitalist, who has lent money on interest to a manufacturer, does not himself sell a portion of the manufacturer's produce, the manufacturer assuredly sells it on his account, and pays him the money which he has obtained in exchange for it. No purchaser is in a condition to give money in exchange for a commodity, unless he has previously exchanged away some product of his own for money. It would argue but narrow intelligence on the part of a manufacturer if he were to declare that it is not an abundance of all sorts of produce which really makes the market firm, but plenty of money.

Money purchased with produce.

"It might well be said in reply to him," writes M. Say, "the farmer will buy your goods if his harvest is productive; he will buy so much the more, according as he produces more: he can buy nothing if he produces nothing."

"You, yourself, even, cannot buy his corn or his wool, unless you produce manufactured goods. You pretend that it is the supply of money which is deficient. I tell you, that it is other products. In a word, why do you want money? Is it not in order that you may buy raw materials for your manufactures, or provisions for your own subsistence? You must see clearly that it is produce which is deficient, not money. The silver, for instance, which will have furthered the sale of your own produce, and the purchase of another person's produce, will pass on into other hands a moment afterwards, and serve for a similar purpose between two other dealers, and so on between others, without any limit to its circulation, in the same way as the vehicle, which has conveyed your produce to market, will convey in its turn some other person's produce thither. When you cannot sell your produce readily, do you ever say, it is because purchasers have no vehicles to convey it away? Well! money is the vehicle of value. Its only use is to convey into your hands the value of the produce, which the purchaser of your goods has sold in order to purchase them; and to convey in return into his hands the value of the produce, which you have already sold to others.

Money the vehicle of value.

"It is thus with the value of your own produce transformed for the moment into a sum of money, that you purchase, in a word, that all the world purchases the articles of which each is in want. Otherwise, how could it be possible to purchase, now-a-days, in France, six or eight times the quantity of articles during the year, that were purchased in the miserable reign of Charles VI.? It is evidently because six or eight times more articles are produced, and that one commodity is purchased with another commodity."

Scarcity of produce makes the market dull.

Whenever, therefore, it is said, "the market is dull, because money is scarce," the means are mistaken for the end. For the market is dull, not because money is scarce, but because some particular kind of produce is scarce, which would exchange for the produce which is abundant. There is always money enough for the purposes of a circulating medium, or in its absence convenient substitutes will be adopted to facilitate the exchange of values, wherever those values really exist. Money is never long wanted for mercantile transactions, for such transactions imply an abundance of valuable commodities, and with some portion of these the particular commodity, which serves the purposes of money, may be procured to satisfy the emergency.

But money will always be scarce in countries where the labour of the people is badly organised, as there will be little, if any, exchange of values, because there will be scarcely any variety of products to form the basis of an exchange.

Production opens outlets for produce.

It might at first sight seem paradoxical to assert that it is production which opens outlets for produce, yet when it is called to mind that the value of an article can only be appreciated and paid for where there are the means of acquiring it, and that these means consist in other values, the fruits of production, the seeming paradox assumes at once the character of a self-evident truth. It will thus follow, that the more numerous the producers, and the more varied their productions, the readier will be the market. A product, when completed, creates at once, to the full amount of its own value, a market for other products, and the producer becomes anxious to exchange it away as soon as possible, that its value may not be lost to him. But he is for the same reason equally anxious to exchange away again in its turn the money which he may have happened to receive for his product; and this second exchange will not be for money, but for some other product. Hence every addition to the stock of one man's produce creates a demand for another man's produce. Hence a good harvest is not merely advantageous to the cultivators of the soil, but to the producers of all other commodities than food. The cultivator can buy more if he produces more. It is the same with the industrious arts: each new article of manufactured produce enlarges the market for raw produce, whilst increased supplies of raw produce in their turn create an increased demand for manufactured goods.

In illustration of this position, that production itself opens outlets for produce, it may be observed that before the discovery of the spinning jenny, there were only 5000 wheel spinners and 3000 hand-loom weavers of cotton in Great Britain, altogether 8000 hands employed in the manufacture of cotton, whilst in 1836 upwards of 800,000 hands were employed in England only. Every improvement in machinery, as it renders labour more efficient, thereby fosters indirectly the demand for produce, since the diminution of cost allows more favourable terms of exchange to be offered to purchasers, and consequently, the market will be brisker.

Results of improved machinery.

But it may be asked, How comes it to pass that at certain periods the circulation of the market seems to suffer a check, and there ensues what is termed a glut, when no purchasers can be found? How happens it that one portion of the produce brought to market does not exchange for some other portion, and so keep up a demand for it?

Origin of gluts.

The answer is obvious. There is a surplus of one sort of produce, because there is a deficiency of some other kind. The demand for one description of produce does not depend upon the will of a consumer, but on his power to offer an equivalent for it. Commodities are brought to market with the view of exchanging them for other commodities, and the fact that any commodity is in excess, is evidence that there is a corresponding deficiency in the supply of those, for which the merchant would be willing to exchange it. Thus we may remark, that the periods when certain articles are heavy in the market, are precisely those in which other articles are at exorbitant prices; and as such prices would naturally tend to stimulate production, there must be certain artificial causes in operation which control the supply, and so produce a glut of certain articles. These causes are found to consist for the most part in unwise regulations, which the cupidity of Governments has suggested, and their inexperience has sanctioned, by which industry has been lured into favoured channels to the neglect of others equally important, and so with respect to the latter production has lagged behind. It will rarely happen that one branch of industry will outstrip others to such an extent as to render its produce a drug in the market, if all branches are equally exempt from interference on the part of the Government.

Faulty application of productive power.

"It is clear," writes Mr. M'Culloch, "that a glut cannot originate in a too great aggregate production, but that it is in every case a consequence of the faulty application of productive power; i. e. of the production of particular commodities, which either do not suit the tastes of those with whom we wish to exchange them, or which we cannot ourselves consume.

"If we attend to these two great requisites — if we produce such commodities only as can be taken by those to whom we offer them for sale, or such as are directly available to our own use, we may increase the power of production ten or ten thousand times, and we shall be quite as free of all excess, as if we diminished them in the same proportion. Miscalculation, and the too great ardour of speculation, occasionally divert capital into channels in which it ought not to have flowed: but if Government do not interfere to relieve the parties concerned from the effects of their own improvidence, a regard to their own interest will make them withdraw from the losing business in which they have engaged, and will, sooner than any artificial remedy, correct the improper distribution of capital, and reproduce the natural equilibrium between the price and the cost of producing commodities. Unproductive expenditure is not, therefore, necessary to prevent the overloading of the market; and to maintain that it contributes to increase national wealth in any other way, is really quite the same thing as to maintain that wealth would be increased by throwing a portion of it into the sea or the fire."

The interests of individual producers reciprocal.

It would follow, if the principle above advanced be correct, that each individual has an interest in the prosperity of his neighbours, and that the prosperity of one branch of industry contributes to the prosperity of all around it. Whatever be our calling, it is evident that we shall find more employment, and derive more profit, in proportion as we are encircled with a greater number of persons productively employed. A man of talent who would pine away in inactivity in a country where industry was stagnant, will find a thousand opportunities for exerting his powers in the midst of a productive community, where he can find employment, and be remunerated for his services. A merchant, settled in a rich manufacturing town, will sell a much larger amount of goods than one who inhabits a dull country district. It would be in vain for an active manufacturer, or a skilful merchant, to establish himself in one of the half peopled towns of Spain or Poland: though he would have no competition to dread, yet he would find no purchasers, because his neighbours, producing nothing, would not have wherewithal to purchase his goods; whilst in Paris or London, in spite of a hundred competitors on all sides, he may succeed in establishing an enormous business; for he will be surrounded with persons who produce every variety of commodity, and who can make purchases with their own produce, or, in other words, with the money resulting from the sale of it.

Relation of the arts to agriculture.

In the same manner, it is of the highest importance to the farmer that the arts should prosper, as it is reciprocally to the artisan that agriculture should flourish. A town situated in a rich territory finds a large body of purchasers amongst the neighbouring agriculturists, precisely as farmers, who dwell near a flourishing town, find an excellent market for their produce amongst the artisans. Too long has a narrow and mistaken selfishness arrayed interest against interest, and class against class. If the agriculture of a country flourishes, it is a reason why its manufactures and commerce should flourish, just as the prosperity of its manufactures and commerce must exercise a beneficial influence upon its agriculture.

Interests of nations reciprocal.

The case of nations does not vary in any essential particular from that of provinces or cities. Every nation is interested in the prosperity of its neighbour, and is certain of benefitting by it. The United States of North America, for instance, have found it to be for their interest, that their Indian neighbours should abandon the habits of savage life, and adopt the sedentary occupations of civilised industry, and thus several tribes on the banks of the Mississippi, who had only a few furs in former times to offer in exchange for the manufactures of the States, have become producers of beans and maize, and work the lead mines within their own territory, and so buy largely in the markets of the States. Europe, again, is interested in the tea crop of China, and the cotton crop of Carolina and Virginia, for the more productive the harvest in those countries, and the greater the quantity of raw produce brought to market, the more brisk will be the demand for the silks of France and the cottons of England. Yet it has been the aim of statesmen to exclude, systematically, foreign produce from the home market, and the effect has been that the hands of the home producer have been thereby tied up.

M. Say's beautiful theory, to use the language of Professor Blanqui, founded as it is entirely upon a scrupulous examination of facts, has proved that nations can only pay for produce with produce, and that prohibitions against buying are obstacles to selling.

LECTURE VIII.

No calamity can directly befall one member of the great family of nations, without other members feeling it indirectly: when the harvest is deficient in one quarter of the globe, the manufacturer suffers in another, and when prosperity reigns throughout a country, all its neighbours share in its effects, partly by reason of the demand which it causes, partly on account of the cheapness which results from the abundance of its produce. Nations thus are bound in sureties for one another (*solidaires*) in good as in evil fortune. Wars are follies, which ruin even the conqueror, and it is the general interest of mankind to give aid to one another mutually, instead of doing harm, as a blind policy has too long driven them to do. We begin to comprehend the consequences of this truly wise and noble doctrine, and we may already infer from the solicitude of governments to avoid war, that the principles of M. Say have penetrated into the council chambers of kings. His most glorious distinction is that of having demonstrated as a positive and practical truth, what had hitherto appeared to be a philosophic Utopia, and his merit is the greater inasmuch as Montesquieu, Voltaire, and La Fontaine, the brightest geniuses of France, have maintained the opposite error.

Nations stand surety for one another.

Montesquieu.

Montesquieu has a chapter (l. xx. chap. 23.) expressly entitled, "A quelles nations il est désavantageux de faire le commerce," and he points to Japan as a country with which a highly profitable commerce might be carried on. "The great quantity which it is capable of receiving, produces the great quantity which it is capable of exporting: things will thus be kept in equilibrium, just as if the importation and exportation were moderate, and in other respects this gorged condition (énflure) will produce a thousand advantages to the state: consumption will be increased, there will be more objects for the arts to practice upon, more men employed, more means of acquiring power. Contingencies, likewise, may arise, when there is need of prompt succour, which, a state gorged with produce, will be enabled to supply sooner than another. It is difficult for a country not to possess superfluities, but it is the nature of commerce to render superfluous things useful, and useful things necessary." Yet Poland, according to the same author, was ruining itself by exporting its grain, and importing superfluities. "If Poland," he writes, "had no foreign trade, its people would be more happy." "A rich country," again, according to Montesquieu, "could alone gain any thing by commerce; a poor country would infallibly ruin itself. A country," he writes, "which always exports less than it receives, maintains an equilibrium by impoverishing itself; it will continue to receive less, until it will have reached a state of extreme poverty, when it will cease to receive any thing."

Opinion of commerce.

The same author elsewhere (l. xx. chap. 2.) writes, "the natural effect of commerce is to carry peace with it. Two nations which trade together, render each other mutually dependent: if the one has an interest in buying, the other has an interest in selling, and all alliances are based on mutual wants." Yet, in the conclusion of the same book, he says, "It is not for me to decide the question, if Spain, not being able to conduct the trade of the Indies alone, had better leave it open to strangers. I will only say that it would be advantageous for her to set as few obstacles in the way of this branch of commerce as her political system will allow her to do. When the goods, which different nations carry to the Indies are dear, the Indians give a great deal of their merchandize, which is gold and silver, for a small quantity of foreign merchandize: the contrary result takes place when the former are cheap. It would, perhaps, be

LECTURE VIII.

desirable, that these nations should hurt one another, in order that the merchandize which they carry to the Indies should be always cheap in the Indian market." Here, he seems to suppose that the opening of the trade with the Indies would create so great a competition amongst foreign merchants, that they would injure each other by lowering their prices, and at the same time benefit the Indians. This seems almost to square with Voltaire's doctrine, as set forth under the article "Patrie," in his "Dictionnaire Philosophique," quoted by M. Say. "Such is the condition of humanity, that to wish the greatness of one's own country, is to wish evil to one's neighbours. It is clear, that one country cannot gain, except another loses." "Il est clair qu'un pays ne peut gagner sans qu'un autre ne perde." It has been thought worth while to refer to this passage, as well as to the extracts from Montesquieu, in order to show how great a gulf separates these writers from M. Say, and how the most powerful intellects of the eighteenth century were quite unequal, by à priori reasoning, to grapple with the questions which the experimental method of the nineteenth century has thoroughly elucidated.

Voltaire.

So far from the truth is it, that the operations of foreign commerce are prejudicial to what Montesquieu terms a poor country, under which head he classes all countries exclusively agricultural, that on the contrary, the importation of foreign produce must favour the sale of home produce. For such foreign produce must be paid for, either directly or indirectly, with home produce, and so effectively stimulate production. For, if it be said, foreign commodities will be paid for with money, let it not be overlooked that the gold or silver, which is given in exchange for foreign commodities, is exchanged away as a *commodity*, and not as *money:* the sovereigns of England,

Foreign commerce.

for instance, and the dollars of Spain, enter into foreign commerce, not as money, but as metal of a certain purity and weight: and if it be true, that certain branches of commerce entail an export of gold and silver, other branches of commerce promote an influx of those commodities. Let us consider, for a moment, the true condition of an agricultural country, in its relation to other countries. Do the exports of grain from Odessa impoverish the southern provinces of the Russian empire? Is it not notorious, in the case of what Montesquieu terms poor countries, that gold and silver form a much larger item of their traffic with foreign nations, than in case of rich countries, and that a very small quantity of bullion is required to adjust the dealings of rich countries? We must never lose sight of the fact, that gold or silver, strictly speaking, is never productive when discharging the functions of money, but only when it is exchanged as a commodity; and that it is in the character of a commodity, that gold or silver becomes an article of foreign commerce.

Nations interested in one anothers' prosperity.

A prosperous nation ought rather to be regarded as a useful friend, than a dangerous rival. We ought, no doubt, to protect ourselves against the ambition or anger of a neighbour, who may misunderstand his own interests so, as to be anxious to embroil himself in war; but after taking the necessary measures to secure ourselves from unjust aggression, it is not our interest to weaken other nations. It has been said that merchants, at London and Marseilles, were alarmed at the prospect of the independence of Greece, and the competition which they would, in consequence, be exposed to. But what profitable commerce could Greece carry on with France or England, that would not encourage the industry of those countries? Could the Greeks import their produce into France or England without exporting in return the full equivalents of it? Could they force British merchants to trade, or would French merchants consent to deal, on terms which were not favourable to themselves? On the contrary, if the Greeks were ever to acquire a high station amongst nations, they would have wherewithal to pay for the gratification of new wants, and they would become important customers to the other European states. It is not a wild and indiscriminate philanthropy which suggests such a result, but a pure regard for self, operating upon an enlightened appreciation of one's own true interest.

Cause of occasional gluts.

The objectors to M. Say's views on this subject cite as a proof that production may be carried too far, the occasional glut of British produce in foreign markets. This superabundance, however, is only a proof that production itself is behind-hand in those countries, where such a glut happens to be experienced. If the Brazils raised sufficient produce wherewith to purchase the goods which are imported from England, there would be no glut of the latter; but it may be possible that there is no natural deficiency, but only an artificial dearth of Brazilian produce, suitable to be exchanged for British goods, which the Custom-House regulations of England alone create, by prohibiting or restricting the importation of certain produce of the Brazils.

Modern evils of restrictive system.

The bearings which restrictions on commerce exercise upon the industry of a country, have assumed a totally different aspect since the adaptation of steam power, as an agent of production. The combination of machinery, worked by steam, with a restrictive system of customs, has entailed the sacrifice of the labourer to the capitalist. The restrictive system, by blocking up certain inlets of trade, closes up certain outlets for produce; machinery, meanwhile, creates a redundancy of produce, and the market becomes glutted.

Hence suspension of employment, or diminution of wages, and the consequent demoralization of the labouring classes. Thus it results that the restrictive system makes man's ingenuity hurtful to himself, and changes into instruments of harm those wondrous inventions, which Providence has intended for the amelioration of the condition of the masses, and the general advancement of civilization.

International division of labour.

From these considerations it would appear, that as the interests of the individuals, which compose a nation, are furthered by everything which facilitates the mutual exchange of the fruits of their separate labour, so the interests of nations, which make up the great human family, will be best promoted by analogous facilities of commercial intercourse. And as the field of international commerce is enlarged by everything which extends the international division of labour, so reciprocally with freedom of international commerce, each nation will be at liberty to employ its capital and labour to the greatest advantage, according to the natural peculiarities of its soil and climate, and the genius of its people. But considerations of national policy are held to forbid that mutual interdependence of nations, which an unrestricted commerce would tend to produce, and it is urged that the evils which would ensue from the interruption of international trade by war, would more than counterbalance the good which could accrue during intervals of peace. But may it not with more reason be contended that the greater the mischief which would result from war, the more indisposed will nations feel to sanction that ruinous pastime of princes?

Commercial neutrality.

An enlightened philanthropy has indeed suggested, that it would be consistent with the free action of nations to adopt universally the principle of a commercial neutrality, viz. of perpetual peace for all legitimate purposes of trade and friendly intercourse,

LECTURE VIII.

even in the case of war, and experience has been appealed to as confirming the feasibility of this suggestion, on the ground that the principle has been tried on the two most difficult points of Europe, the two centres of all great strategic operations, viz. in Switzerland and Belgium. But surely it cannot be necessary, in the nineteenth century, to humour the passions instead of appealing to the understanding of mankind, as may have been needed in that period of social disorganization, when the passionate throb of northern barbarism had not yet come to beat in accord with the steadier pulse of Roman life, and it was requisite for the civilizing power to accommodate its advances to the lingering prejudices of savage life. I allude to such institutions as the Judicial Combat, and the Truce of God, by which a regulated indulgence was substituted for an unbridled licence of revenge.

Institution of middle ages.

Such a proposal, indeed, as that above alluded to, of a universal commercial neutrality, would certainly tend to establish a mode of deciding international controversies, more closely analogous to the wager of battle, than that which is already in use, viz. the substitution of regular troops for the ancient national levies.

But it seems more than questionable whether the establishment of such a commercial neutrality would not tend to perpetuate the recourse of nations to arms, rather than to discourage it. It cannot be denied that there is a tendency in civilization to substitute the constitutional for the despotic form of government, and that wherever a constitutional government exists, the will of the intelligent majority sways the national councils. Whatever, therefore, tends to make it the interest of that majority to maintain peace with its neighbours, will influence the will of the government to prevent war. If, then, the interests of nations were thoroughly interwoven by unre-

Unrestricted commerce.

stricted commerce, the interruption of their commercial relations by war would produce incalculable evil to all parties, and war would consequently be loathsome to the industrious population of every country. Freedom of commerce would thus tend to extinguish war, whilst a commercial neutrality would only palliate its evils; freedom of commerce would foster the growth of a pacific habit of mind, whilst a commercial neutrality proposes only to moderate the exercise of a warlike disposition.

Diversification of natural products.

The globe has surely not been encircled with zones of different temperatures in order that the inhabitants of the temperate should be independent of the products of the torrid zone; nor have different regions been endowed with such diversified gifts without an object in such diversification beyond the mere fact. In one country we find boundless plains of inexhaustible fertility; in another mountains which contain imperishable stores of precious metals; in a third green pastures covered with countless herds and flocks; in a fourth veins of coal and mineral treasures accessible to the ingenious approaches of man. Can it be then the interest of any one of such countries to encircle herself as it were with a brazen wall of prohibitions, and to restrict her own command of the commodities, which her neighbours produce, by impeding the reciprocal exchange of such varied gifts of climate and soil? Must it not be prejudicial to her to abridge the productiveness of her own labour and capital by diverting it from the employment, for which nature has fitted her out so bountifully, to one in which she has no natural advantages?

Dr. Friedrich List.

Yet, indeed, within the last ten years, a treatise has been put forth, entitled "The National System of Political Economy" ("Das Nationale System der Politischen Oekonomie"), by Dr. Friedrich List, in which doctrines, dictated by the narrowest and most short-

LECTURE VIII.

sighted selfishness, are attempted to be palmed off upon the German nation, as the conclusions of an enlightened and comprehensive philosophy. This writer would substitute for that natural freedom of international commerce, which M. Say has shown to conduce to the mutual interest of nations, by enabling them to employ their respective labour and capital most productively, what he terms a cosmopolitical division of labour and confederation of powers, "Kosmopolitische Theilung der Arbeit und Kräfte-Confederation." According to this theory, which is really too extravagant to require any serious discussion, the countries of the temperate zone are, in respect of their natural resources, more especially called to the development of manufacturing power, for the temperate clime is the zone of spiritual and bodily exertion. On the other hand, the countries of the torrid zone have on their side a natural monopoly of valuable products of agriculture, and it is upon the exchange of the manufactured products of the temperate for the agricultural products of the torrid zone, that Dr. List founds his great system of international commerce. It is not necessary to examine the arguments by which he attempts to support his views. There is an excellent paper on the subject in the "Edinburgh Review," No. CLII. (July 1842).

Cosmopolitical division of labour.

Edinburgh Review.

His treatise, indeed, is well described by the writer of the paper just alluded to, as "the work of a zealous and unscrupulous advocate, striving to establish a given practical conclusion, and not the production of a dispassionate inquirer, seeking to promote the improvement of a science or an art." To such as may be desirous of examining into the subject more closely, I would recommend the perusal of a treatise by H. F. Osiander, entitled "Enttäuschung des Publikums über die Interessen des Händels, der Industrie, und der Landwirthschaft, oder Beleuchtung der Manufac-

Osiander.

turkraft-Philosophie der Dr. List, nebst einem Gebet aus Utopien," published at Tübingen in 1842, as well as of two articles by Professor Karl Heinrich Rau, of Heidelberg in the first and second parts of the fifth volume of the "Archiv der Politischen Oekonomie und Polizeiwissenschaft." Heidelberg, 1842.

Professor Rau.

One position, however, of Dr. List's is so extraordinary, that a few moments may be excusably bestowed upon its examination (p. 24.). "The production of raw material and food (rohstoffen und nahrungstoffen—which latter word seems to be the German equivalent of the American phrase "breadstuffs,") is of high importance amongst the great nations of the temperate zone only with regard to their internal commerce. By the export of grain, wine, flax, hemp, wool, and such like, a rude or poor nation, in the infancy of its civilization, may signally raise its agriculture; but a great nation has never thereby arrived at wealth, civilization, and power.

Raw material and food.

"One may lay it down as a rule, that a nation is so much the more wealthy and powerful the more it exports manufactured products, the more it imports raw material, and the more it consumes the products of the torrid zone."

Dr. List's criterion of a wealthy nation.

The old leaven of the exploded error is evidently working in the writer's mind, if his words are a true criterion of his thoughts, which attributed to manufacturing industry an exaggerated productiveness, when contrasted with agricultural labour, and which was employed with great effect by Melon and the writers of his day, in support of the prohibitive system. ("Essai Politique sur le Commerce, par Melon," c. x.)

If Dr. List, in the passage just cited, means merely to say that a nation which has a flourishing import and export trade, and consumes colonial wares, is a rich and powerful nation, he propounds a truism in

Refuted by experience.

LECTURE VIII.

an unnecessarily complicated form: but if he means, that no state which exports raw materials and imports manufactured goods, and does not consume the produce of the torrid zone, is a wealthy and powerful nation, experience contradicts him. Montesquieu had attributed to economical causes, in the case of

Poland.

Poland, what was really to be referred to its social system. It was not the exportation of its agricultural produce that was injurious to the serfs of Poland, but the distribution of the foreign produce that was imported in return; and if Poland had not had any foreign commerce, its people would not have been more happy. Montesquieu assumed that, on this latter supposition, the corn would have been distributed by the proprietors amongst their serfs, and the fleeces and hides would have remained at home to clothe them, and the nobles would have employed them to produce articles of luxury, as they would have no longer procured such articles from foreign countries. But if the stimulus to the agricultural proprietors were withdrawn, as long as the same social system prevailed, so long production would flag, in the absence of a demand for it from other countries, that would influence the proprietors, and, in the absence of sufficient inducements to industry, that would affect the cultivators.

United States of North America.

Montesquieu had not the opportunity, which Dr. List has neglected to profit by, of studying the development of the United States of North America. Until the commencement of the present century, these states were purely agricultural countries; yet their capital accumulated with unexampled rapidity, and, though manufactures were already established in the New England States, yet, previously to the tariff of 1828, they were of no great consequence; and, if we look to the foreign commercial relations of the States in the present day, they are still those of a purely agricultural country, exporting raw material to a vast extent, and importing manufactured and other goods in return, with a tendency at the present moment to become more and more exporters of that primary article of agricultural produce, which Dr. List contends is only of importance to the nations of the temperate zone, with respect to their home commerce. Yet, according to Dr. List, poverty and rudeness are inevitable accompaniments of the agricultural state, because they coexisted with it in certain European countries during the 17th century.

One consequence of the doctrine of M. Say seems to be, that there is no limit to the amount of produce which may result from the labour and capital of a country being judiciously employed. For, if increased production supplies a demand for produce, it will be possible for an unlimited amount of produce, if sufficiently varied in kind, to find a market. Still there are circumstances peculiar to each country which will limit the consumption of produce. Either the tastes of the people may be not sufficiently civilized and refined to enable them to appreciate the product; or the process of production may be too costly to allow of a general demand; or state regulations may control the manufacture and augment the necessary expenditure by exorbitant duties; or population may have reached that limit when a day's labour will not procure a day's subsistence, from the natural powers of the soil being overtaxed, and in consequence a check will be given to the progress of population, and thereby to the further growth of demand. The three first obstacles, some or other of which are of every day occurrence, may be removed: the last, when it occurs, will be beyond our control, but its occurrence may be indefinitely deferred by the practical sagacity of an enlightened statesmanship.

Limits to consumption.

LECTURE VIII.

The advocacy of these doctrines, as to international commerce, which M. Say was the first to propound systematically, has entailed upon their supporters the reproach of basing the peaceful relations of nations upon sordid motives of self-interest, rather than upon the generous dictates of benevolence. Such, however, is an imperfect view of the subject. On the contrary, whilst the advocates of restriction maintain that self-interest forbids a nation to listen to the dictates of benevolence, in regard to its dealings with other nations, the supporters of an unrestricted international commerce contend, that the dictates of self-interest, when rightly apprehended, are in perfect accordance with those of benevolence, and that an enlightened self-interest is one of the most effective engines to promote the welfare of mankind. It is by no means unfrequent to hear doctrines condemned as being of an utilitarian tendency; but persons who indulge in such idle declamation, seem to forget that self-interest is one of those mysterious moving principles, which Providence has implanted in man, and to whose dictates he is disposed to listen more implicitly than to any other guide. He was assuredly no ordinary benefactor to the human race, who first pointed out that the interest of the producers was intimately bound up with the interest of the consumers; and that by neglecting to consult the interest of the consumers, the producers would invariably inflict the greatest injury on themselves. It was at one time supposed that the secret of foreign commerce consisted in selling to foreigners more than you bought from them; in other words, in giving to them more than you received from them in exchange. The patent of this discovery has happily expired. Another sophism is gradually losing its influence before the growing convictions of the age; namely, that the produce of foreign labour cannot be admitted into

Enlightened views of self-interest.

Reproach of utilitarianism.

Exploded sophisms.

the home market without superseding a proportionate quantity of domestic labour. But it is clear that, for that produce, an equivalent must be given, which must be supplied by some one or other kind of domestic labour. There may indeed be a displacement of domestic labour, as is the inevitable consequence of the invention of a new machine, but there will be a new demand created for some one kind of labour, which will be employed more advantageously than the other kind of labour, which was formerly in demand. Where, indeed, domestic labour is what is familiarly termed *protected*, it is employed disadvantageously, otherwise it would not require to be defended from foreign competition: where, however, labour is left to its own resources, it will direct itself to those pursuits in which it has some natural advantage: it will thus be employed with the greatest efficiency, and be most likely to afford, after the consumption of the labourer has been satisfied, the greatest possible surplus to be exchanged away for any other commodities, which are produced more easily and more abundantly, or of better quality, in other districts of the world.

LECTURE IX.

LECTURE IX.

THE events of the concluding portion of the 18th century, and the earlier portion of the 19th, whilst they gave rise to new combinations of circumstances, which served to test existing theories, furnished at the same time subject matter for fresh scientific discussion, and so led to the determination of many new and important laws of Political Economy. The question of Public Credit, for instance, had not assumed at the time when the "Wealth of Nations" appeared, that overwhelming importance, which subsequent circumstances have attached to it. The first establishment of a bank of circulation in England dates no further back than 1694, at which time the Governor and Company of the Bank of England were incorporated by Act of Parliament, and up to the year 1758, no notes had been issued of a less value than twenty-pounds. It is a curious coincidence that in this latter year the first instance occurs of the forgery of a bank note, being one for twenty pounds, the smallest amount then in circulation. The bank commenced in the next year issuing notes and post-bills of 15*l.* and 10*l.*, and during the Seven Years' War, which did not terminate till 1763, the Government contracted loans to the amount of 51,000,000*l.* A brief respite from foreign expenditure ensued; but the breaking out of hostilities between the mother country and her North American colonies led to the contraction of further loans to the amount of 75,000,000*l.*, between 1776 and 1784. During this latter period the commercial interests of this country were unavoidably exposed to great

Public Credit.

Bank of England.

Seven years' war. Government loans.

American war.

embarrassment; but the return of peace afforded at last an opportunity for setting in active operation the great productive power, which the inventions of Watt and Arkwright had given birth to, just as the expenditure of the war, having been thrown upon the future resources of the country, furnished occasion for its activity. No sooner then was peace re-established than these inventions, by increasing the efficiency of British labour in producing exportable commodities, enabled it to obtain at a diminished cost and sacrifice an adequate supply of foreign commodities, amongst which of course the precious metals may be ranked. This advance in the manufactures of England could not but exert a favorable influence upon her agriculture and commerce, and with the increasing activity of all branches of industry, public confidence was revived, a spirit of enterprize was awakened, and increased facilities were sought for in Public Credit to enable the operations of peace to be conducted on an enlarged scale, commensurate to the demands which had been entailed by the burdens permanently imposed upon the labour of the country. The result of this was the establishment of a bank of circulation in every market town, which discounted bills of exchange as readily, or, I may say, as greedily as the drawers could present them. All sorts of notes were thus put into circulation, and were held in nearly the same estimation; and as they were not issued in exchange for money, but in the form of loans, the notes of individuals and the coin of the country circulated side by side. The first and inevitable result of this was a rise of prices, and as prices rose, the spirit of speculation was further stimulated, as all purchases for the purpose of resale would be advantageous. This tendency of profits to rise would dispose persons to purchase readily. The general rise of prices would meanwhile render it profitable to import many foreign

Return of peace.

Banking mania.

Rise of prices.

LECTURE IX.

commodities, which hitherto would not have borne the expense of transport; whilst many articles of home produce would no longer be in demand for foreign markets, from their enhanced price. The necessary result would be, that the exports of produce would fall off, the exchange become what is termed unfavorable, and gold and silver would be exported to make up the balance; the more so, as these commodities would be depreciated in the home market. Such seems to have been the condition of things in 1792. The currency had become redundant, the exchanges were unfavorable, and the Bank of England was obliged in consequence to contract its issues. The check which this measure gave to the accommodation, hitherto so recklessly afforded, entailed a stoppage of payments upon one or two large firms. Their failure created a panic, and the result was what is termed a run upon the country banks. When this reaction commenced, there are said to have been about 350 country bankers in England and Wales, of which not fewer than 100 stopped payment, and of these more than 50 were totally ruined. Mr. Gilbart, in his "History of Banking," states that in this year twenty-two commissions of bankruptcy were issued against country bankers.

The currency redundant.

Reaction.

Gilbart's History of Banking.

"The ease," writes Mr. M'Culloch, "with which supplies of paper were procured from the country bankers, naturally occasioned its employment in an immense number of transactions that had previously been carried on by means of specie, and ultimately occasioned that overflow of the currency and fall of the exchanges which led to the crisis. It is obvious, however, that but a very small portion, indeed, of that frightful mass of bankruptcy and ruin, whose accumulation signalised the close of 1792, and the beginning of 1793, can be fairly ascribed to that contraction of the currency which had become necessary to restore the exchange to par; and that by far the greater portion of it was really occasioned by the unsubstantial and worthless foundations on which many of the country banks rested, and the consequent want of confidence in these establishments. Had the bankers possessed adequate funds to meet the claims upon them, and had the public been aware that such was the fact, the contraction of their issues could not have caused any panic or run, and would have been effected with very little difficulty and embarrassment."

It may be perfectly true that the extent to which any reaction will be felt from a contraction of the circulating medium, must very much depend upon the soundness or hollowness of the system upon which the commercial transactions of a country are based, and that in the instance just alluded to, the system was so unsound that the failure of one or two houses, from whatever circumstance it might have arisen, would have entailed indiscriminate discredit upon all: but there is no doubt that on this occasion the ruin of several great establishments was caused by the Bank of England contracting its issues. Mr. H. Thornton, in a note to his well-known Inquiry into the Nature and Effects of the Paper Credit of Great Britain, states positively, p. 174, that at the time of the distress of 1793, some great and opulent country banks applied to the Bank of England for aid, in the shape of discount, which was refused on account of their not offering approved London securities: some immediate and important failures were the consequences. The purport of which seems to be, either that the Bank of England refused to issue notes for the relief of the country banks, excepting upon securities that could be readily realized, but which were not forthcoming; or the Bank was unwilling to part with its specie, lest it should be unable to satisfy the

Thornton's Inquiry into Paper Credit.

LECTURE IX.

demands to which its own extended circulation might at any moment subject it.

It has been maintained by some writers that this crisis was not occasioned so much by the excessive abuse of a paper currency, as by the interruption to which the commercial circulation, both foreign and domestic, of England was unavoidably subjected on the breaking out of hostilities with France. But a fall in the exchanges with foreign countries, attended with an exportation of bullion, had been experienced in the early part of 1792, considerably before hostilities were declared between the two countries; and Mr. Chalmers in his estimate of the comparative strength of Great Britian, states that none of the great houses that failed at this period had suffered damage by the war, but that the onus of the distress and ruin fell upon the country bankers, and the country traders dependent upon them.

Fall in the exchanges in 1792.

Experiment of M. Necker in France.

In the mean time the experiment had been made in France, originating with the genius of M. Necker, which was calculated to exhibit in striking outline, from the enormous scale upon which it was conducted, the mischievous effects upon prices of a redundant paper currency. Necker had originally supported the state expenditure by borrowing from the Caisse d'Escompte, which being secured from all prosecutions by virtue of an arrêt de surséance, had lent him a sum in its paper, exceeding its entire capital by about four millions sterling. Controlled in the financial scheme, which he had presented to the Constituent Assembly in 1789, and baffled by the unproductive results of the Contribution Patriotique, which had been substituted for his proposed income tax of one-fourth, he projected an extension of the Caisse d'Escompte which Turgot had instituted with a special object, (Bailly, Hist. Financière de la France, ii. p. 212.), so as to adapt it to the purposes of a national bank. His plan, having been variously objected

Caisse d'Escompte.

LECTURE IX.

to and remodelled, led ultimately to the great financial bubble of the French revolution, the issue of assignâts. The Minister of the United States (Gouverneur Morris), resident at that time in Paris, in a letter to George Washington, writes (January 24. 1790), "By way of giving some base to the present operation, it is proposed and determined to sell about ten or twelve millions sterling of the crown and church lands: both which are, by the resolution of the assemblée, declared to belong to the nation: but as it is clear that these lands will not sell well just now, they have appointed a treasurer to receive what they will sell for hereafter, and they issue a kind of order upon this treasurer, which is to be called an Assignât, and is to be paid (out of these sales) one, two, or three years hence. They expect that on these assignâts they can borrow money to free the engagements of the Caisse d'Escompte, and they are at the same time to pay some of the more pressing debts with the same assignâts."

Gouverneur Morris.

The state of monetary affairs in France at this period is well described by M. Thiers in his Histoire de la Revolution Française, c. 5.: — "Another consideration was decisive: there was a want of money, and the dearth of it was ascribed to the emigration which carried out of the country a considerable stock of coin, to the payments which were required to be made to foreign countries, and to the malice of individuals. It is by its circulation that money shows itself. When confidence reigns, exchanges become active; money passes rapidly from hand to hand; displays itself in all directions, and its quantity is supposed to be great, because the use of it is general; but when political troubles spread alarm, capital languishes, money circulates slowly, and it is supposed to be absent from the country, because its presence is concealed.

M. Thiers, Histoire de la Revolution.

" The desire of supplying the place of the metal money, which was supposed to have been drained

LECTURE IX.

away, of giving the public creditors something better than an unproductive title, the necessity of providing for a host of pressing wants led to a forced circulation of these assignâts. The creditor was paid by them, as he could oblige others to accept the paper which he had received, and so could discharge his engagements. If he did not wish to purchase lands, those who received the paper from him, in the course of circulation, must be the eventual purchasers of them. These notes were to be destroyed as soon as they found their way back to the public treasury—whilst, as long as they remained in the hands of the holders, they bore interest."

Opinion of Bailly.

Shrewd observers were not backward in predicting the failure of this plan. However good the security, it was manifest that the paper was not like specie, a reality, or, according to the expression of Bailly, "a physical actuality." Specie, indeed, bore its own value; but the paper, on the contrary, would require a further operation, viz., a purchase of land, to realise it. It would, therefore, of necessity on this account bear a lower price in the market. In addition, the representative of land would not bear so high a value as the universal representative of all commodities, for various reasons; such as the greater trouble of management, the contingency of outgoings, and the increased difficulty of conversion. Money, therefore, could not be raised upon such paper, except at a considerable discount; and as no one would be willing to cash such paper at par, its forced circulation would drive money still more out of the market. This would create a greater demand for paper, and with the increased supply, the evil would become more intense, until at last the difference between the nominal and real value of the assignâts would become so great, that public confidence would be destroyed, and a great crisis ensue.

An observer of passing events at Paris, describes the progress of this great financial juggle in these words: — "There is a plan for paper money now before the Assembly. The Assembly is divided in their opinion, and so are the commercial towns; but the people, who fill the galleries, and who surround the Assembly House, often in crowds, seem to be unanimous in favour of it. Mirabeau undertakes to prove that it is not paper money. It is true, that it is a paper which you may force the creditor to receive; but still he swears, and so do many others, that it is not paper money, because it has land for its pledge. Some insist on calling it 'papier-terre,' and the idea was near passing." — *William Short to Gouverneur Morris, Sept.* 12, 1790, *Paris.*

Mirabeau.

Necker had now resigned the department of Public Finance, which was entrusted to a less cautious spirit. Gouverneur Morris, to whom the letter, just quoted, was addressed, in reply to his correspondent, who doubted that the Assembly would sanction the project, expresses himself with singular foresight: "It will be long before political subjects will be reduced to geometric certitude. At present the reasoning on them is a kind of arithmetic of infinities, where the best information, the wisest head, and clearest mind, can only approach the truth. A cautious man should therefore give only Sibylline predictions, if, indeed, he should hazard any. But I am not a cautious man. I therefore give it as my opinion, that they will issue the paper currency, and substitute thereby *depreciation* in the place of bankruptcy, or rather suspension.

"Apropos of this currency, this papier-terre: I could tell them of a country where there is a papier-terre, now *mort et enterré*. The Assembly have committed many blunders, which is not to be wondered at. They have taken genius, instead of reason, for their guide, adopted experiment instead of experience, and wander in the dark, because they prefer

LECTURE IX.

lightning to light. I think you are mistaken in supposing that the emission of paper will destroy the proportion of prices. This proportion is independent of the medium of trade. The one results from a relation of things, the other is only an ideal standard, by which to measure those things. Your height and mine would be the same, and consequently the proportion of one to the other the same, although a measure of six inches should be called a foot."

Issue of assignâts.

The first issue of assignâts took place in May, 1790, and the amount was limited, by law, to 400 millions of francs. By September, however, 1200 millions had been circulated. Before three years had elapsed, the sum had been raised to 3626 millions, and by the autumn of 1796, upwards of 45,000 millions had been issued, of which, not more than 12,744 millions had been withdrawn from circulation. The consequences of so enormous a supply of paper money may easily be conceived; its value diminished daily, whilst the price of other commodities was enhanced beyond the existing proportion of their relative supply, by the apprehension of that proportion being still further disturbed. And as these assignâts were circulated with increased rapidity, owing to their liability to deteriorate in value by keeping, there grew up, as it were, a competition amongst the sellers of assignâts, which contributed still more to their depreciation.

Their depreciation.

It was attempted to prevent this constantly increasing depreciation, by a law, which made it criminal to circulate assignâts at less than their nominal value. This law was passed in April, 1793; but before two months had elapsed the paper was depreciated to one third of its nominal value. Two more months had scarcely expired, when this depreciation had increased twofold further, and, in spite of heavier penalties being attached to the transgression of the law, in 1796, an assignât, professing to be worth 100 francs, was currently exchanged for 5 sous 6 deniers; in other words, a paper note, professing to be worth 4*l.* sterling, passed current for less than threepence in money. The assignâts were at last called in, and were replaced by a new species of paper money, termed mandâts, being, as it were, orders upon the confiscated estates. Such, however, was the distrust of the public in all kinds of paper money, that they came out at a discount, and sunk, in the course of three or four months, to less than a seventieth of their nominal value,—when they were extinguished.—*Storch, Cours d'Economie Politique*, note 16.

Mandâts.

Storch, Cours d'Economie Politique.

Causes of their depreciation.

The depreciation of the assignâts, and the subsequent paper substitutes for them, was referable to two causes. They were, strictly speaking, paper money, consisting, indeed, of engagements for the payment of specific quantities of land, but issued, not strictly speaking, upon the credit of the land, but in compulsory payment of the expenses of the state, and circulating under its sanction and authority. The issuing of such paper, then, on the part of the government in payment of its debts, was in the nature of a forced loan, which in itself implied a want of credit. From this circumstance alone, then, its value fell at once below par; and this original depreciation was soon increased by the necessity of augmenting the issues in proportion to their diminished value, and thus the excess of the issues co-operated with public mistrust to augment the depreciation.

The Bank of England.

Great Britain, in the mean time, was rapidly approaching to a great crisis in the history of its paper currency. The promissory notes of the Bank of England had now for more than a century formed a very large proportion of the circulating credit of the country. These notes, being engagements for the payment on demand of a specific sum of money, from the

LECTURE IX.

general confidence resulting from such engagements being punctually fulfilled, had come to be substituted for money in the domestic commerce of the country. From the first establishment of the Bank, in 1694, down to the year 1797, there had been no interruption to the convertibility of its notes into money, nor had the state ever interposed its authority to promote or check the issue and circulation of them. The Company were simply the Bankers of the State, and its agents for the payment of the interest of the national debt.

In 1797, however, a combination of circumstances, partly commercial, and partly political, led to an interference of the legislature, which gave for a time a totally new character to Bank paper. Owing partly to the greatly increased foreign expenditure of the government by reason of the war in which England was then engaged, and partly to the enlarged issues of notes in consequence of advances made by the bank to the government in 1794, the exchanges became unfavourable in 1795, and in that and the following year there was a call upon the Bank for large quantities of specie. These and similar causes were of a commercial character, and had they alone operated, the directors would have discovered, in all probability, an effectual method of checking the drain of specie. But political causes supervened. Mr. Huskisson states that the directors tried and found unavailing all those means of checking the demand for gold, which had been efficacious on previous occasions, and that instead of abating, the drain increased every day in spite of their contracting the amount of their issues. Alarms of invasions, and reported descents of the enemy upon the English coast, were in continual circulation during the latter part of 1796 and the commencement of 1797. And thus many of the small farmers and tradesmen became

Exchanges unfavourable in 1795.

Political causes.

anxious to convert as much as possible of their property into cash, which they might carry away with them. This feeling led to heavy demands upon the country banks, and the stoppage of some of the northern banks gave an impulse to the panic.

Run upon the Bank.

The result was a general run from all quarters upon the Bank of England; and the stock of specie in her cellars, which had amounted in March, 1795, to 7,940,000*l.*, was thereby reduced to 1,272,000*l.*, on Saturday, February 25th, 1797, with every prospect of an increased demand upon the following Monday. In this embarrassment the Bank had recourse to the interposition of the government. A meeting of the privy council was held, at which it was resolved to authorise the directors at once to forbear issuing any cash in payment, and an order to that effect was issued on Sunday, the 26th of February—so pressing was the emergency.

Order of Council.

Immediately afterwards, the House of Commons appointed a Committee to inquire into the affairs of the Bank; and on March 3rd, the Bank was authorised to issue notes under the value of five pounds. In the following May an act of Parliament was passed, continuing for a limited time the restriction of cash payments, and indemnifying the directors against all proceedings under the previous Order of Council.

Restriction of cash payments.

Mr. Huskisson's view.

Mr. Huskisson has well observed, that this act made no fundamental alteration in our previous monetary system, neither did it make Bank notes, strictly speaking, a legal tender; but it suspended for a time the liability of every debtor, who should have made a tender to his creditor of the amount of his claim in notes of the Bank of England. It was no doubt intended and supposed by the legislature that this expedient would be but of temporary duration, so that Parliament did not trouble itself to inquire into the remote and possible consequences of stamping

LECTURE IX.

so large a portion of the circulating credit of the country with the character of paper money. This restriction, however, after some intermediate continuations, was ultimately extended to six months after the conclusion of the war, and continued actually in force for nearly a quarter of a century, viz. down to 1822. The result of which was, that in the year 1810 every creditor, to whom the law had secured the payment of a pound weight of gold for every 46*l.* 14*s.* 6*d.* of his just demand, was obliged to accept, in full satisfaction, about 10¼ ounces, or not more than seventeen shillings in the pound.

Value of gold in 1810.

The means by which this result was brought to pass may require explanation. Under the monetary system established by 39 G. III. in this country, one pound or twelve ounces of gold is divided into 44½ guineas, or 46*l.* 14*s.* 6*d.* A pound of gold, therefore, and 46*l.* 14*s.* 6*d.* being equivalent, being in fact the same thing measured in the one case according to a standard of quantity, in another according to a standard of number, any circulating credit which purports to represent 46*l.* 14*s.* 6*d.* ought, by the law of this country, to be exchangeable at will for a pound of gold. Now the object of the statute of 37 G. III. c. 45. was not to diminish the quantity of gold, for which a specific amount of circulating credit should be exchangeable, but merely to suspend for a time the option of the exchange. There was therefore nothing in the Bank Restriction Act to alter the existing relation between a pound's weight of gold and the sum of 46*l.* 14*s.* 6*d.* in Bank paper; yet it resulted, that in 1810 the sum of 46*l.* 14*s.* 6*d.* in Bank paper would only exchange for 10¼ ounces of gold, and that a pound of gold was exchangeable for 56*l.* in paper currency. Any commodity, therefore, which was of equal value with a pound's weight of gold, was of equal value with 56*l.* in paper.

LECTURE IX.

Mr. M'Culloch's account.

Mr. M'Culloch states, "that the first fall in Bank paper, as compared with gold, began in the latter part of 1800. The deficient harvest in that year caused a considerable exportation of the precious metals; but instead of contracting their issues, as they ought to have done, had they acted on sound principles, and as they would have been obliged to do had they been paying in gold, the directors added to the quantity of their notes afloat, and the consequence was that they fell to a discount of about eight per cent, as compared with gold bullion. But they soon after recovered their value, and from 1803 to 1808, both inclusive, they were only at a discount of 2*l.* 13*s.* 2*d.* per cent. In 1809 and 1810, however, the directors seem to have lost sight of every principle by which their issues had been previously governed. The average quantity of Bank notes in circulation, which had never exceeded 17½ millions, nor fallen short of 16½ millions in any one year from 1802 to 1808, was raised in 1809 to 18,927,833*l.*, and in 1810 to 22,541,523*l.* The issues of country bank paper (for the country banks had commenced issuing notes of 1*l.* in 1798) were increased in a still greater proportion, and as there was no corresponding increase in the business of the country, the discount on Bank notes rose from 2*l.* 13*s.* 2*d.* in 1809 to 13*l.* 9*s.* 6*d.* in 1810."

At this time the greatest difficulty was experienced in England in obtaining a supply of gold from foreign countries, in consequence of the interruption to our foreign commerce, which the Milan and Berlin decrees of Napoleon had produced in conjunction with the general extension of the war, whilst there was an increasing demand for bullion, as the readiest remittance to foreign countries, partly to defray the subsidies granted to foreign powers, and to cash the bills drawn upon London by our own commissariat abroad, partly

LECTURE IX.

to purchase foreign corn in consequence of the deficiency of the harvest at home. Had our currency been exclusively metallic, the result would have been an unfavourable exchange, an export of gold, and an enhancement of the value of the portion retained. As, however, a large proportion of the currency was inconvertible paper, a difference inevitably ensued between the Mint price and the market price of bullion, and the exchange must have been depressed at least to the extent of that difference, had the issues of paper been kept at a fixed level. But, as we have seen, the issues were increased, and the price of bullion continued to rise under the operation of both these causes.

Mr. H. Thornton's Enquiry.

It was not to be expected, but that great difference of opinion would prevail upon the subject of this extraordinary depreciation of Bank paper. As far back as 1802 Mr. Henry Thornton had published his "Enquiry into the Nature and Effect of the Paper Credit of Great Britain," the object of which was to show that the excess of the market price over the Mint price of gold, was to be referred to the unfavourable state of the exchanges with foreign countries, and that these exchanges were unfavourable in consequence of the balance of trade being against England. "The immediate cause," he writes, p. 139, ch. v., "of the exportation of our coin has been an unfavourable exchange, produced partly by our heavy expenditure, though chiefly by the superadded circumstance of two successive bad harvests." The improvement of the exchange he considered to have been delayed by the opinion of foreigners being affected by the circumstances of the war, but that as long as the main sources of a country's wealth were unimpaired, gold could not be permanently absent from it. In the mean time, "to alter materially the old and accustomed system of paper credit, and, in particular, to restrain in any very extraordinary degree the issues of paper of more responsible banks, would be to deprive the country of those means of recovering itself, which it naturally possesses." The return of gold was thus to be promoted, not so much by any legislative measure directed to that immediate object, as by cherishing the general industry, and attending to the higher and more leading interests of the country. That the return of gold had not been precluded by the law which authorized the continuance of the suspension of the cash payments of the Bank, he inferred from the circumstance, that since that law had been in force gold had flowed back into the country during one season with a remarkably strong tide. On these grounds, though he admitted the tendency of too great an issue of Bank paper to produce its own depreciation, he contended that the Bank Restriction Act had been wisely renewed. At the same time he maintained that it was unreasonable to suppose "that the degree of fluctuation which is now apt to subsist between the market price and the Mint price of gold could by any efforts of the Bank be materially lessened," p. 209, on the ground, as already observed, "that these fluctuations in the price of gold resulted from the fluctuations in the exchange, and those fluctuations, in general, proceeded from variations in the markets of Europe, which affect the balance of trade, and cannot by any management of Bank paper be exactly counteracted."

Whether, indeed, it would be expedient for the general interests of the country that its circulating medium should be exactly regulated to meet the fluctuations of the foreign exchanges, is open to discussion, but the possibility of such a regulation seems unquestionable, if the currency is to be considered as a commodity, the price of which will fluctuate according to the proportion of the supply and demand, and

LECTURE IX.

the Bank be supposed to have the power of regulating the supply of the circulating medium.

Lord King on the Bank restriction.

In the following year a writer of a different school stepped into the field. The negotiations between France and England had just terminated, and hostilities had been renewed, when Lord King published his "Thoughts on the Effects of the Bank Restrictions." It was not indeed till the conclusion of 1803 that the restriction was continued until six months after the definitive settlement of peace; but in the early part of the year the act had been renewed for a short time, and the discussions in the House of Lords on the subject gave rise to the publication of Lord King's work. Mr. Thornton had impugned several of Adam Smith's doctrines, as to the tendency of an excessive issue of Bank notes to send gold out of the country, and it is very possible that Adam Smith did not take into consideration the possible effect of an enormous foreign expenditure, such as the war with Napoleon entailed upon England, in influencing the exchanges; but Adam Smith was dealing with such facts, as the experience of the past supplied him with, and he was warranted in attributing the excess of the market price above the Mint price of bullion in the instances under his consideration, to over-issues of Bank paper. Lord King on this occasion took up the view which Adam Smith had laid down in the following words: "When, under all occasional fluctuations, the market price, either of gold or silver bullion, continues for several years together steadily and constantly either more or less above, or more or less below the Mint price, we may be assured that this steady and constant, either superiority or inferiority of price, is the effect of something in the state of the coin, which at that time renders a certain quantity of coin either of more or less value than the precise quantity of bullion which it ought to contain. The constancy and steadiness of this effect supposes a proportionable constancy and steadiness in the cause." Lord King maintained that this observation, which Adam Smith had made in respect of a metallic currency, was equally applicable to a paper currency not convertible into specie; the depreciation of the Bank note in this latter case would correspond to the degradation of the coin in the former case.

"During the course of more than four years past," Lord King observes, "an extraordinary and rapid advance has taken place in the price of bullion, and the general course of exchange with the continent of Europe during that time has been unfavourable in the same degree. Within the same period the paper currency of the Bank not convertible into specie, has increased to an extent of which we have had no former example. It may be assumed, therefore, on probable grounds, that the bullion has not become dear, but that the paper for which it is exchanged has been rendered cheap, because every commodity is cheap or dear in proportion to the abundance or scarcity of the supply." Lord King then proceeds to illustrate his reasoning by reference to fluctuations in the price of bullion, and contends that in certain instances, e. g. in 1802, the difference between the market and Mint price of bullion could not be possibly produced by the state of the exchange, and further, that the variations in the price of bullion and in the state of the exchange corresponded in a remarkable manner with the variations in the quantity of Bank notes."

Whilst the cause of the depreciation of the Bank paper was thus a matter of controversy, the steady progress of the depreciation excited great alarm, particularly amongst those who attributed it to a superabundance in the quantity of notes. The attention of the public was meanwhile arrested by some letters which appeared from the pen of Mr. Ricardo, in the

Mr. Ricardo's letters in 1809.

LECTURE IX.

columns of the "Morning Chronicle," in September, 1809, supporting the view which Lord King had taken of the question, and at the conclusion of the year Mr. Ricardo was induced to set forth his views in a more systematic form, and throw down the gauntlet to the Bank directors in a pamphlet, entitled "The High Price of Bullion, a proof of the depreciation of Bank notes." The subject was shortly afterwards taken up by the House of Commons, and in February, 1810, a committee was appointed to inquire into the cause of the high price of bullion, and the unfavourable state of the exchanges. Their report embodied a complete refutation of the statements and doctrines of those who contended that the unfavourable state of the exchanges and the high price of bullion were entirely to be ascribed to the large foreign expenditure of the country, and our peculiar relations with foreign powers, and were in no degree to be attributed to the superabundant issues of paper. This opinion of the committee gave a sanction to Mr. Ricardo's views, and invested them at once withan authority, which they might not otherwise have so readily obtained. Mr. M'Culloch has prefixed to his edition of Mr. Ricardo's works an interesting notice of his life and writings, in which, speaking of this pamphlet, he observes, that "Mr. Ricardo showed that the redundancy and deficiency of currency are only relative terms, and that so long as the currency of a country consists exclusively of gold and silver coin, or of paper convertible into coin on demand, its value can neither rise nor fall below the metallic currencies of other countries, by a greater sum than will suffice to defray the expense of importing foreign coin or bullion, if the currency be deficient, or of exporting a portion of the existing supply, if it be redundant. But when a country issues inconvertible paper notes (as was then the case in England), they

Pamphlet on the the High Price of Bullion.

Bullion committee.

cannot be exported to other countries in the event of their becoming redundant at home; and whenever, under such circumstances, the exchange with foreign states is depressed below, or the price of bullion rises above, the Mint price by a sum more than the cost of sending coin or bullion abroad, it shows conclusively that too much paper has been issued, and that its value has been depreciated from excess.

"Amongst those who entered the lists in opposition to the principles laid down, and the practical measures suggested, in Mr. Ricardo's tract, and in the report of the Bullion Committee, a prominent place is due to Mr. Bosanquet. This gentleman had great experience as a merchant, and as he professed that the statements and conclusions embodied in his "Practical Observations," which are at variance with the Report, were the result of a careful examination of the theoretical opinions of the Committee, by the test of fact and experiment, they were well fitted to make, and did make, a very considerable impression. The triumph, however, of Mr. Bosanquet was of short duration; Mr. Ricardo did not hesitate to attack this formidable adversary in his stronghold. His "Reply" was published in 1811, and is one of the best essays that has appeared upon any disputed question of Political Economy. In this pamphlet, Mr. Ricardo met Mr. Bosanquet on his own ground, and overthrew him with his own weapons. He examined all the proofs which Mr. Bosanquet had brought forward of the pretended discrepancy between the facts stated in his own tract and the theory laid down in the Bullion Report, and showed that Mr. Bosanquet had either mistaken the cases by which he proposed to test the theory, or that the discrepancy was only apparent, and was entirely a consequence of his inability to apply the theory, and not of any thing erroneous or deficient in it. The victory of Mr. Ricardo was

Mr. Bosanquet.

LECTURE IX.

perfect and complete, and the elaborate errors and mis-statements of Mr. Bosanquet served only, to use the words of Dr. Copleston, "to illustrate the abilities of the writer who stepped forward to vindicate the truth."

Report of committee not sanctioned by House of Commons.

The House of Commons, however, on this occasion, clung to the popular view, and refused to sanction the suggestion of the Bullion Committee, that the Bank should be required to resume cash payments in two years; and in the face of the double fact, that guineas were bought at a premium, and Bank notes were current at a discount of 10 per cent, they adopted, by a large majority in the following year, a resolution, proposed by Mr. Vansittart, to the effect that Bank notes were not depreciated, but gold enhanced in value; and that the political and commercial relations of Great Britain with foreign states were sufficient to account for the unfavourable state of the foreign exchanges, and the high price of bullion.

Mr. Mushet on the Bank Restriction Bill.

I have omitted to state, in order not to confuse the subject, that the opponents of Mr. Ricardo, amongst whom I may cite Mr. Mushet, of the Mint, the author of an "Inquiry into the Effects produced on the National Currency and Rates of Exchange by the Bank Restriction Bill," maintained, "that since Bank notes were declared a legal tender, the price of gold in bullion had no longer been rated in gold coins, but in Bank notes, and its price, accordingly, in Bank notes, was *4l.* 13*s.* per ounce; and that gold was no longer the principal measure of property, but Bank notes." In other words, it was contended that Bank paper was the real and the fixed measure of all commodities, and that gold was only one of the articles, of which, in common with others, the value was to be ascertained by a reference to Bank paper, as the invariable standard and universal equivalent. Mr. Chambers, one of the witnesses examined before

Mr. Huskisson's pamphlet.

the Bullion Committee, a gentleman, whose reputation for intelligence and information stood very high in the commercial world, declared that "he did not conceive gold to be a fairer standard for Bank of England notes than indigo, or broad-cloth." Mr. Huskisson, who had been one of the most active members of the committee, and who published, in October, 1816, a most elaborate and successful vindication of the principles and conclusions set forth in the Report, did not fail to notice this extraordinary and most erroneous notion.

"Now I recall to any man's recollection the obvious, and, as I till lately imagined, undisputed grounds on which the precious metals have, not in this country only, and by our system of laws, but in all civilised countries, and in all ages of the world, been received by the common consent of mankind as the fittest standard for measuring the value of all other commodities, and employed as the universal equivalent for effecting their exchange. That the precious metals are less bulky in proportion to their value; that they are accurately, easily, and almost infinitely divisible; that they are less subject to decay, less likely to fluctuate in their supply, less liable to be counterfeited or adulterated, more homogeneous and uniform in quality than either indigo or broad-cloth, or any other known commodity.

"Gold in this country (as silver in Hamburgh) is really and exclusively the fixed measure of the rising and falling value of all other things in reference to each other. The article itself which forms this standing measure, never can rise or fall in value with reference to this measure, i. e. with reference to itself. A pound weight of gold never can be worth $1\frac{1}{4}$ pounds of gold; and being divided, in this country, into $44\frac{1}{2}$ pieces, called guineas, an ounce of this gol will always be worth $\frac{1}{12}$th of this sum, or 3*l*. 17*s*. $10\frac{1}{2}$*d*.

LECTURE IX. The truth of these propositions, which cannot, I conceive, be called in question, would not be affected by any imaginable increase or diminution in the quantity of gold in the country. By such an increase or diminution, indeed, the value of all other things (the quantity of those other things, and the demand for them continuing the same) would be increased or diminished in the same proportion, with reference to gold; but gold itself would still remain, just as much as before, the fixed measure of the rising and falling value of all other commodities in reference to each other.

"A Bank note is not a *commodity;* it is only an engagement for the payment of a certain specified quantity of *money.* It cannot vary its value in exchange for any commodity, except in reference to the general increase or diminution of the value of such commodity in gold, and in the precise proportion of that increase or diminution. Gold therefore is the test by which the value of Bank notes must be tried, and if a one-pound note, being an engagement to pay 5 dwts. 3 grs. of gold is worth in the market only 4 dwts. 8 grs., as stated by Mr. Chambers in his evidence, it is equally worth only 4 dwts. 8 grs. in exchange for any other commodity.

"It follows from this, that a general increase of prices in all the ordinary commodities of any country, is not, in itself, an indication of the depreciation of the currency. Such an effect may arise from other causes. It could not fail to be produced by an increase of the precious metals. But any considerable or durable increase in the price of the precious metals, which forms the standard of that currency, cannot be ascribed to any thing but the depreciation of such currency, even if the price of all other commodities should be falling at the same time. This would happen in any country, if, at the same period, when its currency is depreciated in any given proportion, the supply of the precious metals was diminished, or the demand for them increased, in a greater proportion."

LECTURE IX.

Depreciation of currency.

There are only two ways in which a currency can become depreciated, e. g., either when the coin is debased or degraded, and, consequently, contains a less quantity of the precious metal than it is certified to contain, or when the entire currency is redundant. The latter depreciation will soon right itself, if the currency consists exclusively of the precious metals, as they would be profitable articles of foreign commerce, and would be exported, till their value was restored to the general level. But if the currency consists partly of gold, partly of paper, the depreciation resulting from a superabundant issue of paper cannot right itself by the exportation of the paper. The gold, consequently, will be exported, because its relative value, as a commodity, remaining unaltered with regard to other commodities, its *price*, as a commodity, will have risen in the same proportion as that of other commodities; whilst, in the state of coin, it can only pass current according to its legal denomination.

"When paper is thus augmented in any country, the exportation of the gold coin will take place; not because gold as a commodity has become more abundant and less valuable with reference to other commodities in such a country, but from the circumstance of its value, as currency, remaining the same, whilst its price in that currency is increased in common with the prices of all other commodities. So far as such exportation takes place, the diminution which it effects in the total amount of the currency has a tendency to support the value of the remainder, just as much, and for the same reason, as if in the case of a currency consisting wholly of

LECTURE IX.

gold, first an augmentation, and then an exportation to the same amount had taken place." Such was Mr. Huskisson's view.

Earl Stanhope's Act.

The result of the resolution of the House of Commons, followed as it was by Earl Stanhope's Act, which was passed to defeat Lord King's memorable address to his tenantry, encouraged the Bank of England to increase its issues, and at the same time relieved it from all apprehension as to state control. The country banks hastened to follow in the wake of the National Bank, and an unbridled licence was afforded to speculative enterprise throughout the country by the facility of obtaining discounts from the country banks, which were thoughtlessly bent upon forcing their notes into circulation. There can be no doubt that the excessive issues of country bank paper was one of the main causes of the unprecedented rise of rents and prices prior to 1814.

Rise of rents prior to 1814.

Corn had maintained an extraordinary price in the interval between 1809 and 1813 inclusive, having, in the latter year, found a market at *4l.* 15*s.* the quarter. A luxuriant crop, however, in 1813, coupled with the cessation of hostilities, and the opening of the Dutch ports in the following year, produced a rapid fall in prices, which could not but cause alarm to the country banks, and their customers, and give a check to commercial credit. This was quickly followed by a general want of confidence in the country bank paper, which led to a scene of commercial failures, far more disastrous than that which had been witnessed in 1793, in proportion as the scale of transactions upon credit was more extensive. Mr. M'Culloch states, that in 1814, 1815, and 1816, no fewer than 240 country banks stopped payments, and 92 commissions of bankruptcy were issued against these establishments. The misery, that was experienced on this occasion throughout the country, was declared

Sudden fall of prices in 1814.

Stoppage of country banks.

in the House of Commons, by Mr. Horner, a most competent judge, to have had no parallel in history, with the exception, perhaps, of that experienced in France, on the bursting of the Mississippi Bubble.

The diminution, however, in the amount of paper currency, consequent on the stoppage of so many country banks, was indirectly beneficial, by raising the value of the currency, and so far facilitating the return to cash payments; and, at last, the soundness of the principles, which the Report of the Bullion Committee advocated, and which had been so ably enforced by Mr. Ricardo, was acknowledged by the Legislature, in its adoption of Mr. Peel's Bill, in 1819. By this Bill (59 Geo. III. c. 49.) the return to cash payments, on the part of the Bank of England, was provided for, according to a graduated scale, extending over three years. In consequence, the notes of the Bank of England were declared, in 1822, to be once more convertible into gold, at the rate of 3*l.* 17*s.* 10½*d.* per ounce.

Mr. Peel's Bill in 1819.

Resumption of cash payments in 1822.

Although, however, the Bank note was once more declared to be convertible into gold, we must not suppose that the recognition, on the part of the State, of its convertibility, would, of itself, secure its convertibility. The law imposed, once more, upon the directors of the Bank the liability of payment on demand; but it did not secure to the public that the Bank should have the means of discharging that liability. The providing of those means was left to the discretion of the directors, and their experience, it was considered, would enable them to meet all emergencies.

On the abolition of the Bank Restriction Act, it had been provided that the country bankers should discontinue issuing notes under 5*l.*, as soon as the Bank should have resumed cash payments. With this object, the Bank had been required to procure

LECTURE IX.

gold, not merely for the payment of its own 1*l.* notes in circulation, supposed to be about 7,500,000*l.*; but also for paying off the small country bank notes, in 1825, amounting to seven or eight millions more. In addition, it was under the necessity of maintaining a fund of about five millions surplus bullion, to insure the convertibility of its own large notes, so that an aggregate of 20 millions of gold was to be provided within the space of four years after 1819.

In 1822, however, the Government thought proper to authorize the circulation of the country small notes until 1833. The consequence, according to a memorandum delivered by the Bank directors to a Parliamentary Committee, in 1832, was to leave in the possession of the Bank an inordinate quantity of bullion (14,200,000*l.*, in January, 1824), and further, to afford the power of extension to the country bankers' issues, which, it is believed, were greatly enlarged from 1823 to 1825.

I have already, I fear, entered too minutely into particulars in regard to the disastrous consequences of a redundant paper currency, on two occasions. But there are few questions that seem to require facts to elucidate them, so much as those connected with currency and credit; a third occasion now presents itself. In 1824 and 1825 a speculative frenzy once more pervaded the country, resulting in the formation of no less than 626 joint stock companies, whose projects would have required a capital of more than 372 millions. In addition to domestic schemes, foreign loans, to the amount of more than 55 millions, were contracted for in England. The consequences of such extravagance are well known. The course of the exchange began to be unfavourable, in October, 1824, and gold began to be exported. The Bank, however, did not thereupon contract its issues, nor was it until the autumn of 1825, that the continued drain

LECTURE IX.

of bullion, at last induced the directors to do so. Mr. Harman's evidence before the Committee explains very clearly the views which the directors then took of the duty of the Bank. In the month of December *the Panic* commenced upon the failure of a London banking house, and the tragedy of 1793 was a third time repeated, on a far grander scale than on the second occasion. Seventy banking establishments were now swept away in less than six weeks, and, according to Mr. Harman's evidence, the Bank of England itself owed its own preservation to the accidental discovery of a box of one-pound notes, which had not been destroyed, and were forthcoming at the moment of greatest pressure.

The panic of 1825.

Three great monetary panics had now occurred within the memory of a single generation, the intensity of which had increased on each successive occasion. It was evident that there was some great defect in a pecuniary system, which did not obviate the recurrence of such disastrous revulsions. "A system," as Lord Liverpool declared in the House of Lords, in 1826, "was wanted, which would exclude the possibility of discredit and bankruptcy, by preventing every individual or association from issuing notes without an adequate guarantee;" in other words, a system was required that should secure the convertibility of the Bank note. I do not propose to enter minutely into the various steps by which the state has endeavoured to secure this object, partly by measures calculated to reduce the liabilities of the country banks, such as the abolition of country notes under 5*l.*, partly by provisions, likely to ensure the solvency of banking establishments, from the number of partners in them being increased.

Lord Liverpool's Declaration in 1826.

The extension of branch establishments from the Bank of England into the country, and the concession

LECTURE IX.

of charters to joint-stock banks of issue were amongst the peculiar features of the act of 1826. Subsequent experience, however, has proved the inadequacy of these measures to secure the desired end. At last the great change by which the convertibility of the Bank note into gold has been most effectually guaranteed, was accomplished in 1844, by what has been termed Sir Robert Peel's Bank Charter Act, the nature and purport of which may be briefly considered. Hitherto, no limit had been imposed by law upon the Bank as to the amount of its issues, but it was left to the judgment of the directors to regulate their issue of notes according to the ordinary principles of banking under the obligation of paying them on demand in gold. The Bank of England, as observed in a previous Lecture, unites in itself the character of a bank of issue and a bank of discount; and its notes circulate partly upon the faith of deposits, partly upon the credit of securities. Now it has been found by the experience of private banks, that a reserve in specie of one third the amount of notes in circulation will be sufficient to meet the ordinary demand for gold (Lect. iv. p. 108), so that, as a matter of fact, two thirds of the capital of a bank of circulation may be invested in securities without endangering the convertibility of its notes. Supposing, therefore, a bank to have 21 millions of notes in circulation, if it has seven millions of specie deposited in its coffers, it will be enabled to meet all ordinary demands upon it for specie, and the convertibility of its notes will be guaranteed by such a proportion being maintained between its reserve and its circulation.

Sir Robert Peel's Bank Charter Act in 1844.

Convertibility of Bank notes guaranteed.

Security against depreciation of currency.

In addition, however, to a practical guarantee of convertibility, it was advisable to provide, if possible, a like guarantee against the depreciation of the currency. Now the best index of fluctuation in the value

LECTURE IX.

of the currency, which in almost every country consists of coin and bank notes, is to be found in the rate of exchange with other countries: for example, if the rate of exchange on Paris is high in England, it is evident that a given amount of the currency of England will not buy the same amount of the currency of France, and the currency of England is so far depreciated; if, on the other hand, the exchange is at par, then the currencies of the two countries will be at par. If therefore it be supposed, that the exchange between England and France has been at par for a certain time, whilst the circulation in England has been maintained at a certain level, the presumption will be, that as far as prices are affected by the value of the currency, the maintenance of that amount of currency will prevent any disturbance of prices, at least on that account. The Bank Charter Act consequently provided that there should be an absolute limit to the amount of notes issued upon securities, such an amount being taken as would keep the currency at par with foreign currencies, according to past experience. It combined a further provision for an expansion of the currency to suit the convenience of commerce, upon a basis which should preclude the depreciation of it; namely, by allowing an unlimited issue of notes upon bullion. These appear to be the distinguishing features of Sir Robert Peel's bill, and the present condition of monetary affairs in England appears likely to test most severely the working of it. If it should be found by experience that no monetary panic takes place after the extravagant speculation of last year, (1846), it would seem that one great evil at least has been obviated by it: but it seems probable that a greater benefit may result from it, namely, that the difficulty of procuring money will be recognised sooner than heretofore, and that the spirit of rash spe-

Probable results.

culation will thereby be controlled, so that amidst the general pressure which must follow the reaction, the disastrous cases of individual ruin will be less numerous than on any of the previous occasions above alluded to.

INDEX.

A.

B.

D.

E.

F.

G.

H.

I.

J.

K.

L.

M.

N.

O.

P.

Q.

R.

S.

THE END.